Modern Indian Interpreters of the *Bhagavadgita*

Sri Garib Dass Oriental Series-No. 127

Edited by ROBERT N. MINOR

Modern Indian Interpreters of the *Bhagavadgita*

SRI SATGURU PUBLICATIONS
A DIVISION OF
INDIAN BOOKS CENTRE
DELHI-INDIA

Published by :
Sri Satguru Publications
Indological and Oriental Publishers
A Division of
Indian Books Centre
40/5, Shakti Nagar,
Delhi–110007
(INDIA)

The Publication of this Book in India is made by permission of State University of New York Press.

First Indian Edition : 1991

ISBN 81–7030–295–1

Printed at
D.K. Fine Art Press, Delhi

PRINTED IN INDIA

Contents

Preface

Two hundred years of translation and study of the *Bhagavadgita* in the West and two *thousand* years of study and translation in India have produced a vast body of literature. This volume is a study of significant Indian interpreters of the modern period whose interpretations have affected others in India and the West. It is representative, of course, not exhaustive, and we hope it will promote the study of scriptural interpretation in the modern period, so as to clarify the continuity and change in modern definitions of religious traditions. Although we wish, like most authors, that ours were the definitive study of these matters, we would be pleased if this volume became a new benchmark for further research.

The project began with the preparation of papers presented at a research conference on Modern Interpreters of the *Bhagavadgita* at the University of Kansas, Lawrence, in conjunction with the Midwest Conference on Asian Affairs, October 7–8, 1983. The conference was supported by a research conference grant from the National Endowment for the Humanities and by the University of Kansas, particularly the Department of Religious Studies, the Center for Humanistic Studies, and the General Research Fund of the Graduate School. Special appreciation is due to Professor Robert Shelton, Chairperson of the Department of Religious Studies and Professor James Woelfel, Acting Chair for 1983–84, to Susan Gronbeck-Tedesco of the Center for Humanistic Studies, and to Professor Daniel Bays, Director of the Center for East Asian Studies.

Introduction

ROBERT N. MINOR

Most religious traditions, though they have placed a strong emphasis upon the oral, also have texts which function as scriptures or sacred writings. These scriptures function differently for different members of the tradition. Some revere these texts while otherwise ignoring their content. A few both know their content and practice their teachings. But many read the scriptures exclusively in terms of their own experiences, even though these readings were unknown to the original authors, and then practice what the text means in that light. Believers are often unconcerned with what a text meant in the original author's (or authors') historical context, for they see it as the embodiment of a living truth with which they identify. To believe the scripture is true and to know what that truth is in a different context from that of its human author, easily results in seeing that scripture in ways unseen by others in the tradition who know truth differently. The religious traditions of India are no exception.

In India a distinction is regularly made between two types of religious literature, *śrūti,* "that which is heard," and *smṛti,* "that which is remembered." *Śrūti* is theoretically more authoritative, for it is thought of as directly obtained truth, while *smṛti* is mediated tradition. Yet the works which are designated *smṛti* have functioned as scripture more often in the lives of Indians than have *śrūti. Śrūti* designates the Vedas, a vast collection of religious texts which reflect a variety of religious positions that existed in India from 1400 B.C. to 300 B.C. Except for the latter portions of the Vedic corpus, known as the *Upanishads,* the Vedic material came to receive more reverence than it did following. This meant that *smṛti* had to claim that it was Vedic, that what it taught was found in the Vedas when they are rightly understood, or that it was an authoritative addition to the Vedas. Thus, the *Mahabharata* epic (400 B.C.–400 A.D.) claimed authority as the fifth Veda, an addition to the four original Vedas of the collection.[1]

The *Puranas,* from 200–1200 A.D., with their stories of the gods, became more well-known than Vedic literature. They too claimed authority as fifth Vedas or as official commentaries on the Vedas that spoke the words of inspired sages. But one of the earliest works designated *smṛti* which functioned as scripture in India was the short, 700 verse text known as the *Bhagavadgita,* "the Song of the Beloved One."

From the time of its authorship for insertion into the *Mahabharata,* Indian religious thinkers have regularly commented upon, cited, and written about the *Bhagavadgita.* Even in the later portions of the *Mahabharata* itself, the *Gita* was taken as authority for a wide variety of religious ideas and paths to the now traditional goal of liberation from the wheel of rebirth. The earliest extant commentary is that of the eighty-century non-dualist Shankara, who refers to at least one previous commentator. But commentaries on the *Gita* since Shankara's come from nearly the whole religious spectrum, including devotees of the three most popular Indian gods: Krishna, Vishnu, and Shiva.[2]

For reasons unknown, the *Gita* become a part of the *prasthānatraya,* the "triple foundation," the three texts on which it was believed the Indian schools of religious thought called Vedanta were founded. Vedanta, meaning the "end of the Vedas," denoted not only that the *Upanishads,* on which these schools were based, were literally the last works added to the Vedic corpus, but also that the thought of the *Upanishads* and these later schools, each of which believed it best understood the *Upanishads,* was the "end" or goal of Vedic experience. It became standard practice for thinkers identifying with Vedanta to comment on the *Upanishads,* the *Vedanta Sutras* of Badarayana, which are thought to summarize the thought of the *Upanishads,* and the *Bhagavadgita.* Each school believed that all three taught its view of Reality and its path to *mokṣa,* liberation from the eternal cycle of karma and rebirth.[3]

The *Bhagavadgita* itself was created in a period which seemed to evidence a growing variety of religious options seeking *mokṣa.* The Upanishadic schools produced their variety of solutions to the human predicament by about 300 B.C. Liberation was attained, they believed, by experiential identification of one's being with the one permanent Reality, often designated *brahman,* that is behind the flux of karma, of birth and rebirth. Numerous religious personalities wandering throughout India preached other paths to liberation and at times gathered not a few followers. Of these the Buddha (563–483 B.C.) and his contemporary Mahavira became the most well-known. The period also saw the rise of popular religious movements whose concerns centered around *bhakti,* devotion to a personal deity. The gods Vishnu and Shiva, who would dominate Indian religion ever since, were worshipped by followers whose devotion soon found its way into the *Mahabharata* and the *Ramayana,* the other great epic created from about 400 B.C. to 400 A.D.

The *Bhagavadgita* was written about 150 B.C. by a devotee of another Indian deity, Krishna, whose popularity would spread throughout India. It was meant to be included in the *Mahabharata* by a Krishna *bhakta,* in order to show that devotion to Krishna was the key to an understanding of Vedic religion. Its author proclaimed that the correct path to liberation from the cycle of rebirth was the performance of action done without concern for its results; this coupled with meditation would result in a realization that one's true self was not involved in action but was eternally devoted to the Lord of the universe, Krishna.

In one exclusive path the author combined what has come to be called *karma-yoga,* a path of non-attached action, *jñāna-yoga,* a path of intuitive knowledge, and *bhakti-yoga,* a path of devotion.[4] The fact that he combined these elements with Upanishadic terminology and quotations, however, provided the basis for later commentators to emphasize one element or another in their interpretations of the text. The *Gita*'s author also included numerous citations of the Vedic material, reinterpreted for his objectives. These in turn provided points from which later interpreters who did not share the author's path could assert their own positions. A traditional Indian commentarial spirit searches out the *mahāvākya,* the "great saying," in a key verse or phrase or term. By this "saying" the commentator then understands the remainder of the text. The *Gita* provided enough of these "great sayings" to be used, often out of context, to support almost any commentator's understanding of the path. Thus, even though it was called *smṛti,* the *Gita* became a standard authoritative text within a number of schools of Vedanta.

Apparently a number of the religious personalities who gathered followers about them in the period of the *Gita*'s authorship challenged the system of caste or class by which the Vedic texts structure society. According to the Theravada tradition the Buddha did so as he set up his monastic order. Central to the *Gita* is its concern that the caste structure be maintained. Declaring that the fourfold caste system was created by Krishna (4.13), it also held that it was better not to teach the truth to people if it caused them to depart from their duties *(varṇa-dharma),* which were determined by their place in the social structure, i.e. their caste (3.26,29).

One of the heros of the *Mahabharata,* Arjuna, provides for the work's author a paradigmatic case in which to promote the performance of *dharma.* Arjuna is a *kṣatriya,* a member of the class of warriors. To abandon his duty by not fighting in the battle to come, even though his reluctance is prompted by his concern that he would kill his relatives if he fought, is a violation of *dharma,* Krishna argues. Though Arjuna's own argument in *Gita* chapter one was also an attempt to preserve the class structure with its duties, Krishna argues that he must fight because that is his class-duty. Twice the *Gita* declares that it is better to do one's own *dharma* poorly than to do another's well (3.35; 18.47). Thus, the author sought to maintain the structure which would be reinforced by the law books, the *dharma-śāstras,* that would soon appear. On these matters the traditional commentators would agree.

Beyond the commentaries and essays of the intellectual elite, it is difficult to determine how popular the *Gita* has been. Many scholars believe it had little popularity and non-literary evidence seems to support this view. The earliest illustrated manuscripts of the *Gita* available are from the 18th century, and earlier artistic representations are rare. While the Krishna of the very popular *Bhagavata Purana* and scenes from the rest of the *Mahabharata* are to be found regularly, only two illustrations of the Krishna of the *Gita* are known: one in the 14th century at a temple at Pushpagiri in Andhra Pradesh and another from a frieze on the late 12th century Halebid temple.[5]

However,, the *Bhagavadgita* clearly assumes a place of importance in the India of the nineteenth and twentieth centuries, both popularly and among its elite religious thinkers. One modern Hindu defined this place as follows: "For the Hindu it is now the *one book* of books. . . . The Gita is as fresh as ever and just as to the Christian is the Bible [sic] . . . the Gita is to the Hindu."[6] It played a part in Indian nationalism, in the rise of a 'Hindu' consciousness and the definition of a 'Hinduism', and in the growing interest in oriental studies.

At the same time, it drew the attention of the West, beginning with its first translation into English by Charles Wilkins 200 years ago. Many Westerners found their religious vision in the *Gita* as well. The American Transcendentalist Ralph Waldo Emerson and others were enthusiastic about it, as reflected in Emerson's mistaken reference to the *Gita* as "the much renowned book of Buddhism."[7] Translations into Western languages abound, making it the most translated text after the Bible. In the 1960s and 1970s its popularity in the West increased dramatically with the rise of an Eastern-looking counter-culture, both within that counter-culture and among others interested in similar products of Eastern spirituality.

Within India, however, the modern period (used here to designate the nineteenth and twentieth centuries) was a time of great ideological, political, and sociological upheaval. Foreign domination of Indian soil moved from the last vestiges of Moghul rule to the British raj, with Queen Victoria proclaimed Empress of India and suzerain over the Indian Princely States in 1876. Various opinions about the type of education to be offered to colonial India culminated in 1835 in the acceptance of the British educational system over the study of Indian subjects. Thomas Babington Macaulay's famous "Minute on Education," with its low evaluation of classical Sanskrit and Arabic literature, won the day in spite of Macaulay's almost complete ignorance of Oriental knowledge. Among those presented in this volume, the result of this decision was profound since they were in many ways direct products of that system and the values it taught.

Indians were also exposed to the criticisms of 'Hinduism,' which was now being treated as a reified entity, by Western critics, particularly teachers and missionaries. Gandhi's characterization in his autobiography is representative of the feeling of many: "In those days Christian missionaries used to stand in a corner near the high school and hold forth, pouring abuse on Hindus and their gods. I could not endure this."[8]

The modern Indian interpreters studied in this volume took the presuppositions behind these criticism to heart. In their arguments they did not outwardly grant the objections of the critics. 'Hinduism,' they felt, was not essentially guilty as charged. Yet, the assumptions behind the charges were ones that, in many cases, these modern interpreters shared. Thus, they did not respond to them indifferently as people from worldviews which were traditional to India and other than those of the critics might have. Instead they defended their positions in their critics' terms, since the criticisms were rooted in ideals they also accepted. As such, criticisms that Hinduism is fatalistic, passive, lacking in concern for social ethics, otherworldly, idolotrous, etc., found a hearing in these thinkers, based on their 19th and 20th century backgrounds as well as their own ancient traditions. They did not respond that these criticisms were unimportant or that the critics simply misunderstood Reality or that the criticisms were precisely the virtues of their traditions. Rather, they defended 'Hinduism' as incorrectly indicted. 'Hinduism,' they believed, must be evaluated in its purity, its essence, and not in the historically debilitated forms popular among the common people.

The *Gita* thus provided a basis for an active response to British rule. Its author had placed the text at the beginning of the battle which is central to the *Mahabharata.* One of the epic's heros, Arjuna, refuses to fight because he has been painfully reminded that it is a battle between two sides of his clan, the Bharatas. As Arjuna surveys the battlefield, he sees relatives and teachers on both sides, and by the end of the first chapter of the *Gita,* he has dropped his weapon and decided not to fight. Krishna, who is acting as Arjuna's charioteer, calls for an active response on Arjuna's part. He is to do his duty and fight, without concern for the outcome of the battle. This exhortation to action from the god Krishna suited well the aspirations of Indian nationalists in their struggle for *swarāj,* independence from British sovereignty. Likewise, Krishna's call to Arjuna rejected renunciation of action as a solution to the human predicament, and thereby provided support for social action and Indian social reform to modern thinkers who wished to show that Indian religions are concerned with these matters. They regarded Krishna as the karmayogin *par excellence,* working unceasingly and with total selflessness.

Yet the *Gita* itself was also an object of pride for India. As it captured the praise and interest of the West, it symbolically provided a counter to Western criticisms of Indian culture. The British may provide products of Western technology to India, but India, they said, provided the harvest of its spirituality to the world. For some, like Aurobindo, India was thereby the world's guru. That praise of the *Gita* was praise for India and 'Hinduism' which was not lost on the thinkers whose ideas are presented in this volume.

The popularity of the *Bhagavadgita* is evidenced by the growth in the number of translations and essays in modern India which continues without abatement and seems to be growing in momemtum. Selecting from among the many who have interpreted the *Gita,* this volume concentrates not on contemporary productions but on those who have been most influential and whose influence has been felt beyond India. A number of these interpreters are culture heroes today for whom the centrality of the *Gita* is seldom noted. Moreover, how they understood or used the text is rarely investigated. Many subsequent interpretations, both Indian and Western, result from the influence of the interpreters studied in this volume.

The first chapter studies both Western and Indian thinkers associated with the Theosophical Society. Many interpreters, such as Gandhi, first read and even personally discovered the *Gita* in the translation of Edwin Arnold which was current among the Theosophists; the Theosophical Society itself, with Annie Bésant as its spokesperson, provided support for the Indian cause and praise for the religious traditions of India. The Theosophists believed the Hindus were unsurpassed spiritually and, thus, a superior people. Such a people, it followed, should have political independence. Accordingly Annie Besant, along with B. G. Tilak, founded the all-India Home Rule League in 1915–16 and was president of the Indian National Congress in 1917. Through the Theosophists, pride in Indian spirituality increased among many modern Indians who had been trained in Western institutions. Though Theosophy was founded in the West, by 1879 its two founders, Colonel Olcott and Madame Blavatsky, had arrived in India. Their presence, together with Theosophy's praise of things Indian and reverential interest in texts like the *Gita,* was in sharp contrast to the disdain for or condescension to Hinduism expressed by other Westerners. Before 1900 most publications on the *Gita* from the Society were by Indians such as Subba Row and M. M. Chatterjee. Even Annie Besant's authorized text in 1904 was produced through Indian assistants. But Judge's translation and study and her 1906 *Hints on the Study of the Bhagavad Gita* continued to show a Theosophical interest which encouraged the exaltation of the *Gita* as a lasting contribution to world-wide spirituality in the minds of many of these thinkers. Though it represents for them a high point of Hindu spirituality, and in many cases essential Hinduism, they believed it is of broader human significance as a universal scripture when understood in terms of the eternal truths it teaches.

Bankim Chandra Chatterji (1838–1894), sometimes known as the father of modern Bengali literature, was an administrator in the government of Bengal and a man of letters. Though he took no part in politics, his appeals to Indian language, history and literature provided a basis for Indian national pride. His famous poem *Bande Mataram,* "Hail to the Mother," which wedded the concept of the female deity to the nation of India, became an inspiring hymn for nationalists throughout India. His unfinished Bengali commentary on the *Gita* reflected his interest in defining 'Hinduism' not on the basis of *śrūti* but through the *Gita*.

The Maharashtran Bal Gangadhar Tilak (1856–1920), after receiving his B.A. and Bachelor of Laws degrees, refused to enter government service. Instead he turned to journalistic pursuits, attempting in the Western area of India known as Maharashtra to develop the people's sense of pride in their history and religion. The government accused Tilak of inciting anti-British activities and sentenced him to an eighteen month jail term. He soon became the greatest leader of the extremist wing of the Indian nationalist movement, which advocated militant overthrow of the British. During his six year imprisonment in Mandalay, Burma, Tilak continued Sanskrit studies and wrote his commentary and study of the *Bhagavadgita* and so provided an active ethic and even violent precedents for anti-British activity.

After studying in England another Bengali, Aurobindo Ghose (1872–1950), returned to participate in the leadership of the extremists. He edited a journal entitled *Bande Mataram* that advocated extremist causes in Indian nationalism. The British arrested him for conspiracy in 1909. After a year in prison he emerged with a central interest in his religious experiences and yogic practices. He retired to French Pondicherry in southeast India to develop his "Integral Yoga," and there the well-known Sri Aurobindo Ashram grew up around him. It now has branches throughout the world. The *Gita* was a part of much of his life and his *Essays on the Gita* in English were reprinted in a number of forms.

India's most well-known figure, Mohandas Karamchand Gandhi (1869–1948), returned to India with his law degree from London and with experience in nonviolent resistance from South Africa. He was a man of action more than a thinker, and the *Gita* was his favorite text, his "spiritual dictionary." Having discovered it in London through Theosophical Society friends, he translated it into his native Gujarati and afterward centered much of his advice on the *Gita*.

Gandhi's most well-known disciple was Vinoba Bhave (1895–1982), India's "walking saint." After Gandhi's death he emerged from the shadows and continued the life of action focusing on Gandhi's goal of *sarvodaya,* the welfare of all human beings. His campaigns in independent India for economic reform through land, village and monetary donations were actions tied to his understanding of the message of the *Gita,* on which he had lectured earlier while imprisoned by the British for his participation in Gandhi's campaigns.

After receiving a Western education and after a mental and religious struggle with himself, Swami Vivekananda (1863–1902) became a disciple of the mystic and spiritual teacher Ramakrishna (1836–1886). In 1893 he addressed the World Parliament of Religions in Chicago and, after lecturing in America and Europe, returned to India as a cultural hero. Through his dynamic personality he established the Ramakrishna Mission, known in the West as the Vedanta Society. His definition of 'Hinduism' has influenced Indian and Western understanding since, with its emphasis upon the active life of social service, the 'tolerance' of the Indian tradition and a neo-Advaitin metaphyisic. His lectures on the *Gita* indicate his interest in it as a tolerant text calling for an active religion.

Vivekananda's definition and defense of 'Hinduism' restored the confidence of Sarvepalli Radhakrishnan (1888–1975) in his own tradition. Trained as a philosopher, Radhakrishnan used the *Gita*'s call to action to argue against Western claims that there was no basis for ethics in Hinduism. As a philosopher who taught at Oxford University as well as in prestigious academic positions in India, and as Vice President and President of the Indian republic, Radhakrishnan wrote that the *Gita* taught a universal "religion of the spirit" that provided what the modern world needed. His writings on Indian thought have influenced Western understanding of India widely.

Swami Sivananda Sarasvati (1887–1963) received a British medical education, but after practicing medicine he renounced that life style to become an ascetic and recluse, was initiated into the Shankaracharya order and became a guru with one of the largest mass appeals in India. Though his ashram is in Rishikesh in the foothills of the Himalayas, his disciples have touched thousands, in both India and the West. Sivananda published 340 books and pamphlets, including a popular 800 page translation and commentary on the *Bhagavadgita*.

Another popular guru, Swami A. C. Bhaktivedanta (1896–1977), did not remain in India but came to the West, where he established the International Society for Krishna Consciousness. Though he received a Western education, more formative was the training and subsequent initiation from his guru, Swama Bhaktisiddhanta Sarasvati Gosvami in Calcutta in the devotion to Krishna. Steeped in the tradition of devotion to Krishna alone, he began writing in English on the *Gita* while still in India, criticizing "impersonalists" such as Radhakrishnan who, he felt, obscured its true teaching. In 1965 he came to New York City to fulfil a mission given him by his master, and in 1972 his *Bhagavadgita As It Is* appeared as an attempt to correct the misinterpretations of previous commentators, academic and religious, who were outside the "true" line of gurus.

These philosophers, leaders, and thinkers, then, are among the leading modern Indians who have received training in Western institutions and who have believed that their traditions represent the truth, a truth found in a correct understanding of the classical Indian text known as the *Bhagavadgita*. Though it has been called *śrūti,* it functioned as a touchstone for them as they identified, defined, and defended their own traditions.

CHAPTER ONE

A Lesson in Allegory: Theosophical Interpretations of the Bhagavadgita

RONALD W. NEUFELDT*

If we accept the widsom of recent scholarship on the *Bhagavadgita,* this classic became a popular text for religious self-understanding and scholarly debate and interpretation at about the same time in India as it did in the West. It has been suggested that the *Gita* was not really a popular scripture in India before the nineteenth century, that it was known mainly to the spiritual elite who treated it as another Upanishad. In the West, with the earliest translations appearing near the end of the eighteenth century, the *Gita* came to be known as a poem of beauty and universal wisdom. Surprisingly, however, in the writings of the founders of the Theosophical Society, the *Bhagavadgita* did not appear to draw much attention as a book expounding esoteric teaching or occult wisdom. To be sure, there are isolated references to the *Gita* in Blavatsky's magnum opus, *The Secret Doctrine,* and in her *Collected Writings* and even the promise that *The Theosophist* would begin to expound the meaning of the *Gita.*[1] After 1885, however, much attention and energy was given to interpreting and understanding the *Gita* by writers directly or indirectly associated with the Theosophical Society. It is not surprising this happened given that a concern of the Theosophical Society has always been to recover the esoteric teachings wherever these may be found in the religious history of humankind. Thus as the *Gita* became popular in both East and West, it was bound to receive special attention as a vehicle *par excellence* of occult widsom or the perennial philosophy.

The concern of this study is to uncover the understanding and the use of the *Gita* in Theosophical writings. It will be my contention that there is in Theosophical literature a fairly consistent understanding of the *Gita,* brought about by an overarching commitment to Theosophical teachings as found in the writings of H. P. Blavatsky. If outstanding differences do appear, they will usually appear on the level of the use to which the *Gita* is put, but not on the level of understanding or interpretation.

WORKS ON THE GITA

Works on the *Gita* from the perspective of Theosophical teachings are indeed numerous. The beginning of the period of special attention seems to be the 1880's, particularly in the work of Subba Row who, according to Eric Sharpe, functioned for a time as the *Gita* expert for the Society.[2] There follows a long list of monographs which takes Theosophical interpretations of the *Gita* up to the present day. These monographs are of various kinds—translations, recensions, studies, discourses, essays, notes and indexes.

In addition to monographs one can also point to a plethora of articles appearing for the most part in Theosophical journals. These would probably run into the hundreds and are too numerous for consideration in this paper. There is, of course, some overlap between monographs and journal articles inasmuch as some of the monographs are compilations of series appearing in Theosophical journals. For example, *Essays on the Gītā* by William Q. Judge appeared originally as a series of studies in *The Path* in 1887–88 and 1895–96 under the penname William Brehon.[3] *The Yoga of the Bhagavad Gītā* by Sri Krishna Prem originated in a series of articles written for *The Aryan Path* of Bombay.

A number of the monographs are also compilations of lectures delivered at meetings of Theosophical Societies. *The Philosophy of the Bhagavad Gītā* by Subba Row, for example, was delivered in four lectures at the annual convention of the Theosophical Society held in Adyar in 1886. *Thoughts on the Bhagavad Gītā* by A. Brahmin was originally a series of twelve lectures delivered before the Kumbhakonam Branch of the Theosophical Society in 1892. *Hints on the Study of the Bhagavad Gītā* by Annie Besant was a series of four lectures delivered at the thirteenth anniversary meeting of the Theosophical Society at Adyar in 1905. *The Doctrine of the Bhagavad Gītā* by Paṇḍit Bhavāni Shankar represents talks given in 1914 and 1925 in Calcutta and Madras respectively. *Discourses on the Bhagavad*

Gītā by C. Jinarajadasa were originally lectures delivered in Bangalore in 1946.

The approach in this study will be to present an overview of a representative sampling of the early monographs from 1885 to 1920. Consideration of the monographs will be divided into two parts, the first dealing with Indian works and the second dealing with Western works.

Indian Works

The stage for Theosophical interpretations of the *Gita* is set by Subba Row's influential 1888 work, *The Philosophy of the Bhagavad Gītā.* As Eric Sharpe points out, Subba Row had already been active in the pages of *The Theosophist* expounding the true meaning of the *Gita.*[4] His approach to the *Gita* is that it is essentially practical, designed to give directions to humanity for spiritual guidance in the evolutionary drama in which man realizes more and more his essential immortality.[5] It teaches nothing more than the premises which have been the basis of every system of philosophy and scientific endeavor.[6] The *Gita* is proposed as the path to true spirituality over against other Hindu, particularly Sankhyan paths, which have degenerated into superstition and demoralized India by leading people away from practical action. In making this criticism he sounds a note which is a familiar one in the writings of Hindu reformers of the nineteenth and early twentieth centuries.

> If you examine these customs by the light of Krshna's teachings, it must appear to you that, instead of having Hinduism we have assimilated a whole collection of superstitions, beliefs and practices which do not by any means promote the welfare of the Hindu nation, but demoralise it and sap its spiritual strength, and have led to the present state of things, which, I believe is not entirely due to political degeneration.[7]

It is interesting to note that Subba Row, in his discussion of the philosophical basis of the *Gita* adopts a fourfold classification of the cosmos and humanity, rather than the traditional sevenfold classification usually found in Theosophical works. The sevenfold classification is seen by him to be misleading, unscientific, and contrary to Hindu works.[8] This rejection of traditional theosophical numeration and his appeal to quite traditional approaches to the study of the *Gita,* appear to have played a role in his subsequent departure from the Society.

The fourfold classification of the principles of the cosmos, according to Subba Row, is as follows. *Parabrahman* is the first cause, omnipresent and eternal, subject to periods of activity and passivity. From it springs a center of energy, the Logos, not different from *Parabrahman* but individualized. Essentially this is the Ego of the cosmos of which every other ego is but a manifestation or reflection. *Mūlaprakrti* is the veil thrown over *Parabrahman,* the basis of material manifestation in the cosmos. *Daiviprakrti* is the light emanating from the Logos and acting on *mūlaprakrti.*[9] The evolution of the cosmos is described in language reminscent of *Sankhya.* Everything occurs through the light emanating from Logos and acting on *mūlaprakrti.*

The human being is also seen as a quaternary; thus there is a correspondence between the individual and the cosmos. According to the Vedantins and Krishna, the individual is physical body *sthūla śarīra)* corresponding to the manifested solar system, astral body *(sūkṣma śarīra)* corresponding to the light emanating from the Logos, higher individuality *(kārana śarīra),* corresponding to the Logos and *ātma,* corresponding to *Parabrahman.*[10]

The individual's goal is to identify more and more through successive incarnations with the Logos through the development of the *kārana śarīra,* the real ego, and its physical frame, to the point where one lives as an immortal being, a manifested *Īśvāra.*[11] Subba Row states:

> The *Logos* is, as it were, the pattern, and emanating from it is this light of life. It goes forth into the world with this pattern imprinted on it, and, after going through the whole cycle of evolution it tries to return to the *Logos,* whence it had its rise. Evolutionary progress is effected by the continual perfecting of the *upādhi,* or organism, through which this light works. In itself it has no need of improvement. What is perfected is neither the *Logos,* nor the light of the *Logos,* but the *upādhi* or physical frame through which this light is acting.[12]

In the *Gita* proper, Krishna is seen as representing the Logos. For the benefit of humanity, the Logos descends in rare cases to the human plane to associate itself with a soul, which then *has* the Logos rather than being a mere reflection of it. Indeed, Subba Row suggests that the whole of the *Gita* could be classified as a book of the philosophy of the Logos, explaining its activity as it incarnates in *yuga* after *yuga* for the sake of humanity.[13]

Arjuna on the other hand is the human monad in the process of evolution. He is a representative human being who has reached the stage in the evolutionary process where he must decide whether to identify with his higher individuality or his lower passions. Essentially, it is a decision to identify with the Logos, the light which enlightens or brings life to all matter. The *jīva,* the real individuality of the human being, is the light of the Logos, which, becoming differentiated, forms the individual ego in combination with *karanopādhi.*[14] This identification, however, should not be understood as a loss of individuality. Such a culmination is seemingly viewed with horror by Theosophists. According to Subba Row, the doctrine of complete extinction of individuality has spoiled Advaita philosophy, led to the present deplorable condition of Buddhism in Asia, and made immortality into a meaninless term.[15] Rather than become extinct, human individuality becomes the individuality of the Logos; what is extinguished is merely *punarjanmam.*[16]

The purpose of *Gita* study is the attainment of immortality in these terms and the use of this knowledge of immortality for the sake of helping one's countrymen.[17] Krishna as Logos becomes the guru who teaches Arjuna, the student, how this immortality is to be acquired. The battle becomes a battle between the higher and lower elements, the human monad versus the lower passions, which go to make up the constitution of the human being. It is this view which comes to dominate in Theosophical interpretations of the *Gita* from Subba Row onward.

Equally as important as Subba Row's work, at least in terms of lasting impressions, is the translation and commentary by Mohini M. Chatterji entitled *The Bhagavad Gītā* or *The Lord's Lay.* There is uncertainty concerning the first edition of this work. Certainly an edition was current by 1888. Chatterji suffered the same fate as Subba Row in his relationship to the Society, in that he fell out of favor after a promising beginning.

Contrary to Eric Sharpe's judgement that Chatterji's work contains little interpretation,[18] the copious notes yield, in fact, much interpretation, some of which runs counter to generally accepted Theosophical teachings on human destiny. In keeping with general Theosophical teachings, however, Chatterji puts the *Gita* in the framework of belief in progress through an evolutionary process in which the ego progresses through a series of kingdoms—vegetable, animal, human, and divine.[19] He also affirms that the *Gita* teaches nothing but those truths which are taught by all scriptures and systems of thought if one understands them correctly. In this context, the peculiar chracteristic of Chatterji's work is the frequent reference to Biblical, particularly New Testament, passages. Thus in speaking of the God of the *Gita,* he proclaims that the same god is proclaimed in all scriptures, and this is followed by references to Job 10.7, Romans 11.33–34, and John 1.1–9.[20] John 1 is of course a natural text to cite given its use of the term Logos. If one follows through on Chatterji's suggestions, one reads the Bible in effect alongside the *Gita.*

Since his commentary runs chapter by chapter and, in some cases, verse by verse, Chatterji's interpretation is more specific and more sophisticated than Subba Row's. In general, the allegorical approach is the same: the *Gita* is understood to be speaking about the human being in general and his spiritual travels in the evolutionary development of the cosmos. However, not only is Arjuna made to stand for humanity or a certain type of human being, but so is the opposition. Thus Duryodhana is seen as the incarnation of pride, injustice, and jealously, and Bhishma comes to stand for success in experience, the mainstay of the existence of evil.[21]

Arjuna, on the other hand is taken to represent one who is thrown into doubt as a result of being assailed by the internal enemies represented by such opponents as Duryodhana and Bhishma. This was to become a frequently stated position in Theosophical interpretations. In commenting on *Gita* 1.30 Chatterji states:

> Whenever a man loses faith, these three evils, grief, fears, and weakness, attack him, and he begins to delude himself into the belief that it is fruitless to persevere on the upward path.[22]

The subsequent injuction to fight in chapter 2 of the *Gita* is to be understood as "a statement of Arjuna's mental state, which has been temporarily clouded by doubts."[23] The concern of the *Gita* then, in the injunction to fight, is not to propose a specific course of action, but rather to highlight the internal enemies which one must overcome in order to achieve the extinction of conditioned existence.[24]

In two important respects Chatterji's interpretation departs from the generally expressed views in Theosophical literature. In his views on action and non-dualism he follows Shankara rather than Theosophical thought. First with respect to non-dualism, Chatterji agrees with the Theosophists that in reality the human monad is divine or at least a manifestation of the divine. However, this manifestation is one of appearance only and not of reality. In commenting on chapter 2 of the *Gita* he states:

> In this chapter as well as in those succeeding, it is taught that the only reality is Consciousness, or the Supreme Spirit, which, being absolute, has no relation to any object or action. But there is a mysterious power, which though really non-existent, except in identity with the Supreme Spirit, yet appears as if possessed of a co-oordinate being. . . . The one pole is the personal God . . . the other, man.[25]

The whole universe is to be understood as illusions which "simulate the One Reality."[26] The human goal then becomes not simply the overcoming of conditioned existence but the elimination of any individuality whatsoever. In general, Theosophists would insist on the reality of the universe and the evolutionary process, and on movement to higher and higher states of individuality.

In his view of action Chatterji takes the same view expressed by Shankara, that the path of action is a necessary antecedent to the path of knowledge. In his comment on *Gita* 2.39 he states

> . . . although the knowledge of the philosophy of action does not by itself remove "bondage of action," yet it renders man pure enough to receive the knowledge of the Spirit which does cut asunder the knot of action.[28]

Work and forms, although necessary for the human being at one stage in his life at some point become unnecessary. According to Krishna therefore, action is inferior to knowledge.[29] The injunctions for right action are meant only for those who are still bound by egoism.[30] This position would appear to be quite different from that taken by Theosophists in general, who assert that there is a real involution of the absolute, a real evolutionary process in which action is essential and not a matter of choice, and that knowledge of the true nature of reality dawns in ongoing activity rather than apart from activity, as one aligns oneself with the evolutionary process. Activity is simply not seen by Theosophists to be either antecedent to or inferior to knowledge, nor is the loss of individuality seen to be a desirable goal.

An obscure treatment of the *Gita* is found in *Thoughts on the Bhagavad Gītā,* a series of twelve lectures delivered to the Kumbhakonam Branch of the Theosophical Society by an author known simply as A. Brahmin, F.T.S. in 1893. It has received little or no mention in Theosophical writings, possibly because it is so badly written and has relatively little to do with the *Gita,* notwithstanding the title. The book includes more reference to Puranic teaching and to *The Secret Doctrine* than it does to the *Gita.*

The author purports to give a non-sectarian treatment of the *Gita* along Puranic lines rather than the usual one-sided treatments given by Europeans, karma-yogins, Advaitins, and Vishishadvaitins. The *Puranas* are put forward as containing almost everything occult. The difficulty is that they are written in symbology which can be understood in broad outlines only through the work of Blavatsky.[32] Consequently there is more emphasis on teaching basic Theosophical ideas than on teaching about the *Gita.*

There are, nevertheless, some interesting developments in this treatment. Perhaps the most outstanding is the attention given to historical issues such as the time and place of the war and the appearance of Krishna within human history, something which is barely mentioned in previous works. The war is alleged to have taken place about 5,000 years ago at the beginning of the present Kali Yuga as a karmic punishment for the selfish spirit which had developed in the previous cycle. The situation demanded the appearance of a great soul, a *jagat-guru,* to adjust things.[33]

Following this, however, there is a resort to the standard allegorical treatment of the *Gita.* Although the war is real and actually took place, it is to be understood as a war which went on in human hearts and minds. The war symbolizes what takes place at an important juncture in human evolution, a battle between the divine and gross elements or the higher and lower selves in human beings.[34] The injunction to fight in the cause of justice and to do so in a spirit of renunciation, without grief or doubt, is an injunction given for the student of *Brahma-vidya* rather than an injunction literally to kill people.[35]

Krishna is to be understood on various levels. On the one hand, he is the "ray of dark glory that dwells in the lotus of the human heart."[36] As the unmanifested Logos, he is "the spirit of all consciousness in the entire universe," the individualized ray in the Jivatma."[37] On the other hand, Kṛishna as *avatāra* is simply "one of those divine beings who, living in the noumenal planes of nature, watch over and protect the field of human evolution."[38]

Arjuna is simply a human monad who has reached a certain stage in the evolutionary process requiring that he bid good-bye to a previous stage of life and all of its affectations in order to enter into a higher, less personal stage in the evolutionary process. Arjuna's doubt and anguish is caused by his lack of knowledge of the course of the evolutionary process and not literally by the prospect of doing away with his own kinsmen. His conflict must be understood symbolically. Rather than recognize that both *pravṛtti* and *nivṛtti* are two aspects of the ongoing evolutionary process, Arjuna shrank in ignorance from the task at hand of growth in consciousness and threatened to lead an ascetic life.[39]

The central message of Krishna to Arjuna is that he must act according to the laws of cosmic development and perform those duties required at this stage of development in human life. Such activity, furthermore, is to be done as *yajñā,* that is in a spirit of service to all, recognizing that all have their place in the great unfolding of the evolutionary process towards universal oneness.

> . . . The fundamental keynote of true theosophic teaching is the key-note of the Gītā and that is act, act, act. Act how? To render service to cosmic yajñā, mentally indifferent to the blissful fruit of it.[40]

This emphasis on sacrificial action leads to some interesting conclusions. It means to take seriously the plight of the famine-stricken whether in India or elsewhere,[41] to love others, to work for others to alleviate the cruel blows of nature,[42] and to do so within one's own tradition, not to denounce such traditions or seek to convert people from one tradition to another; all traditions, practices, and nationalities have their own peculiar functions to perform. This is what is meant by being true to one's own *dharma* or caste.

The Brahmin, however, does take pains to reject what are seen as false notions of oneness. On the one hand modern advaitins come under attack as nihilists who do not discriminate properly between *ātma* and non-*ātma* or world evolution.[43] To suggest that there is such a thing as eternal rest and that all manifestation is falsehood is to reject puranic lore.[44] On the other hand, neither is the divine to be personalized, a tendency which has led in India to enormous waste of energy and money on temples and adornments and the growth of evils or *rakṣasas* like religious hatred and bitter disputes while millions suffer from poverty and ignorance.[45]

An influential series of studies of the *Gita* by The Dreamer, a pseudonyom for Rajendra Lal Mukerjī, was published in 1902–1904.[46] The purpose of the *Gita* is seen as teaching Sankhya Yoga, which, incidentally, is standard theosophical teaching concerning the origin and destiny of man. A great deal of time is spent setting "the record straight" in order that we might understand the *Gita* properly. Consequently there appears to be more reference to the writings of Blavatsky than to the *Gita* itself.

The interest is in the timeless meaning of the *Gita* as a guide book for the student on the path of non-attachment (*nivṛtti*), service, love and sacrifice.[47] The message has meaning only for the crucial point in human evolution, for "the great battle where the human soul has to conquer the *human* in it and cross over to the other side of immortality and service."[48] Considerable attention is therefore given to Arjuna's despondency and the problems symbolically presented in chapter one. It depicts the critical stage of the life of an aspirant when he or she is struggling to forge links with and move on to a higher level of life. It is a struggle between a well-developed personal self, which was fit for the current stage in the evolutionary process, and the higher life or self to which one is to move.

Arjuna, though a highly evolved being who has purified his life to the extent that his personal self no longer has a voice in the regulation of his conduct, is still bothered by spiritual powers and virtues which he has evolved but must now give up. The lower self, once evolved, is bent on securing a separate existence for itself, and will not easily give way to the evolution of higher forms of life.[49] Thus, The Dreamer says, the virtues of *rāga,* attachment to formal life, *yoga,* desire of possession, and *kṣema,* extreme compassion for forms of life which were once

> . . . the very *sine quā non* of evolution and growth, are now used as dead weights to stop his further progress. His intellect becomes confused; he cannot distinguish between the form and the life. He loses sight of the great fact, that every Ego has to give up all likes and dislikes, *all love for life in form* as well as *all attraction for formless* life; that the Ego's progress henceforth lies in recognizing itself as merely an aspect and a mode of the Diving energy instead of being a separate centre by itself.[50]

The lengthy allegorical treatment of Arjuna's problem sets the stage for similar treatment of other aspects of the *Gita.* Such is the case, for example, in the treatment of Arjuna's basic argument against fighting—caste confusion. This receives special treatment because of the efforts of Hindus towards spiritual regeneration and freedom from caste restrictions.[51] Caste has its proper role to play in the economy of cosmic evolution to allow for infinite variety and specialization, and to indicate the most efficient lines for individual development.[52] The ego must evolve slowly in vehicles appropriate to its stage of development. Otherwise the result will be discord (caste-confusion) and pollution (the vitation of women). In an obvious warning against attempts to reform the caste system too quickly the Dreamer states:

> When, however, the body follows a different line of evolution—when there are built into it materials incongruous to the stage of evolution of the Ego—when the body goes one way with its lines of heredity and the Ego the other way, there is war and discord. There is then what the Gītā calls "Caste Confusion"—when the vehicles of man, instead of being instruments to express the inner Life in a way most suited for growth (which is called duty), are vitiated by the effects of actions incongruous to the needs of the inner Man—when by such actions forms of matter of different planes hostile to the life of the Ego are drawn and built into the bodies, then these vehicles become polluted, or, as the Gītā puts it, "the women become vitiated," there is what is called confusion of caste.[53]

Thus he allegorized caste confusion, pollution of women, and *dharma*. Outward forms, particularly *dharma,* have efficacy. Their primary role is to allow for the unfolding or manifestation of the potentialities of Life or the Deity within the individual, the gradual realization of the true nature of the "individualized Self" within.[54]

The idea of the *avatāra,* too, is rendered in terms of the conflict between stages in the evolutionary process. The *avatāra* appears when the law of growth changes from one that emphasizes separation, concentration, and self-centeredness to one that emphasizes expansion and surrender to the larger life of which we are all a part.[55] Such a change however, means conflict that at times threatens to overwhelm the forces for evolutionary progress or good. In such a situation the *avatāras,* as manifestations of the One Life, appear to restore a proper equilibrium. The forces for good (expansion and surrender to larger life), the Devas, combine to beat back or subdue the forces of self-assertion or resistance, the Asuras.[56] The vehicle whereby such a manifestation is made possible is the Yogi, the purified and perfected individual who, having unified his life with the "Supreme Life," becomes a vehicle for a special manifestation or descent of the Unmanifest.[57]

A more recent Indian interpretation of the *Gita* is that done by Pandit Bhavani Shankar, published in 1966. The volume is actually based on lectures given in 1914 and 1925. These lectures were not an attempt to deal with the whole of the *Gita,* but only with chapters 4, 13, and 15, which are regarded as key chapters.

With frequent reference to the *Voice of Silence* and the *Light on the Path,* Shankar described chapter 4 as having to do with the successive initiations of the *jīvātma* on its way to *jñāna* once it enters the human realm. Arjuna's dilemna is described as follows:

> He has not yet killed what in "The Voice of Silence" is called the Raja of the senses, the "slayer of the real," and despondency possesses his mind when at last he has to pass through the experience. He is now called upon not only to kill the 11 Akshauhinis of Kinsmen formed of his five senses and six passions (Kama, Krodha, etc.) but to slay even the Dharmacharyas to whom he was looking up hitherto for guidance.[58]

The successive initiations through which Arjuna and all human monads are to travel are the realization that the physical ego or center is an expression of divine life, the realization that the astral body is a reflection of the one life, the realization that the spiritual ego or causal body is a mere reflection of divine light, not limited by any form, and finally the realization of transcendence over the neutral point of isolation from all matter or the death of the individual and birth of a regenerate human being not limited by the bonds of matter. It is this last initiation which is said to be the real *kurukṣetra* battlefield of the *jīvātma* which does not end in the loss of individuality and passivity but leads on to yet further progress. This, however, is thought to be difficult indeed as indicated by the verses which suggest that the real *mahātman,* the true *jñānin,* is indeed hard to find.[59] Here again one comes across the criticism of advaitins that says that they are wrong because they reject individuality while Krishna teaches the perfection of individuality.[60]

An interesting twist is given to the concept of *avatāra.* The seeker after *jñāna* becomes a participator in the incarnation of the Divine in that the incarnation is a response from *Īśvara* to some individual's developing the virtues entitling him to union with *Īśvara.*[61] The *Gita* should therefore be seen as a treatise dealing with the high doctrines of the origin, trials, and destiny of humanity and should not be used to feed the questionable neo-theosophical preoccupation with past lives of the Mahatmas and sensational stories of personal loves and hates of previous incarnations of particular monads.[62]

WESTERN INTERPRETERS

An early and influential treatment of the *Bhagavadgita* on the American scene is that written by William Q. Judge. He offered both a recension and a series of essays dealing with the first seven chapters and intended as a non-academic exposition. His work influenced some later treatments in the West coming out of the Theosophical movement.

He spends a great deal of time discussing the proper approach to take to the *Gita* to avoid inappropriate interpretations. As might be expected, he places the *Gita* in the optimistic evolutionary framework so typical of much Theosophical literature. The *Gita* is to be understood as an account of the evolutionary development of humanity. Therefore, like the Indian interpreters, he takes an allegorical approach. While admitting that there may be interesting historical material in the *Gita,* Judge suggests that to dwell on this, as do many European scholars, is to overlook the Hindu psychological system underlying the work.[63] To find the inner sense he argues, we need to move beyond the disclosed word or the historical facts and read between the lines. This is possible, he maintains, even if we don't know the language, because we have a faculty which should allow us to do this.[64] At any rate, brahmins, Orientalists, and Western Sanskritists are all at fault for fixing our minds on the lowest or literal meanings of key words and references.[65]

Reading between the lines for the higher, more psychological meaning leads to some interesting but not unexpected interpretations of specific characters and terms. Dhrtarashtra, for example, is taken to represent the material side of existence, the human body, or senseless matter acquired by the immortal monad for its evolutionary journey. His blindness represents the fact that the material body has no inherent power of sight or feeling; rather, it is the Self which is the final support of every phase of consciousness and form.[66] In general, the Kurus are seen as representing the material side of life while the Pandus represent the spiritual side.[67] Accordingly, the battle is to be understood as a battle between the material and spiritual forces residing in every individual. Indeed, the battle is necessary to the course of evolutionary progress in order to prepare the spiritual for taking over from the material the rule of life.

> The hostile armies, then, who meet on the plain of the Kurus are these two collections of the human faculties and powers, those on the one side tending to drag us down, those on the other aspiring towards spiritual illumination. The battle refers not only to the great warfare that mankind as a whole carries on, but also to the struggle which is inevitable as soon as any one unit in the family resolves to allow his higher nature to govern him in his life.[68]

As might be expected, Arjuna represents the human being standing at the threshold of the development of higher powers. But further development comes at a price: the lower faculties, old tendencies and habits must be left behind to make way for the new. This is the real meaning of the enumeration of all the generals and commanders—they are really "a catologue of all the lower and higher faculties in man," the powers of our being.[69] We are all Arjuna, and the battle we fight is the battle with ourselves, or more specifically, with our lower nature. Kurukṣhetra, then, is not India, or a certain spot in India, it is the sacred plain of the human body, Indian, Hindu, American, Christian, or otherwise wherever it is found, and the words of Krishna are the universal message given to help us conquer our lower selves.

Krishna's concern—the concern of the higher self—is to reveal oneness, and in the light of that oneness, to teach a correct view of selflessness and action. Thus Judge says of the purpose of the *Gita:*

> The Bhagavad-Gītā tends to impress upon the individual two things: first selflessness, and second, action; the studying of and living by it will arouse the belief that there is but one Spirit and not several, that we cannot live for ourselves alone, but must come to realize that there is no such thing as separateness, and no possibility of escaping from the collective karma of the race to which one belongs, and then, that we must think and act in accordance with such belief.[70]

Our situations and bodies are to be understood as the product of nature's law, which is also our law; in evolutionary terms this means that we have those bodies and tendencies, and are born into those situations necessary to give us the experiences we need for further growth. This is what is to be understood by the fact that Arjuna is a warrior.[71] It is also to be expected that in this upward path we will sometimes despair and feel despondency, as Arjuna did since any action bent on further progress will naturally arouse tendencies antipathetic to further development from previous evolutionary stages.[72]

Particularly in the Western world today, there are blocks to further progress just as there were in the *Gita's* time. These range from hedonistic concerns like the pursuit of money and external enjoyment,[73] engaging in actions to bring the favor of the Mahatmas or which will result in good karma,[74] to false doctrines such as the Christian notion of securing happiness and prosperity on earth and bliss in heaven.[75] Particularly pernicious is the worship of the spirit of individualism, which flies in the face of the *Gita's* message of sacrificial action. Judge states:

> With the culmination of the dark age it was, however, natural that the last vestiges of sacrifice should disappear. On the ruins of the alter has arisen the temple of the lower self, the shrine of the personal idea. In Europe individualism is somewhat tempered by various monarchical forms of government which do not by any means cure the evil; and in America, being totally unrestrained and forming in fact the basis of independence here, it has culminated. Its bad effects—vaguely as yet shadowing the horizon—might have been avoided if the doctrines of the wisdom-religion had been also believed in by the founders of the republic.[75]

There is, however, a note of hope and optimism injected by Judge. According to natural law, evil can only grow to the point where there is demanded its opposite by way of reaction—the personification of good to oppose rampant evil. This is how the notion of Krishna as *avatāra* is to be understood.[77]

Annie Besant's work on the *Gita* is difficult to place. While she was a Westerner, she identified thoroughly with India and Indian causes. Her interpretation of the *Gita* is equally as influential at Adyar as Judge's has been in North America. I include her here because of her Western origins. Her influential work published as *Hints on the Study of the Bhagavad Gītā* is based on four lectures delivered at the thirtieth anniversary meeting of the Theosophical Society at Adyar in 1905. She also contributed two translations, one together with Bhagavan Das.

For Besant, the *Gita* is not a Hindu text, nor even an Indian text. Rather it is a universal text acclaimed by all nations[78] and a mirror of the complex history of the world.[79] Moreover, the *Gita* is not simply a text to be read, but one to be lived as well, for it is by living it that it comes finally to be understood.[80]

Given her view of the *Gita,* it is expected that she will seek out the allegorical meaning in the text. Besant, however, makes a distinction between two related meanings: the historical which has reference to "the working out of the plan of the Logos" or "the evolution of a World-Logos," and the allegorical, which has reference to a smaller history, the history of some individual who exemplifies the larger picture.[81] It is this double meaning that one should look for in the *Gita.*

The larger historical view sees Krishna as the *jagat-guru,* the *avatāra* or Logos of the world system who appears in physical form at a critical point in the evolution of the world system.[82] However, this Logos is not something separate from the individual but a part of the human spirit.

> He comes as the *Logos* of the system, veiling himself in human form, so that He may, as man, outwardly shape the course of history with mighty power, as no lesser force might avail to shape it. But the Avatāra is also the Ishvara of the human Spirit.[83]

Besant at this point becomes somewhat prophetic. Krishna's role has practical implications for our understanding of human history and India's place in it. India was destined to serve as world model and savior. But this could only come about through suffering and humiliation, in other words, through a crisis which necessitated the leadership of an *avatāra.* Ironically, his work destroyed the *kṣatriyas* and opened India up to a series of invasions, that nation's "passion" and "crucifixion," which nonetheless fertilized India and resulted in a life-giving stream of wisdom flowing to other lands. Thus, Besant concludes, the *avatāra* is a loving guide bringing unceasing good.[84]

Arjuna's dilemna is that he doesn't understand the larger sweep of history. He stands for the preservation of an old order, unable to accept what is about to happen because he sees only ruin, not the rise of a new and mightier India. Nor does he understand his own role as a bridge from old to new forms until the cosmic plan is revealed to him. What is the larger lesson in all this? Besant says

> And so in all history, if only we can see aright in the history around as, in the history of Arjuna on Kurukshetra; if only we can learn the spirit of the great unveiling, the meaning of life behind the veil and of the little lives on this side, their cooperation, their relations one to the other, then in every struggle we can throw ourselves on the right side, and fight

> without doubt, without illusion, without fear, for the Warrior who really fights is doing all, and we are but the cells of His body with our wills harmonised into unity with His.[85]

It is not just a call to activity, but activity in world affairs, and a call to optimism in this activity.

The allegorical meaning mirrors the larger historical one. On the allegorical level, the conflict is between *manas,* or the "unfolding mind" and *kāma,* the passions symbolized by the relatives and their ties to the past. Early in his evolution Arjuna experiences no struggle but follows naturally his own appetites and the teaching of the elders. This, however, gives way to a time of struggle and confusion, when *kāma* becomes unsatisfying. But this struggle results in the triumph of *manas,* "illuminated, with the light of the Self, clear, radiant, decided; the delusion destroyed."[86] In either case, the historical or the allegorical, the lesson is the same struggle to move on to higher levels of development, historical or individual.

Given this emphasis on struggle, Besant sees action as the central teaching of the *Gita*—its nature, its binding force. Thus it is also a book about yoga, for yoga is mastered on the field of activity, a lesson she feels, on the basis of her experience, modern India still needs to learn. Krishna's teaching of skill in action rather than seclusion is a lesson which has been largely forgotten and this has led to the decadence of India.[87]

Since the name of the game is action, one does what needs to be done at the moment, whether it is fighting, or discarding the body, so that something new and better can arise out of the old.[88] Certainly this is a call to radical change, if not revolution. Whatever action is called for however, must be done, as the *Gita* commands (4.15; 18.23), without attachment, as a sacrifice.[89] This is, however, not possible unless one is able to see the union of the many in the One, as chapter 11, the heart of the *Gita* teaches.[90] This teaching of the unity of the many in the One is given an interesting ethical twist in that it applies to evil as well as good. Indeed, Besant argues, in the nature of things there is no good or evil. We create these categories through our own ignorance, folly and passion.[91] Thus, conventional views and practices of good and evil must be transcended by realizing unity and living within it, whatever one's walk of life may be.

The call to skill in action—action done in complete dispassion—is for the ascending path of the evolutionary cycle, the *nivṛtti mārga.* This is different from the *pravṛtti mārga,* not because activity motivated by man's various temperaments ceases, but because the goal of activity changes. Thus one's desire is directed to Self rather than *kāma,* one's activity is directed to sacrifice rather than objects, one's knowledge is directed to the One rather than separate outer objects. In each case there is desire, a necessary force for the realization of the evolutionary process, but the direction and goal of desire shifts from acquisition of things and knowledge to desire and activity for, and knowledge of the One. This Besant sees as the gist of 13.24.[92] The outcome of the reorientation of desire is the realization of unity, and this leads to yet more activity rather than cessation of activity:

> We shall then see that out of one universe rises, in this Body of Light, the Lord of another universe, and we, parts of His Body, shall work with Him in that new universe more perfectly than we have worked here. Thus on from age to age, from universe to universe, and where, I say again, where is grief, where delusion, when thus we have seen the Oneness?[93]

A somewhat different look at the *Gita* or at least a different emphasis is found in Charles Johnston's translation and commentary of 1908. It is different in that more attention is given to the Indian background to the development of the text. However, Johnston remains true to what Theosophical writers perceive as the universalist message or import of the *Gita.* Thus Arjuna's despondency and doubt, the resolution of these doubts, and Krishna's majesty are universal in their import. Similarly, the *Gita*'s insight into human hearts, the concentration on the conflict of natures, the fetters of selfishness, and the subtle evasions to which humanity is given, also have a universal application.[94] In spite of its Indian background, the *Gita* is to be understood as a symbolic scripture with many levels of meaning and truth.

The attention to the Indian background reflects an acknowledgement of the various strands or systems of Indian thought that the *Gita* tries to reconcile, all of which address the issue of the soul and immortality. These strands or systems are identified as the work of the four castes or races—the rajput or red, the brahmin or white, the vaishya or yellow, the shudra or black.[95] From each of these the *Gita* inherits something important. From the rajput it inherits the key message of the *Upanishads,* that the human being is an immortal being subject to rebirth and capable of liberation. From the brahmin it inherits the genius of abstract reasoning. From the vaishya, it may have inherited the way of works, of fulfilling every duty as a ritual. And from the shudra, it may have inherited the devotional path, the path of emotion or exaltation of the heart.[96] The comments of the *Gita* on *dharma* or caste mixture, Johnston argues, have to do with the rights and duties of each race. These are emphasized because children from parents of different castes fail to inherit the better qualities of either parent.[97]

Johnston also acknowledges that the *Gita* has the flavor of a local martial epic or a bardic cycle derived from a war, a flavor which is apparent in spite of the universal message interpolated into the basic bardic structure. It is these martial aspects which supposedly belong to the earliest parts of the *Gita.*[98] The movement from local epic to universal message is seen as early as chapter one when Krishna's epithets take on an increasingly universal tone.[99] The universal message has, of course, to do with the evolution of the human monad. This is how Arjuna's references to fratricide, destruction of families, destruction of women, and mixing of castes are to be understood. He is standing at the threshold of further spiritual development, a breakthrough that inevitably involves the same kind of conflict to which Jesus alluded when he stated that he had not come to bring peace.

> There is a spiritual significance to all this, and the situation of Arjuna is well chosen to bring out great spiritual truths. He stands for the personal self, beginning to grow conscious of the Higher Self; touched and enkindled with the spiritual light of that Higher Self, yet full of dismay and terror from the realization of what obedience to the Higher Self must mean . . . Against the still, small voice of the Soul are arrayed the strong forces of the material nature, the passions, the mind. These are the opposing brothers on the field of Law.[100]

Like the Bible, Krishna teaches the necessity for losing or sacrificing life in order to live, for giving up structures which have carried us thus far in order to allow for higher, more spiritual structures, for, in effect, a new heaven and earth.[101] The path to this transformation is the path of disinterested work, the undoing of bondage to works through work itself. By this means we gradually transcend the plane of selfishness and desire and begin to hear the voice of immortality within. In effect we are "born again from above," to live under the "commands of infinite love."[102]

This conflict between self-seeking and sacrifice, or the personal self and Higher Self is the key to understanding the juxtaposition of fire and smoke, light and night, the moonlit and moonless nights in *Gita* 8.24–26. The first side represents the positive pole of a series of ascending planes, while the second represents the negative pole. The self-seekers, or those living by Vedic or ritual religion, are drawn to the negative pole and are destined to be reborn in this world, while those who have given up self-seeking, who live by the mystery teaching are drawn to the positive pole and thus ascend to eternal worlds from which they do not return.[103]

This conflict also provides the key for understanding the dramatic situation in chapter eleven of the *Gita* that parallels the book of Revelation.

> The truth would seem to be that, at a certain point in spiritual life, the ardent disciple, who has sought in all things to bring his soul into unison with the great soul, who has striven to bring his will to likeness with the Divine Will, passes through a marked spiritual experience, in which the great soul draws him upward, the Divine Will raises his consciousness to oneness with the Divine Consciousness; for a time he perceives and feels, no longer as the person but as the Oversoul, gaining a profound vision of the divine ways of life, and feeling with the infinite Power, which works through life and death alike, through sorrow and joy, through union and separation, through creation, destruction and recreation.[104]

Again we are back at what is considered the essential message of the *Gita*—selflessness or self-forgetfulness, a "ridding oneself of the heresy of separateness, self-centred vanity and egotism."[105]

CONCLUSION

This survey of theosophical treatments of the *Gita* points to remarkable continuity in the understanding of what are to be considered the essential teachings of the *Gita*. There is perhaps something here akin to a controlling orthodoxy—notwithstanding the early claims of the society that crucial for membership in the society is not what one believes but simply a commitment to the search for truth. The issue here is not creedal commitment but the overriding influence of particular ideas owing much to the writings of Blavatsky, and in the view of the society to the instruction of the Mahatmas. This is supported by the many references to the writings and ideas of H.P. Blavatsky and to the use of terminology found in Blavatsky's writings.

The commitment to particular ideas through which one is to read the *Gita* is also found in the basic view of Theosophical interpreters that the *Gita* teaches the ancient esoteric knowledge that is the fountain for all major scriptures and systems of thought. This ancient esoteric knowledge is, of course, to be found in the writings of Blavatsky which in turn are said to be based on the findings of the ancient Greeks, Chaldeans, Egyptians, and Eastern traditions. For some interpreters, the *Gita* becomes in effect a jumping off point for the explanation or expounding of Theosophical teaching, moreso than one would normally expect for scriptural interpretation or commentary. The outcome is similar to that of Shankara's *bhasya* of the *Gita*—that is, one has the feeling that a system is primary and that the *Gita* is simply being filtered through the system. The single exception to this is Chatterji's interpretation, which is viewed favorably by Theosophists even though some of its ideas run counter to what one might expect in Theosophical literature.

Aside from commitment to particular ideas, or a system of thought through which one reads the text, there is also consistency in the approach to understanding the *Gita,* that is, the allegorical approach, which remains dominant throughout. Given this, the changes one will perceive as one moves chronologically through the interpretations will not be found so much in the basic teachings which are seen in the *Gita,* as in the level of sophistication or detail in the use of the allegorical method. Thus one will move from very general lessons concerning the state and travels of the individual monad represented by Arjuna to a much more detailed use of allegory in which significance comes to be attached to the various characters on both sides, to the epithets used, and even to the weapons used.

Given the predominance of the allegorical approach, it is the esoteric or philosophical import of the *Gita* and not the historical concerns that receives the emphasis. While the historical material is sometimes acknowledged, for the most part it is passed over for the sake of getting to the real essence of the text. Thus Subba Row in his early interpretation points out that Vyasa, the author, "looked upon Arjuna as a man, or rather the real monad in man; and upon Krishna as the Logos, or the spirit that comes to save man."[106] The real import of the *Gita* faithfully repeated by Theosophical interpreters from 1881 on is that we are all Arjuna called upon to do battle with our lower selves. To quote Subba Row:

> We are each of us called upon to kill out all our passions and desires, not that they are all necessarily evil in themselves, but that their influence must be annihilated before we can establish ourselves on the higher planes. The position of Arjuna is intended to typify that of a chela, who is called upon to face the Dweller on the Threshold. As the guru prepares his chela for the trials of initiation by philosophical teaching, so at the critical point Krishna proceeds to instruct Arjuna.[107]

It is this lesson which is developed in greater and greater degrees of detail and sophistication by Theosophical interpreters. We come back again to the basic Theosophical position concerning life and the human being. Life is an evolutionary process in which individuals evolve from lower to higher, from grosser more physical forms of being to more spiritual forms of being. It is a process which involves constant conflict between those powers and forces which have developed and those which are developing to fit us for a higher plane of life. This evolutionary framework informs the various interpretations of the *Gita*.

Any substantial distinction between the various interpretations would lie in the area of their practical use and social and ethical implications. Here, I believe, we find two broad categories of interpretation. First, all interpretations see the value of the *Gita* in more general terms as reminding individuals that they must join in the struggle to further the process of evolution in order to overcome the forces of ego, desire, and selfishness and to further the development of a human brotherhood characterized by love and selflessness. Second, there are those, particularly Row, Besant, The Dreamer and The Brahmin, who would put the *Gita* to more particular use—that is, as a support for reform efforts and nationalistic aspirations in an India seen as a light that will lead the world to true insight and thus to liberation. This category of interpretations has as part of its agenda the reform and liberation of India. Above all, this liberation of India requires the elimination of slavery to pernicious religious and social customs and religious systems that have caused her to lose sight of the true esoteric teachings of her scriptures. This would characterize the approach of Indian interpreters as well as a few Western interpreters like Besant. The result is a definition or redefinition of Hinduism in terms of Theosophical or primieval teachings that takes issue with a variety of Hindu traditions that are seen to have led India into decadence. Western interpreters, on the other hand, are not so intent to define true Hinduism as they are to spread the gospel of the universal religion, which just happens to be Theosophy. If there is a more specific agenda it is Western in orientation—that is, the value of the teachings of the *Gita* is seen in its potential to rid Western society of the excesses of individualism and of false interpretations of its own religious traditions, particularly Christianity. This would seem to echo a concern that surfaces frequently in Blavatsky's writings.

Whether Indian or Western then, the interpretations tend to proceed on two levels. There is first the general level having to do with the education and evolutionary development of the human monad, a level which transcends any local, national, geographic or particular religious concerns. There is secondly, the more specific level in which the message of the *Gita* is applied to more particular concerns, national, religious, etc. On this level at least the interpreters could be said to be influenced by the particular worlds or societies in which they are raised or have chosen to move. Beyond the more general message, the *Gita* is made to speak to the concerns, the changes, and the ethos of these societies.

CHAPTER TWO

Bankim Chandra Chatterji's New Hinduism and the Bhagavadgita

AJIT RAY

Bankim Chandra Chatterji was born in Kanthalpara, a village of West Bengal, on June 26th, 1838. At the age of 20, he was the first Indian to receive his B.A. degree from the University of Calcutta, having studied languages, History and Geography, Mathematics and Natural Philosophy, Natural History and Physical Sciences, and Mental and Moral Sciences. In the same year he was appointed by the Lt. Governor of Bengal to the post of Deputy Magistrate and Deputy Collector, and while in service took his Law degree from Presidency College, Calcutta. He married twice and had three daughters. In 1891 he retired from Government service, and he died in 1894.

As an administrator, Bankim was efficient. C.E. Buckland in his *Bengal under Lieutenant-Governors* wrote:

> He rendered good service in a number of districts . . . While in charge of the Khulna sub-division he helped very largely in suppressing river *dacoities* and establishing peace and order in the eastern canals.[1]

But it was not for his services as a prominent member of the Provincial Service that he is to be remembered; it was his contribution to the world of letters that made him famous. Nirad C. Chaudhuri praised him as:

> a man who probably had the most powerful intellect and the best intellectual equipment of any Indian in the nineteenth century, and who was the creator of Hindu nationalism and the writer of the *Vande Mataram* song.[2]

In 1864 Bankim started serialising an English novel, *Rajmohan's Wife,* in the *Indian Field.* When the novel was not a success, he came to believe, like his predecessor, Michael Madhusudan Dutt, that he could not fully express his creative drive in a foreign language. He started writing in Bengali, and his first novel *Durgeshanandinī* appeared in 1865. "After that there was no going back for him."[3]

In the beginning of the nineteenth century the criticism by Christian missionaries of some of the social and religious practices of Hinduism prompted leaders among the Hindus into reaction. Some opted for reform while others rallied for the preservation of old customs and traditions. Rammohan Roy (1774-1833), relying heavily on the teachings of Vedanta, defended essential 'Hinduism,' but at the same time he deplored and condemned certain practices which had crept into 'popular Hinduism,' such as image worship, animal sacrifice, and widow-burning. He pointed out that personal gods as mentioned in the *Puranas,* and image worship, were meant for people who could not comprehend the nature of the unqualified and formless Brahman that Advaita Vedanta teaches is the ultimate reality.

During the fifties, the period of Bankim's youth, Calcutta witnessed the phenomenon of Young Bengal, electric with thought and loaded with enthusiasm. Western ideas had already disturbed the placid waters of traditional Indian life, and the rough going, critical thinking, and heavy drinking of early Young Bengal were subsiding gradually. Deeper acquaintance with Western ideas brought new and sustained judgments of what were strengths and weaknesses of Indian tradition. A new appraisal of India's past had already begun, and the men around Bankim were calmer and more temperate. English education and the study of the philosophical systems of Kant, Fichte, Bentham, Mill and Spencer aroused Bankim's critical faculties, and Auguste Comte's positivism deeply influenced his mind, but "neither the Utilitarianism of the Benthamite school, nor the evolutionary Hedonism of Spencer, nor the godless Positivism of Comte satisfied him."[4] His intellect found satisfaction in the study of Hindu philosophy and religion. But the methods of Western philosophy shaped his approach towards religion, and he tried to apply a scientific, critical, and rational method to the great problems of life and society.

Like Rammohan, Bankim was also involved in a religious controversy,[5] and like Rammohan he argued in favour of an understanding of Hinduism. But unlike him he did not rely on the Vedanta. "The whole of Hindu religious philosophy is probably post-Vedic, and serves to mark the end of separation between the ancient and modern religion of India."[6] Instead, he relied on the *Gita* and the *Puranas.* He glorified the personal god Krishna, and even justified image worship. And also unlike Rammohan, Bankim did not take a defensive stand—"Hinduism does not consider itself placed on its defence."[7] To him, "Hindudharma is superior to all other religions."[8] The answer to the problems which beset Hindu society was, he thought, to revive Hinduism to its purity. And as Bankim grew older "the sense of his exalted mission gripped him. He came more and more to believe that the solution of India's problem lay in the revival of Hinduism, the mystical and intuitive religion of the *Gita* reinterpreted for the new India".[9]

BANKIM'S NEW HINDUISM

In a letter to *The Statesman,* Bankim tried to present a brief outline of Hinduism. Like many other developed religious systems, he wrote, it consists of a doctrinal basis, or creed, a system of worship, and a code of morals more or less dependent upon the doctrinal basis. The doctrinal basis consists of (1) dogmas formulated, explained and illustrated in a mass of philosophical literature; and (2) legends which form the legitimate subject of the *Puranas.* The value of the legends is inferior to that of the philosophy "in the depths of which are laid, broad and solid, the foundations of modern Hinduism." The Hindu philosopher Kapila made the distinction between spirit and matter, *puruṣa* and *prakṛti,* and in the hands of the eclectics, this conception has taken its place as the backbone of modern Hinduism. It runs through the whole world of Hindu thought, shaping the legends, prescribing the rites, and even running through the secular literature. As the new religion grew out of the old, the time-honored names of the Vedic gods were retained, but grouped under new ideas. But there were difficulties:

> The Citadel had been stormed and battered down by the Buddhists and the philosophers themselves, and had to be reconstructed out of the old materials but on new and more solid foundations. Pantheism and polytheism, philosophy and mysticism, all lent a hand; and out of this bold eclecticism rose the beautiful religion which I do not believe to be of Divine origin, but which I accept as the perfection of human wisdom.[10]

Much of Hindu ritual, according to Bankim, is mere mummery, and is rejected with deserved contempt, he claims, by educated

Hindus. Idolatry, which is generally treated by Christian missionaries as covering the whole field of Hinduism, is really a small fraction of it, and though it is no doubt a part of Hinduism, it is not an essential part. It is not enjoined as compulsory. The daily worship of the Hindu is not idolatrous, and "a man may never have entered a temple and may yet be an orthodox Hindu". Bankim tried to provide a philosophical justification for the use of images in worship:

> The true explanation consists of the ever true relations of the subjective Ideal to its objective Reality. Man is by instinct a poet and an artist. The passionate yearnings of the heart for the Ideal in beauty, in power, and in purity, must find an expression in the world of the Real. Hence proceed all poetry and all art. Exactly in the same way the ideal of the Divine in man receives a form from him, and the form is an image. The existence of Idols is as justifiable as that of the tragedy of Hamlet or of that of Prometheus. The religious worship of idols is as justifiable as the intellectual worship of Hamlet or Prometheus. The homage we owe to the ideal of the human realised in art is admiration. The homage we owe to the ideal of the Divine realised in idolatry is worship.[11]

Hindudharma should not be identified with the *Dharmashastras.* Whatever is found in the *Dharmashastras* is not necessarily *Hindudharma.*[12] *Hindudharma* is eternal and catholic, while the *Dharmashastras* are of much later origin and are parochial; the degeneration of Hindus, Bankim says, when they mistook the dictates of the *Dharmashastras* as their *dharma.* Religion is nothing but truth, and if there is any untruth in the *Manusmriti,* or in the *Mahabharata,* or even in the *Vedas,* it should be discarded as anti-religion. There are many Hindus who think that the *Vedas* contain infallible truth. Bankim pointed out that his writings were not meant for such persons.[13] Bankim also argued in favour of sea-voyages for the Hindus which were prohibited by the dictates of the *Dharmashastras.* In a letter to Kumar Binayakrishna Deb, he wrote that whatever was good for the people was *dharma,* and if something was good for the people, why should they shun it because of some silly injunctions of the *Dharmashastras?* Sea-voyages were beneficial to people, and therefore, there was nothing wrong in them as far as *dharma* was concerned.[14]

Bankim incorporated his ideas of regenerated Hindu religion in the two volumes of *Krishnacaritra* (1886) and the *Dharmatattva* (1888). In the *Krishnacaritra* he discussed not only the religious teachings of Krishna but also their relevance to the advancement of Hindu society. Krishna was the ideal man, "the Wisest and the Greatest of the Hindus."[15] His teaching was as sublime as his personality. The center of his doctrine was selflessness and purity of mind. His objective was to bring about the moral and political regeneration of society, spread religion, and establish a kingdom based on religion. And "if religion is the source of true happiness," Bankim wrote in his *Dharmatattva,* "the whole human life should be governed by religion." Most of the religions are concerned with only God and life beyond. But the Hindu religion emcompasses this life, the life beyond, God, man, all living beings, the whole creation. "Is there any other religion," he asked "so all-encompassing, so full of bliss and so pure?"[16]

In the process of formulating the picture of an ideal Krishna, Bankim retained from the *Puranas* what appropriate details could be gathered about the childhood and youth of Krishna, rejecting and interpreting symbolically all the passages which did not serve his purpose including those he considered indecent morally. For the adult Krishna he accepted only the testimony of the original *Mahabharata,* refusing to accept the legends about him. Bipin Chandra Pal mentioned that in his act of interpretation and readjustment, Bankim very closely followed the canons of Renan in his studies of the life of Jesus and the early history of Christianity:

> Like Renan who had formed in his mind a picture of Jesus Christ in accordance with the moral and spiritual ideals presented through the Gospel narratives and then applied the picture of Christ to critically examine the Gospel narratives themselves, accepting as true only such portions of these narratives as seemed to be in consonance with his own fancy picture, and rejecting as false and spurious additions all these things in these narratives that were inconsistent with this picture of the character of the Master, Bankim Chandra also first formed in his own mind a picture of Shree Krishna as the Ideal Man; he applied this picture to his examination of the Krishna legend current among our people, and rejected everything that did not harmonise with it.[17]

BANKIM'S ŚRĪMADBHAGAVADGĪTĀ

The *Śrīmadbhagavadgītā,* Bankim's commentary on the *Gita,* was first published in the Bengali journal *Pracāra,* and afterward appeared in book form in 1902, eight years after his death. It was an unfinished work; he commented on the *Gita,* up to the 19th verse of chapter four. He pointed out in the introduction that though it might seem superfluous to bring out another commentary on the *Gita* when there were so many, he realized that one along the model of Western argument and logic was necessary. The Western educated Bengalis, acquainted with Western types of thinking since their childhood, could not often comprehend the implications of ancient Indian thoughts and beliefs, and consequently, could not properly understand the sayings of the sages even when they were translated. Bankim had decided to bring out the message of the *Gita* to this new elite group in a way which they could understand and appreciate. The commentary was part of Bankim's program of re-explanation and readjustment undertaken to revive Hindu purity.

The *Gita* preaches *svadharma* (duty of a person in a community) and *nishkāma karma* (selfless action). Action is the law of life, and selfless action is the essence of religion. Hinduism is a religion of action which lays down duties for each individual. In his commentary on *Gita* 2.11, Bankim thus explained *svadharma.* The work in a community can be classified in three broad categories: (1) production; (2) organisation (including revenue collection); and (3) protection, or security. Groups involved in these three types of work are, in Hindu terms, Shudra, Vaishya, and Kshatriya respectively. And those who earn knowledge to know the Ultimate Reality *(Brahman)* are the Brahmins. To perform one's own duty is a meritorious act which leads one to his Spiritual world. There is *svadharma* also in non-Hindu societies, according to profession (i.e. a cobbler is a Shudra, an academic is a Brahmin etc.) With the change in profession, the classification changes (i.e. a cobbler becomes a Kshatriya when he is elected the president of the country). The only difference is that in a Hindu society *svadharma* is hereditary, while in the others it is not.[18]

Bankim's elaborate commentary on the two verses 2.12 and 2.13, gives his views on the immortality of the soul and its transmigration, or reincarnation—the two fundamental ideas of Hinduism. A person is made of a body and a soul. While the body is subjected to death and decay, the soul is immortal and indestructible. Death signifies the end of the body but not of the soul which is everlasting. Almost all the religions believe in the conception of a soul which is separate from the body. The opponents of this belief are the scientists who say that there is nothing more than the body, and that there is no proof of the existence of the soul. Here Bankim tried to be objective in his argument and quoted Mill *(Three Essays on Religion)* to present the views of scientists on the topics of body and soul:

> Thought and consciousness, though mentally distinguishable from the body, may not be a substance separable from it, but a result of it, standing in relation to it, like that of a tune to the musical instrument on which it is played; and that the arguments used to provide that the soul does not die with the body, would equally prove that the tune does not die with the instrument but survives its destruction and continues to exist apart.

For the knowledge of a thing science relies on direct perception *(pratyakṣa)* only; it avoids assumption *(anumāna).* A body is visible, therefore science believes its existence. A soul, on the other hand, is invisible, has never been an object of direct perception, and so science does not believe in its existence. Science is, no doubt, sincere in its investigation, but its field of investigation is rather narrow; it cannot go beyond a certain point. Consequently, science cannot comprehend things which are outside its limited area. Take the example of a diver in a deep sea. He can descend only as far as the rope allows him to go; what is beyond is out of his reach, and he will never know the existence of the treasures which lie in the deep. So are the scientists. Their knowledge is confined to this visible world only; beyond that nothing exists.[19]

If we believe in the soul's existence and its immortality, there then arises the question of what happens to it after the death of the body. To this there can be found answers; the soul (1) becomes a spirit (belief of many primitive tribes); (2) goes to heaven or hell (Christians and Muslims); (3) transmigrates to a new body (Buddhists); and (4) becomes one with the Eternal Soul *(paramātman).* The last three beliefs are part of Hinduism. The Hindus believe that in this world the individual soul *(ātman)* separates itself from the Eternal Soul *(paramātman)* under the influence of an iilusionary power *(māyā),* and involves itself in a cycle of birth and death. It can free itself from the influence of that power in three ways: (1) by acquiring knowledge regarding the nature of the world and the Reality (i.e. by *jñāna*); (2) by selfless action in this world (i.e. by karma); and (3) by deep devotion to the Supreme Being (i.e. by *bhakti*).

When *ātman* frees itself from the bondage of *māyā,* the individuality of the soul vanishes, the cycle of birth and death ceases, and the soul itself becomes one with the Eternal Soul which is nothing but pure consciousness *(caitanya).* In Hindu terms this is liberation *(mokṣa).* Those souls which are still under the influence of *māyā,* and are not destined to be free, take new bodies after the death of the previous ones after being in heaven or hell for a length of time determined by their actions *(karma)* in this world. And the cycle of birth and death goes on. The Christian belief in eternal heaven or eternal hell, raises some problems. There is nobody in this world whose actions are absolutely good, or absolutely bad. If somebody has done some good deeds and some bad, where should his soul go? If it goes to heaven permanently, why is he not punished for his sins? On the other hand, if the soul goes to hell permanently, why is he not rewarded for his good deeds? So Bankim backed the theory of transmigration as the more reasonable explanation. Anticipating that his skeptical, Western-educated Bangali readers would not be very convinced by his argument, he quoted several Western scholars like Tylor *(Primitive Culture),* Carpenter *(Mental Physiology)* and Samuel Johnson *(Oriental Religions)* to support the theory, and he concluded that (1) it was difficult to disprove transmigration; (2) there was a strong case in its favor; and (3) belief in the immortality of the soul naturally led to the belief in its transmigration.[20]

Hinduism inherited from the *Upanishads* the concept of an unqualified, unmanifested Brahman, and the *Gita,* the first principal work on *bhakti,* brought into Hinduism the conception of a qualified, manifested Ishvara (i.e. Krishna). Are these two conceptions contradictory? Bankim did not think so. The realization of the nature of an unmanifested Brahman and the devoted worship of a manifested Ishvara are two different ways to the same goal. They are not contradictory but complimentary, and together they complete the idea of the divine in Hinduism.[21] But Bankim himself seemed to favor the idea of a manifested, personal god when in his *Dharmattattva* he quoted Krishna's reply to Arjuna on the same topic:

> The difficulty of those whose thoughts are set on the Unmanifested is greater, for the goal of the Unmanifested is hard to reach by the embodied beings.[22]

Conclusion

For his reformation of Hinduism, Rammohan relied more on the *Upanishads,* and never took the *Gita* seriously. In the latter half of the century, when the idea of nationalism was establishing itself firmly on Indian soil, the *Upanishads* with their sublime thought of the Supreme, could not stimulate the nationalistic tendencies that were then needed, and it is no wonder that Hindu leaders of nationalism from Bankim and Aurobindo to Tilak and Gandhi all relied on the *Gita,* which depicts Hinduism as a religion of action. In contrast to the *Upanishads,* the *Gita* is amenable to an interpretation that provides motivation for supreme sacrifice at the altar of the nation. And, as M. K. Halder pointed out, it was not necessary for the Hindu nationalist intellectuals to be embarrassed by decidedly non-human, individualistic aspects of Hindu rituals and tradition:

> Bankim's interpretation of Hindu religion and the *Gītā* as containing historical, moral and philosophical doctrines of the highest and best order fitted in very well with the double-faith agglomerative attitude of the Hindus.[23]

The duty of a commentator, as Bankim pointed out, was to interpret the text in the light of prevailing conditions of the time, no matter whether the text belonged to the *Gita,* or to the Bible; whether it was divine, or came from a prophet.[24] The interpretations of the past are not always applicable to the changing world of the present, and to keep a message alive it is necessary to reinterpret it from time to time according to the changing ideas in society. During his time Bankim was convinced that:

> Hinduism is in need of a reformation . . . reformed and purified it may yet stand forth before the world as the noblest system of individual and social culture available to the Hindus even in the age of progress. I have certainly no serious hope of progress in India except in Hinduism—in Hinduism reformed, regenerated and purified.[25]

In his interpretation he intended to convey a message of reassurance to Hindus whose social and religious ideas were badly battered by the incoming ideas of the West. What he accomplished was not a synthesis of two ideas—old and new, but an evaluation of the old in the light of the new, so that it could be understood properly in the mind of modern humanity. The Hinduism which Bankim taught embraced the whole of human life—a synthesis of enjoyment and renunciation. It provided the moral foundations upon which the Hindu society and state were to be built. And the central figure of that reconstruction and regeneration was Krishna—the ideal, the wise, the eternal man, who brought to this world the richness of human virtues,[26] and who proclaimed a religion which was elevating, universal, and beneficial to all.[27] In his admiration, Bankim paid homage to that ideal man who

> by the strength of his arm subdued the wicked and united India by his wisdom, who by the power of his superior knowledge proclaimed a unique self-less religion, and who in the land of the Vedas, could say "Dharma is not in the words of the Vedas, but Dharma is what conduces the well-being of man." I salute him, whether he be god or man, who is the source of all strength, all virtue, all truth, and of all love.[28]

CHAPTER THREE

Tilak and the Bhagavadgita*'s Doctrine of Karmayoga*

ROBERT W. STEVENSON

Bal Gangadhar Tilak wrote his work on the *Gita, Śrīmad Bhagavadgītā Rahasya,*[1] in Mandalay jail during the winter months of 1910–11. At the time he was serving a sentence of six years' deportation imposed by the British colonial government in India for sedition.

That he wrote such a work in such a place points dramatically to those elements of Tilak's life that must be taken into consideration when attempting to evaluate and understand his interpretation of the *Gita.* He was, on the one hand, a devout and scholarly brahmin, steeped in the religious and historical traditions of Hindu India; and, on the other, an ardent nationalist politician whose main objective in life was to bring India Home Rule or *swarāj,* independence from British rule.

Tilak was born in Maharashtra in 1856 into a Vaishnava family of Chitpavan brahmins.[2] This was a caste whose members had played important roles as prime ministers and heads of the great Maratha confederacy, prior to its defeat by the British in 1818. As a descendant of such men Tilak would have no difficulty in combining the roles of brahmin scholar and active politician.

After receiving a solid grounding in Sanskrit, mathematics and Marathi from his father, Tilak continued his education at Deccan College in Poona and at Elphinstone College in Bombay, receiving his B.A. in 1876 and an L.L.B. three years later. His was a mixture of Indian and Western education.

By 1881, Tilak was teaching at the New English School in Poona and editing an English language weekly, *Mahratta.* The latter was openly nationalist, aiming to educate the Maharashtran intelligentsia to the need for independence from British rule. By 1890 Tilak had taken over full ownership of *Mahratta* and also of *Keshari,* a Marathi weekly with similar policies and objectives.

In the meantime two other significant developments had occurred. The first was that Tilak had entered the lists of public debate and activity on matters of social, religious and educational reform through the Deccan Education Society and the newspapers; the second was his involvement in political life.

With regard to the first, the major reform issues of Tilak's time concerned such subjects as female education, the age of female consent in marriage, and widows' rights. Details of his arguments against such reforms are less important here than is the basic position from which Tilak advanced these arguments. Fundamentally, he opposed any reforms that might be imposed upon the Hindu community by British law. He claimed that he did not resist reform *per se,* only that it should arise in conformity with *dharmaśāstra,* out of an educated Hindu community. Thus religious, social and educational reform proposals were to be judged in the light of Hindu religious tradition. Furthermore Tilak's knowledge of Hindu scriptures enabled him to argue authoritatively on the relative merits of existing practices and demerits of proposed reforms. This attitude won him the support of much of the orthodox Hindu community which felt threatened by various reform proposals. He became not only the defender of the tradition but a leader in the counter-attack against foreign interference.[3]

Unfortunately, Tilak's position also obliged him to excuse or depreciate the conditions that had initiated the calls for reform. To many reformers, both British and Indian, these were not condonable under any circumstances, and Tilak's opposition on mainly religious grounds seemed a cynical exercise in political opportunism.

As to Tilak's formal entry into politics, many of the issues that concerned Tilak and on which he expressed himself in *Mahratta* and in his reform activities, had clear political implications. *Swarāj* was the most obvious of these but by no means the only one. It was inevitable then that Tilak should move into the field where he could apply direct action towards the realization of his objectives. In 1889 he participated in the meeting of the Bombay Provincial Conference of the Indian National Congress. He was elected a delegate to the meeting of the Congress itself in the same year, and so began the political involvement that was to last the rest of his life.

From this time on there is constant evidence of Tilak's endeavours to awaken in India feelings of pride and self-sufficiency in her ancient culture and traditions, and to build on these feelings a pragmatic political program.

Aurobindo Ghose was to say of this period:

> To bring in the mass of the people, to found the greatness of the future on the greatness of the past, to infuse Indian politics with Indian religious fervour and spirituality, are the indispensable conditions for a great and powerful political awakening in India. Others, writers, thinkers, spiritual leaders, had seen this truth. Mr. Tilak was the first to bring it into the actual field of practical politics.[4]

A brief examination of some of this evidence will help illustrate the role played by Tilak's work on the *Gita.* The main thrust of Tilak's efforts was towards Hindu India. His attitude towards Indian Muslims has been a source of debate, but we cannot enter into it here.

In 1893 he revived a Peshwa family festival honoring the birthday of the elephant-headed god Ganesha, helping it become a ten day, public festival of speeches, singing, music, and great parades with images of Ganesha—in short a Hindu celebration for Hindu society. Three years later Tilak supported the establishment of a festival in honour of Shivaji, a great Marathi leader who had used deception to defeat an occupying Muslim army in 1659. In his remarks at the inaugural event Tilak claimed that the object was not to encourage an imitation of Shivaji'a deeds; but to develop in the people the spirit and courage that had motivated Shivaji.[5] Nevertheless, it took no great stretch of the imagination to move from the idea of honoring a hero to that of emulating his actions, a point that was not lost on the British and caused the Muslim community concern also.

At the same time, Tilak was stressing his nationalist priorities in a revealing way: the nation was to come before everything else:

> We must raise a nation on [t]his soil. Love of nation is one's first duty. Next comes religion and the Government. Our duty to the nation will be the first.[6]

Unlike earlier reformers who had tended to stress religious, social and educational reforms before political ones, Tilak held that *swarāj* was the first priority; and that only with the power that comes from self rule would other reforms truly be possible.[7] Furthermore he invested the concept of *swarāj* with Hindu religious and traditional values.

To Tilak the word was a *mantra*. He compared *swarāj* to the *Rig Veda,* the origin of the sciences. He claimed that *swadeshi* (the reliance upon home-made goods) and boycott (of British-made goods) derived from *swarāj;* and he likened *swadeshi* and *swarāj* to the *Yajur* and *Sama Vedas* which are formed from the *Rig Veda.*[8] The thoughts of Hindus were directed back to their common heritage—the *Vedas,* the *Gita,* the *Ramayana*—to unite and motivate them:

> If we lay stress on it [the common heritage] forgetting all the minor differences that exist between different sects, then by the grace of Providence we shall ere long be able to consolidate all the different sects into a mighty Hindu nation. This ought to be the ambition of every Hindu.[9]

Yet the nation that Hindus ought to form and to which they owed their duty was not merely a political entity. It had God's support and it *was* in a sense God.

> . . . It is the special divine plan that we must achieve success at some time. God and our nation are not separate, on the contrary, our nation is one of God's forms.[10]

Such an identification can perhaps hold under the Advaita Vedanta system to which Tilak subscribed. In it all things, including one's country, are manifestations of the Supreme Brahman; and it becomes possible to deduce from this that service of country is, in effect, service of God.

As Tilak continued to build popular support with this religious nationalism, he also worked to advance his political program. He became one of the leaders of the "Nationalist" or "Extremist" group in the Indian National Congress. The leaders of the Congress in its early years were products of the English education system established in India and were firm believers in Western ideals of freedom, equality and justice. Their political philosophy was also informed by Western ideas and they were concerned chiefly with political, economic, industrial and social reform, along European lines, to be achieved by constitutional means within the structure of the system of British rule. These "moderates" tended to preserve a distinction between their religious and political views.[11]

Towards the end of the nineteenth century there began to rise to prominence in the Congress men, like Tilak, whose religious nationalism was combined with increasingly impatient political aspirations. They rejected concepts of political activity and government based on foreign ideals and philosophy. What India needed was her own political system, evolved out of her own values and traditions. For her national "self-realization" India needed to be in control of all the constitutive elements of the nation (e.g. judicial, financial, industrial, and political). The aim of the "extremists" then, was not cooperation with British rule and relative autonomy within it, but non-cooperation, complete political autonomy and national independence.

The "extremists" worked to educate the Indian masses in the agitation for *swarāj* and the practices of *swadeshi*, boycott, and non-cooperation. They fomented and seized upon popular reaction against British political moves, such as the partition of Bengal in 1905, and eventually gained control of the Indian National Congress. It was the extremist policies that finally held sway in the independence movement.

So key a figure in the extremist movement was Tilak that Valentine Chirol named him "the father of Indian unrest."[12] The title caught on, for it served both as an accusation by his opponents, and an accolade from his supporters. It is simply not possible to touch even briefly on the varied whirl of activities and events—the newspaper battles, court cases, jail sentences, political struggles, travels, and speeches—that characterized Tilak's life until his death in 1920. The main themes and the rationale of his activities have been set out. They can be summed up in his words:

> I regard India as my Motherland and my Goddess, the people in India my kith and kin, and loyal and steadfast work for their political and social emancipation my highest religion and duty.[13]

THE GĪTĀ RAHASYA

Where in all this does the *Gita* fit in? By Tilak's own account,[14] he first encountered the poem in 1872 when he read a commentary on it to his dying father. It was presumably, then, regarded as an important work, though not much used in the home. Conceiving a liking for the poem, Tilak continued to study it along with commentaries and criticisms in various languages.[15] The many differences he found in interpretations of the *Gita* caused Tilak to doubt the objectivity of the commentators and he therefore undertook an independent study of his own.[16]

Tilak developed his interpretation over many years, for he records lecturing on the *Gita* several times, e.g. at Nagpur in January, 1902.[17] However, it was not until the winter months of 1910–11, in Mandalay jail, that he found time to write it down. It was published in 1915 and was well received across the country. By 1933, it had appeared in five Marathi, eight Hindi and two Gujarati editions, and one each in Bengali, Kanarese, Telegu and Tamil.[18]

This work is not the usual, classical, verse by verse commentary. Tilak begins with an essay of fifteen chapters on subjects and doctrines contained in the *Gita,* together with arguments and comparisons with other religions and philosophies. This is the *Gītā Rahasya,* "the Esoteric Import of the Gītā."[19] In a second section, Tilak then provides a verse by verse translation of and consecutive commentary on the poem.[20] He also presents an Appendix to deal with matters that he considers extraneous to establishing the real meaning of the *Gita.*[21] These include the relationship of the work to Hindu texts and Buddhist literature, its history, its relationship to the Bhagavata sect, and its influence on Christian scriptures. Taken as a whole, Tilak's *Gītā Rahasya* is very much a combination of the "traditional Indian" and "modern scholarship" types of interpretation discussed by scholars such as J. A. B. van Buitenen and S. K. Belvalkar.[22]

The independent, impartial conclusion reached by Tilak is that the *Gita* teaches the philosophy of Energism or *karmayoga.*[23] The latter, he claims, is popularly understood as conforming to the requirements of *varṇāśramadharma,* and refraining from *saṃnyāsa,* the ascetic renunciation of action.[24] Tilak is fully aware, of course, that the *Gita* teaches several possible paths to *mokṣa* and he takes care to try to "locate" them adequately within the teaching of Energism. The following is one example of his efforts (not always clear) to accommodate these paths to the overall requirement of *karmayoga:*

> . . . The Gītā has propounded the device of performing Action in such a way that one ultimately attains Release without committing sin, namely, the Karma-yoga founded on Knowledge, in which Devotion is the principal factor, after it had fully expounded the Philosophy of Action and Non-Action, and also the various paths of attaining Release according to pure Vedānta Philosophy, and had established that no man is free from Action, and that Action should never be given up.[25]

Before proceeding to a more detailed discussion of Tilak's interpretation of the *Gita,* it should be noted that he was a pragmatic politician and an ardent nationalist who strove to motivate his people to political activity on the basis of traditional Hindu values. The *Gita* was a popular text that could serve as a natural focal point of those values, and that could also legitimize Hindu nationalist aspirations and activities. It should be no surprise, then, that Tilak saw in the *Gita* a call to action from God.

The "pure Vedanta Philosophy" which Tilak refers to above is none other than the *Advaita Vedanta* generally supported by the school of Shankara; and Tilak holds that the latter's *Gitabhashya* is more valuable than other commentaries because it accurately identifies the *Gita* philosophy as non-dualistic.[26] Since Shankara's philosophy is relatively well-known, for the sake of brevity, we will point out only that Tilak's exposition of *Gita* philosophy follows that of Shankara fairly closely in such major areas as the concept of Brahman, the theory of creation, the doctrine of the human being, and the nature of bondage.[27] However, on the question of the means to liberation, Tilak maintains that Shankara, who holds that the only means is knowledge *(jñāna),* has forced his own doctrine upon the *Gita.*[28]

TILAK'S DEVELOPMENT OF KARMAYOGA IN THE GITA

To support his contention that the *Gita* teaches *karmayoga,* Tilak is at some pains to develop the history of that doctrine in the Hindu tradition. Briefly, chapters ten and eleven of his essay and part four of his appendix provide most of this history. It is concerned with the development of the *karma-* and *jñānakaṇda,* as paths of spiritual advancement, and with their harmonization in a third path, that of action *and* knowledge *(jñānakarmasamuccaya).* In the *Gita,* claims Tilak, Krishna revives the original Bhagavata doctrine, first taught by Nara and Narayana, and characterized by the attainment of knowledge combined with the performance of desireless action—in other words the *karmayoga* doctrine.[29]

Of more interest here, however, is how and where Tilak develops his *karmayoga* theory within the *Gita* itself. A review of the physical structure of Tilak's commentary shows that the chapters on which he comments at greatest length are, in decreasing order: three, fifteen, four, six, and (approximately equal) two and eight.[30]

Their lengthier commentary is explained in part by the presence of one or more long passages: For example three to three and three-quarter pages each for *Gita* 3.17–19; 6.3; 8 Introduction; and 15.1;

and two to two and two-thirds pages each for *Gita* 2.16, 45, 46; 3.9; 4.1–3; and 8.3–4.

Of the five longest passages, three (3.17–19; 4.17–18; 6.3) show how controversial verses, interpreted by others in support of renunciation or Mimamsa ritual or devotion, do really support *karmayoga.* Of the six somewhat shorter passages listed above, four (2.45, 46; 3.9; 4.1–3) deal with the necessity, history, and efficacy of desireless action.

The lengthy commentary on certain chapters is also generally explained by the opportunities they aford Tilak for *karmayoga* discussion as compared with other subjects. It is hardly a surprise that chapter three, entitled *karmayoga* in the *Gita,* is Tilak's longest. In it he maintains a pattern of relatively lengthy passages (in addition to those indicated in the previous paragraph) e.g. *Gita* 3.4–5, 8.25–26, all discussing the necessity of action and duty and the contribution of action to the world's welfare *(lokasaṃgraha).* Chapter 15 is an anomaly in our list of long commentary in that it gains its place by means of one lengthy comment (on the *aśvattha* tree) in one of the shortest chapters in the poem.

With chapter four the emphasis on *karmayoga* emerges again. It is entitled *jñānakarmasaṃnyāsayoga,* but for Tilak the renunciation here is to be of the fruits of action accompanied by the dedication of that action to the Supreme.[31] The longer passages of commentary (on 4.17–18 and 4.1–3) discuss the nature of action to refute *saṃnyāsa* and Mimamsa positions, and to establish that the *Gita*'s *karmayoga* is that of the early Bhagavata tradition. A series of lengthy passages for 4.22–31 expounds on the nature of sacrifice, understood to include all actions performed selflessly, on the necessity of performing duty desirelessly whether they involve household rituals or world affairs; here sacrifice is identified with *karmayoga.*[32]

While chapter 6 is entitled *dhyānayoga,* Tilak refers to the mental exercises of *Gita* 6.10 ff. as *Patanjalayoga.* Its end result, *samādhi,* is the "highest stage of *Karma-Yoga.*"[33] *Gita* 6.3, has been interpreted by others to mean that *karma* is preliminary to total renunciation of action. In his longest passage of commentary in the chapter, Tilak refutes this interpretation in favor of the necessity of continuing activity. At *Gita* 6.40–45, Tilak argues that desire-prompted ritual purifies one and leads to desireless action—*karmayoga.* The superiority of the *karmayogin* to the *tapasyin, jñānin* (or *saṃnyāsin*) and Mimamsaka is put forward at *Gita* 6.46. And at the next verse Tilak maintains the subordinate position of devotion (there equated with dhyāna), knowledge and Patanjalayoga as methods for attaining the "Equability of Reason" *(samabuddhi)* necessary to *karmayoga.*[34]

The structure of chapter two provides an interesting case for this type of examination. Verses 1–10 set the scene for the two major lines of exposition in the chapter. The first of these, on Sankhya, which is generally associated with knowledge and renunciation, is expounded in verses 11–38 The second, on Yoga, generally associated with action, runs from verse 39 to chapter's end. The average length of commentary per verse increases by about 50 percent from the Sankhya to the Yoga section.

This rather brief summary of a detailed analysis verefies that Tilak concentrates on the development of *karmayoga* far more than on any other theme. Let us now examine his doctrine of liberation.

Tilak understands the *Gita* to show that man is bound in *saṃsāra* because a) he is ignorant of the true identity of Atman and Brahman; b) his accumulated karma holds him in *saṃsāra;* c) he acts with desire as his motive (so will be bound in future).[35] The process of liberation, then, can be understood in terms of counteracting those three factors. The main paths of liberation are *jñāna,* karma and *bhakti;* but before discussing them it is useful to analyze the meaning Tilak gives to three recurring terms: *jñāna, karman, yoga.*

While Tilak sees several kinds of *jñāna* analyzed in terms of the *guṇas* in *Gita* 18.20–22, the most significant one is the highest or *sāttvika jñāna.* This combines not only the knowledge but the actual experience of the fact that there is one fundamental Atman/Brahman/ Parameshvara of which apparent diversity is a manifestation.[36] This liberating knowledge is the common goal of the three paths—though the paths are not consequently considered identical. *Jñāna,* when used in reference to the process of *jñānamarga,* has other meanings.

In the *Gita, karma* extends far beyond the religious, social and moral activity of *śruti* or *smṛti* literature. According to Tilak it includes all conceivable actions of the human being—physical, mental, social, vocational, religious, secular, and so forth; all action in the animate and inanimate worlds; even the mere fact of being alive. The last point is crucial to Tilak's arguments against *saṃnyāsa.*[37]

To Tilak, *yoga* in the *Gita* is primarily "skill" or "device" in relation to performing action. The word is thus synonymous with *karmayoga* (and *yogin* with *karmayogin*). Where either of these appears the meaning intended is of a particular technique for action.[38]

In considering methods for attaining *mokṣa,* Tilak refers to two traditional paths: the active *(pravṛttilakṣana) karmayoga;* and the renunciatory *(nivṛttilakṣana) jñānayoga.*[39] The former, as we have seen, is *the* path in the *Gita* for Tilak. Analyzed in terms of the meaning of its two component words, *karmayoga* is skill in performing any human action whatsoever. But, in the context of Tilak's advaita view it involves, in addition, the actual experience, the immediate knowledge *(jñāna)* of Brahman or Parameshvara as the Absolute Self. Those who attain such a state reach *mokṣa* in this world,[40] or after death, and are variously described in the *Gita* as *sthitaprajña, triguṇātīta, bhaktimat;*[41] they become Brahman *(brahmabhūta)* and attain *brahmanirvàṇa.*[42]

Tilak's theory of action has three fundamental tenets: one cannot avoid performing action; action is normally performed with desire for its fruits; and action so performed has a binding effect on the actor.[43] Tilak understands the *Gita* to teach that the influence of one's accumulated karmic residue upon the *guṇas* determines one's inherent nature, activities, class, duties, taste, religious practices, and so forth.[44] One has, then, certain inherent tendencies to develop desires and act in certain ways as a result of prior desiderative action. Clearly the enemy is desire *(kāma),* and one must neutralize its effect, by working to attain *naiṣkarmya siddhi,* perfection in desireless action, which is *mokṣa.*[45]

The *Gita* teaches, says Tilak, that tendencies and desires are to be controlled, rather than suppressed through fasting and excessive austerities. Control requires steadying and purifying both the mind and reason in order to sever attachment to the fruit of any contemplated action. At the same time the mind must concentrate upon the Lord, because complete control of the senses comes only with knowledge *(jñāna)* of Brahman.[46] Success in this process brings one mental equanimity and steady reason or the *Gita*'s *sthitaprajña.*[47] To attain this "Brahmic state", in which one realizes the identity of Atman and Brahman, and to maintain it at death bring one to merge with Brahman.[48]

The *karmayogin* thus overcomes the three factors of ignorance, desire and binding karma that combine to keep one in bondage. He acts desirelessly and does not create new karmic ties for the future. He attains the knowledge of Brahman, of its identity with Atman, and of the illusory nature of the world. Finally, this knowledge destroys that part of his karma that has not yet begun to bear fruit, i.e. the *anārabdhakārya,* leaving only his commenced karma or *prārabdhakārya* to be lived out.[49]

Two points deserve emphasis here. First, the above process is largely a mental or intellectual one, involving mind *(manas)* and reason *(buddhi)*. Second, Tilak insists repeatedly throughout his commentary that even the realized man should not abandon action, but continue to do his duty desirelessly for universal welfare *(lokasaṃgraha)*. *Jñāna* alone does not effect release. It must be accompanied by desireless action.[50] Janaka is one of the examples Tilak draws on as evidence. He sees the performance of action by Janaka, even though he was a *jñānin,* as a key illustration of the ethical doctrine of the *Gita.*[51]

The second traditional path to *mokṣa* is *jñānayoga,* the way of renunciation of the Sankhyas and *saṃnyāsins.* In Tilak's interpretation the process is much like *karmayoga* in that by mental stabilization through control of the sense organs, one also seeks *jñāna* or the knowledge of Brahman, the Parameshvara.

> . . . as the Spiritual and worldly knowledge *(jñānavijñāna)* necessary in both *[karmayoga]* and the path of renunciation is the same, the practices prescribed for acquiring Spiritual [sic] Knowledge are common to both.[52]

Tilak is most concerned, however, to refute any interpretation that encourages the *jñānayogin* to give up worldly life and renounce all action. While there are such *jñānins,* he argues, the *Gita* favors those who continue to perform their duties *(dharma),* even after attaining knowledge of Brahman, as a benefit to those less advanced than themselves.[53] The *Gita* recognizes, he points out, that the *saṃnyāsin* aims only at release and is not essentially concerned that a universal application of his beliefs would destroy the functioning of society; Krishna presents, therefore, by his teaching and example, the importance of seeking release and maintaining society.[54]

Furthermore, there is a fundamental flaw, Tilak says, in a doctrine tht supposedly demands renunciation of action when it is not possible to do so while alive. He claims that the *Gita* solves this problem by revising the concept of renunciation in the light of its doctrine of action. The true *saṃnyāsin,* then, renounces not action but the desire for its fruits and "performs Actions having given up the Hope for the Fruit of Action." With this interpretation, Tilak holds that in the *Gita* there is no real difference between true *saṃnyāsa* and *karmayoga.*[55]

There remains the path of *bhakti.* The *bhakta*'s goal, according to Tilak, is to realize the identity of Brahman and Atman, ". . . to imbibe, the nature and form of the Parameśvara by Love, and to make one's mind uniform with the Parameśvara."[56] This goal, then, is achieved through the worship of a perceptible form of the Parameshvara. The devotee cultivates desirelessness in order to discontinue the accumulation of karmic effects, by dedicating all actions to the Parameshvara.[57] The actual forms of worship are not much detailed in the *Gita,* beyond *Gita* 9.34 and 18.65–66, but Tilak understands them to be fairly standard as described in various *bhakta* works.[58]

Tilak obviously thinks that the *Gita* teaches *bhakti* as an easier form of *jñānayoga.* Concentrating on the imperceptible Supreme is not an easy task, and the *Gita* compensates by expanding in chapters nine through twelve upon the perceptible form of the Parameshvara and the royal and easy road to knowledge of it—the *bhaktimarga.*[59] Followers of this path seek the steady reason *(buddhi),* the *jñāna* and the desireless action that are, as we have already seen, sought by the *jñāna-* (and *karma-*) *yogin.*[60] The *Gita,* says Tilak, makes only ". . . minor verbal changes in the doctrines of the Philosophy of the Absolute Self in adopting them into the Path of Devotion."[61]

Tilak makes it plain that the monism of the *Gita* is unaffected by this adoption. Whatever deities humanity may worship and by whatever means, "ultimately that worship amounts to a worship of the Parameśvara."[62] Thus, worship of various perceptible forms of the Supreme is not the worship of different objects, but ". . . is the Devotion according to which, there is only one All-Pervasive Parameśvara in all symbols or objects of worship, whatever symbol or object is taken for worship; . . ."[63]

Once the worshipper attains knowledge of the Parameshvara, however, and the latter is understood for what it really is, *bhakti* resolves into *jñāna. Bhakti* is based on duality of the worshipper and the worshipped, a duality which ceases when one experiences the knowledge of the Parameshvara, and all is realized as one. Tilak says, "The ultimate resolution of Devotion is into Knowledge; Devotion is a means for acquiring Knowledge, it is not a goal in itself."[64]

Thus for Tilak, the three main paths to liberation—karma, *jñāna* and *bhakti*—are harmonized in the *Gita.* In fact, as his view of the outcome of *bhakti* suggests, Tilak claims that the *Gita* really deals only with karma and *jñāna.* The idea of three independent paths is dismissed as the invention of "doctrine-supporting commentators."[65]

The foregoing exposition of Tilak's handling of the means to liberation has been considerably simplified and abbreviated for presentation here. One should not conclude from it that Tilak's commentary on the subject is clear and consistent and without difficulties or contradictions. In fact, there are a number of these and they occur frequently and seriously when Tilak is attempting to establish the primacy of *karmayoga* in the *Gita* and its superiority to other paths. Unfortunately, we cannot discuss these problems in any detail here. They have been laid out elsewhere.[66] For our purposes it is sufficient to point to some of them in order to indicate the typc of problems encountered.

In one instance, Tilak says that the way to *jñāna* is through desireless action, while elsewhere he asserts that such action is not possible without *jñāna*.[67] A somewhat similar difficulty arises with regard to the experience of *jñāna* in relation to becoming a *sthitaprajña*. One attains *jñāna* to become a *sthitaprajña*, but the latter subsequently experiences *jñāna*.[68]

Elsewhere Tilak stresses the differences between Sankhya *(jñānamarga)* and *karmayoga*, but insists at another point that it is not appropriate to stress the differences in view of the similarities between the two disciplines.[69] *Jñāna* may be the only thing necessary for release or it cannot by itself give release.[70]

An analysis of Tilak's commentary on *Gita* 12.6–11 and comparison with his claims at 12.12 and at 13.24–25 lead to a hopeless confusion as to what he understands to be the actual correlations between practices such as *abhyāsa*, *jñāna* and *dhyāna* and Patanjala-, Sankhya-, and *bhakti-yoga*. If we take the correlation that is apparently established at *Gita* 12.12 and commentary, *abhyāsa* is a practice of Patanjalayoga, *jñāna* is a practice of Sankhyayoga and *dhyāna* pertains to *bhaktiyoga*. Tilak speaks disparagingly of those three paths (e.g. Patanjalayoga "advocates only the acrobatics of the organs") and pronounces them inferior to *karmayoga*. Yet within a sentence or two he claims that the "equable reason" required for *karmayoga* is attainable through none other than *abhyāsa*, *jñāna* and *dhyāna*.[71]

Finally, Tilak's treatment of Patanjalayoga itself is quite contradictory. It is not one of the only two ways to acquire knowledge of the Parameshvara (they are *jñāna* and *bhakti*).[72] Yet it is a means to "equable reason," like *jñāna* and *bhakti*, and is included with them elsewhere as a path that does lead to knowledge of the Parameshvara and release.[73]

In sum, the consistency of Tilak's interpretation of the *Gita* on the means to liberation has suffered considerably from his championing of the path of action.

Let us now consider how Tilak has interpreted two elements of the *Gita*'s teaching that are intimately related with *karmayoga* and the concept of *varṇa*. Both of these have direct influence on the practical application of the *Gita* in everyday life and they pose problems for Tilak's interpretations.

VARNADHARMA AND STHITAPRAJNA

In his introduction to the *Gītā Rahasya,* Tilak asserts that the beginning and end of the *Gita* indicate that the purpose of the poem is quite clearly to induce Arjuna to perform his *varṇadharma* in a non-attached way and therefore, to fight.[74]

A review of the *Gita*'s basic teaching on *varṇa* (*Gita* 1.41 and 43; 4.13, 18.41 ff.) can be summarized as follows: *Varṇa* is a social classification based upon heredity, and involving a system of duties and obligations incumbent upon its several strata. Its purity and function are maintained by the observance of endogamy and the proper performance of duties in the families and castes of each *varṇa,* or class. The *varṇa* system of four classes was created by Krishna. Within each class its members have common inherent natures *(svabhāva),* the qualities *(guṇa)* of which determine the actions and duties of members of that class as distinct from the others. Since the *Gita* holds that actions performed in a previous life determine subsequent birth (e.g. *Gita* 6.37–45), it follows that one's karmic accumulations influence one's inherent nature, one's *gauṇa* content, social class, and incumbent duties. As to the duties, the *Gita* reiterates throughout the necessity of performing one's own duty and action *(svadharma, svakarma).* Done properly, they can lead to heaven, even to perfection (*Gita* 2.32 and 18.45); straying to someone else's duties can be more dangerous than death (*Gita* 3.35 and 18.47–48). Finally, one's duty is always to be done without attachment to its fruits (e.g. *Gita* 2.47).

Arjuna's dharma is initially interpreted by Tilak to be that, as an unenlightened *kṣatriya,* in the circumstances of the poem he must fight. He must do this in a non-attached manner and should understand that he is blameless, first because the immortal *ātman* of an opponent cannot be slain and there is therefore no cause for grief; and second, the victim's own misdeeds have condemned them to deaths in which Arjuna is only to be the instrument.[75] There might be difficulties enough for a civil authority in accepting the above theory of violent action, but consider Tilak's understanding of the role of the pure and "mentally-stabilized" *sthitaprajña* of *Gita* 2:54 ff.

Egoless, desireless, of pure mind and reason, the *sthitaprajña* is, by definition, sinless and is even, by example, a basis for the laws of behavior for others.[76] In his case, the motive, not the act itself, is the criterion by which an act is to be judged, and ". . . a pure minded person cannot be held responsible . . ." for an act that might seem improper to our worldly view.[77] Tilak uses this rationale to provide an apologetic for Shivaji's method of defeating his Muslim opponents. It is disturbing for ethical theory for it asserts that some men are above the law:

> Was this act of the Maharaja [Shivaji] good or bad? . . . The laws which bind society are for common men like you and me . . . Great men are above the common principles of morality. These principles do not reach the place on which great men stand . . . Shrimat Krishna preached in the *Gita* that we have a right to kill even our own *guru* and our kinsmen. No blame attaches to any person if he is doing deeds without being actuated by a desire to reap the fruit of his deeds . . . get out of the Penal Code, enter into the lofty atmosphere of the *Shrimat Bhagavad Gita* and then consider the actions of great men.[78]

This is strong stuff but Tilak's theory has its controls. To begin with, there are absolute ethical principles such as non-violence, truth, non-stealing, and justice. The *sthitaprajña* is obliged to enter upon any affair in the light of those principles. The initial reaction to a situation in which one may be subjected to violence, or see others subjected to it by evil men should be one of non-violence; but if that fails it is a duty to repay evil with evil, even to kill if necessary.[79] This is a thoroughly practical theory: there are ideals to be observed, but in our imperfect world, for the welfare of others and for the sake of arriving at a state of universal happiness, it is not necessary to labor long under the disadvantages of absolute principles. It is quite proper, *pace* Gandhi, to deal with an unethical opponent in kind.[80]

Another control would be the *Gita's* insistence that one perform *svadharma,* that it is dangerous to follow someone else's *dharma.* Tilak appears to agree with this so that, for example, where violent action like warfare is undertaken it is the responsibility of the *kṣatriyas* and not of the other classes.[81] There is a traditional safeguard here that is particularly useful in the case of violent situations. The duty is the property of those who, according to the *Gita,* are best suited for and born to it by virtue of the qualities of their inherent nature. But Tilak introduces a new element into the concept of *dharma*—the possibility that one's duty may be a matter of personal choice rather than a consequence of one's innate nature:

> When once one has accepted a particular action as one's own, for whatever reason one may have done so, one must perform it, unattachedly, however difficult or undesirable it might be . . .[82]

The statement puzzles Tilak's translator, who explains that actions are acceptable only if ordained *(niyata)* by the Shastras. Tilak himself, in *Gita* 18.48, refers to action that one must not abandon, even though doing it faultily, as *niyata,* required or ordained according to the three *guṇas.* There is a direct reference to the Gita's teaching that our karmic accumulation affects our *svabhāva* and the *guṇas* arising therefrom, which in turn affect the class and the required actions to which we are born. Why, then, does Tilak speak of different reasons for accepting one's duty?

The answer is that Tilak is seeking to universalize the *Gita,* to show that its doctrine of *svadharma* applies outside the *varṇa* system also. He claims that whatever a society's system may be with regard to its members' duties, whether the duties be determined by a four-class system, or the individual is free to choose them, those duties become "one's religion", not to be abandoned or changed.[83]

The immediate consequence of this view would be that the traditional safeguard, which confines certain actions to the class best suited to perform them, is severely eroded. Anyone, whatever one's natural propensities, can choose to be, for example, a *kṣatriya* and try to behave accordingly. The potential is greatly enlarged for people to assume roles for which they are totally unsuited, with all the disharmony and mischief that can result.

The problem of allowing for free choice of one's duties and obligations, however, runs deeper than that. It strikes at the heart of the *Gita's* teaching on reincarnation and the formation of human nature. One may accept the empirical evidence that there are societies in which individuals make a free choice of their *svadharma.* But in the *varṇa* system, according to the *Gita* and as we have seen, individual karmic accumulations, the social classes, the inherent natures of members of each class, and their proper activities, duties, or occupations are causally and inextricably linked together. The *Gita's* teaching on *varṇadharma* is clearly based on this, but it is not at all clear that a social system of free choice can be based on the *varṇa* doctrine. I do not think that it can; Tilak has certainly not made the case.

This discussion of *Gītā Rahasya* was intended to show that the poem appealed personally to Tilak, a man of abundant energy and varied activity, and that it also suited the cause of religious nationalism that he espoused. Tilak's era was one in which India was to be roused to action in the struggle for independence. The opponent was a foreign power so advanced industrially and militarily that its culture, traditions and values tended to overshadow India's and demonstrate the ostensible inferiority of the latter. The need to restore pride in India's cultural and spiritual heritage was not lost on Tilak, as it had not been lost on Roy, Saraswati, Vivekananda and Gandhi.

For Tilak, the *Gita* put forth a doctrine of action that was applicable in every sphere of human activity; it urged activity and yet related that activity to traditional Hindu paths of spiritual release and freedom. In Tilak's mind, spiritual and political freedom were symbolized by the concept of *swarāj.* Without it the Hindu individual or community was not free to follow *dharma* and chaos and disintegration were the result; without it there would be no real industrial, educational or social progress.[84] Thus, the *Gita* was an ideal text with which Hindus could identify and in which they could base and legitimize their religious and political aspirations. Tilak used the *Gita* for those purposes, but not merely as a tool for his own ends. His own life of work and self-sacrifice demonstrates his personal dedication to the path of *karmayoga.*

CHAPTER FOUR

Sri Aurobindo as a Gita-yogin

ROBERT N. MINOR

Though Sri Aurobindo Ghose (1872-1950) never accepted the ultimate authority of religious texts, scholars agree that the *Bhagavadgita* was central to the life and thought of this Indian Nationalist, who left the movement to develop his "Integral Yoga" and establish an ashram.[1] Not only did he write a major commentary on the text called *Essays on the Gita,* but another of his major works, *The Synthesis of Yoga,* is an expansion upon the yoga that Aurobindo believed the *Gita* taught. The title of one of the early journals he founded and edited, the *Karmayogin,* also referred to the person who followed the active yoga advocated by the *Gita.* Likewise, a set of religious experiences central to Aurobindo's life in 1908-9, is described in terms of the teaching and vision of the *Bhagavadgita. Finally, in the Karmayogin* itself, Aurobindo declared that the *Gita* is "our chief national heritage, our hope for the future, our great force for the purification of the moral weaknesses that stain and hamper our people."[2]

Yet, in later letters to his disciples, Aurobindo also cautions restraint in equating his teachings with those of the *Gita:* "Our yoga is not identical with the yoga of the *Gita* although it contains all that is essential in the *Gita's* yoga."[3] This study is an analysis of the place of the *Gita* in the life and thought of Aurobindo as it leads up to and includes his *Essays on the Gita* and after.[4] Though the *Gita* was apparently an important factor in Aurobindo's religious stance, especially his yogic practice, it was not always central. Aurobindo's own personal experiences were authoritative and dictated the rise and fall of the *Gita's* influence, as well as the principles by which it was to be interpreted.

The Gita Discovered

When Aurobindo returned from his studies in England in 1893 to take up positions in the Baroda State Service, eventually at Baroda College, he immersed himself in the literature of his homeland. He learned Sanskrit and other Indian languages, studied the *Upanishads* and the epics, and translated portions of the *Mahabharata* and *Ramayana,* as well as the works of Kalidasa and Ghartrihari. He was also introduced to the *Gita.* What he later calls a lack of interest in metaphysical speculation did not prevent him from affirming a metaphysical position he identified with the *Upanishads* in manuscripts published later: "Philosophy of the Upanishads" and "On Translating the Upanishads."[5] Behind the phenomenal flux which is a datum of experience, he believed, there was a unity identical with one's true Self. This unity, Brahman, is known in the *Upanishads* as *saccidānanda,* pure being, pure consciousness, and bliss. Based upon the yogic experiences of the Upanishadic seers, both the One—the Absolute, Brahman—and the many, are facts; but the highest state of the yogin is total absorption in the Absolute within without the dissolution of the plurality. Thus, Aurobindo's position included the Upanishadic *Tat tvam asi,* "Thou art That," which identified with the true Self the Absolute; but it would not completely eliminate, even in the highest consciousness, the experience of its progressive phenomenal manifestation.

During the Baroda period (1893–1905), Aurobindo wrote nothing on the *Gita,* but his unpublished manuscripts introduce some standard interpretive principles for understanding the text. In a manuscript entitled "The Interpretation of Scripture," Aurobindo first set out his understanding of the value of religious texts. Scriptures, he says, "are guides to knowledge, brief indications to enlighten us on our path, not substitutes for thought and experience. They are *śabdabrahma,* the Word, the oral expression of God, not the thing to be known itself nor the knowledge of Him."[6] In relativizing the authority of scriptures, Aurobindo exalted the authority of experience to an almost absolute position, a principle that he would affirm throughout his life. In this early paper, Aurobindo distinguished three elements of śabda, the Word: the term itself, the meaning of the term (*artha*), and the spirit behind the meaning (*svarūpa*). Even the meaning of the term "is only the indication of something deeper which the thought seeks to convey to the intellectual conception." Ideas, like words, are no more than symbols of knowledge, but these point to the "*svarūpa,* the essential figure of Truth, which we cannot know with the intellect but with a higher faculty." This knowledge is experiential, intuitive, a realization, a knowledge by identification with Truth. What Aurobindo thereby knows is the highest authority and the first interpretive principle for understanding a scripture: "all else is mere idea or opinion."[7] On this basis Aurobindo criticized Sāyaṇa, Shankara, and Max Müller, describing Müller, for example, as "a scholar of wide attainments, great versatility and a refreshingly active, ingenious and irresponsible fancy," who "could not feel the language or realise the spirit behind the letter."[8]

Aurobindo recommends three "standards of truth" in the interpretation of scriptures: the "known," which must be understood in terms of the right word, meaning and spirit; "the knower," the original seer, "with whom we ought to be in spiritual contact"; and the "knowledge," which is the whole truth of which the scriptures show only a part.[9] All three are experiential, intuitive and monistic, and throughout his life Aurobindo will emphasize the supramental experience as an interpretive principle.

Aurobindo's unpublished manuscripts from this period include one entitled "Notes on the Mahabharata." His goal in this study was to disengage the 24,000 or so couplets which could be traced to Vyasa, the traditional author of the *Mahabharata,* from later accretions that brought the epic to around 100,000 verses. Aurobindo treated the *Gita* as a central part of the *Mahabharata.* It was, he felt, the epitome of Vyasa's main emphasis upon the active religious life. "Moreover, the whole piece [the *Gita*] is but the philosophical justification and logical enlargement of the gospel of action preached by Krishna in the Mahabharata proper, the undoubted work of the poet."[10]

Within his discussion, Aurobindo lays down some of the central themes of his interpretation of the *Gita.* The *Gita* is interpreted as a combination of Vedanta, Sankhya and Yoga. "Vedanta" here probably represents Aurobindo's understanding of the teachings of the *Upanishads* and "Sankhya" the teaching of the duality of Nature or *prakṛti,* as ever-active and the soul or *puruṣa,* as eternally inactive and above the continual flux of *prakṛti.* "Yoga" here means the techniques used to attain higher states of consciousness. Vyasa's religion, founded upon these three, Aurobindo says, must be the basis for Hinduism today if it is to endure.[11] It is a combination that reflects Aurobindo's own religious position.

Aurobindo's discussion of the *Gita* centers around 3.4-8, 20-26, which, rejecting renunciation of action as a religious path, teaches the impossibility of inaction and the necessity for and method of non-attached action, i.e. action done without personal attachment to the results. Thus, Aurobindo speaks of actions which are accomplished through "an august and selfless disinterestedness."[12]

Such action must also be "surrendered" to the Divine, which is identified with one's true Self and with an Upanishadic Brahman. Aurobindo equates the deity Krishna with Brahman, identifying him with the "imperishable, undefinable, unmanifest" which the *Gita* actually teaches is, inferior to Krishna himself in 12.1-7.[13] Thus, quoting 12.3-12, he inserts the terms "Me as" in the third verse to read: "They who worship Me as the imperishable, illimitable, unmanifest, controlling all the organs, one-minded to all things, they doing good to all creatures attain to Me . . . "[14] In this attempt to reconcile the personal deity Krishna with the impersonal Absolute of the *Upanishads,* Aurobindo reveals a future emphasis, the doctrine of the "three purushas." Here the topic under discussion is the surrender of all works to the the divine, but this interpretation of the passages indicates his indentification of the personal and impersonal, or at least the acceptance at this early point of the *saguṇa-nirguṇa* distinction of the advaitin position: the Absolute without characteristics (*nirguṇa*) is perceived as containing characteristics (*saguṇa*) when seen on a lower level of consciousness.

The central theme in the Baroda manuscripts is the *Gita* as a gospel of disinterested action. Aurobindo faults past interpreters who have missed this point. They missed it, he says, because of the debilitating emphasis on renunciation of "the heresy of Buddhism" and the subsequent monopoly on the *Gita*'s interpretation by the brahmin class; as the class of knowledge, the brahmins emphasized quiesence. "They have laid stress on the goal, but they have not echoed Sri Krishna's emphasis on the necessity of action as the one sure road to the goal."[15]

NATIONALISM AND THE GITA'S SILENCE

Aurobindo's interest in the political situation in India continued to grow until he became, from 1905-1910, one of the major advocates of the Indian Nationalist movement. He identified with the party that favored immediate independence from British rule and even revolution to achieve that end. In so doing he did not abandon the religious position he had previously defined in Baroda, but temporarily raised a more immediate concern to the level of ultimacy: the independence of India.[16] In order to promote a Vedantic vision for the world, the nation of India must be free to be the world's guru to lead and guide the nations to Vedanta. India is the divine means for spiritualizing the human race. She is the *avatāra;* the "descent" of the Divine, and even the "Mother," the *śakti* of the Divine, the "power" of the Absolute at work in the world, just as the *śakti* of the god Shiva (Parvati, Durga, Kali) is understood as the active power of the god at work. True patriotism therefore, "sees God as the Mother in our country, God as *śakti* in the mass of our countrymen, and religiously devotes itself to their service and their liberation from present sufferings and servitude."[17]

His writings before his imprisonment in 1908 are surprisingly lacking in references to the *Gita,* especially since the *Gita*'s call to the active life of disinterested service sacrificed to the Divine seemed to suit well his active political life, in the thick of the Nationalist battle for India's *swarāj,* 'own rule," and his understanding of the *Gita* revealed at Baroda. On August 6, 1906 *Bande Mataram,* a magazine of political and cultural comment, was founded by Nationalist Bepin Chandra Pal. Aurobindo became joint-editor and its chief contributor. His articles continued until his arrest in May, 1908. Up until 1908 Aurobindo invoked the *Gīta* once to support active resistance to British rule. Any means to *swarāj* that are necessary must be used, even if that means violence. The very battlefield setting of the *Gitȧ* provided support for his argument.

> To shrink from bloodshed and violence under such circumstances is a weakness deserving as severe a rebuke as Sri Krishna addressed to Arjuna when he shrank from the colossal civil slaughter on the field of Kurukshetra. Liberty is the life-breath of a nation; and when the life is attacked, when it is sought to suppress all chance of breathing by violent pressure, any and every means of self-preservation becomes right and justifiable . . . [18]

Aurobindo never accepted a pacifist posture and throughout his life the *Gita* would provide him with support for his position. In the *Bande Mataram* Aurobindo would also speak of the Nationalist movement as the "spirit of the kshatriya" without specific reference to the *Gita,* but clearly calling to mind the activist understanding he held at Baroda.

The period of Aurobindo's life during which he contributed to the *Bande Mataram* is divided, however, by a set of religious experiences which he would later call the first of "four great realisations,"[19] and the discovery of "the foundations of my Sadhana [yogic discipline]."[20] Discouraged by the failure of the more extreme Nationalists to take control of the Indian National Congress from the Moderates at the Surat conference in December, 1907, and by the failure of his own yogic practices, Aurobindo immediately sought out a Maharashtran yogi, Vishnu Bhasker lele. After three days of yogic practice he attained what he later describes as advaitic experiences in which he envisioned the world as unreal: "they made me see with a stupendous intensity the world as a cinematographic play of vacant forms in the impersonal universality of the Absolute Brahman."[21] He did not accept these experiences as final, however for they meant rejection of the reality of the world, and its reality was a belief to which he was fully committed throughout his life. The experiences confirmed the unity but not the plurality. Aurobindo remembers coming away from them with a commitment to absolute surrender to the divine guru within, experienced at times from then on as an inner voice or *adeś*.

This emphasis upon surrender to the Divine within as it works its way in history, a teaching which was partly set forth in the writings from Baroda, is reflected in Aurobindo's speeches and articles from January, 1908 on. Yet, though one would have expected explicit references to the *Gitā* on this subject, as there are after the Alipore jail experiences of 1909, there are only vague allusions to the *Gita*'s teaching. Instead it is supported by references to his own set of experiences with Lele. In his first speech following these experiences (January 9, 1908) Aurobindo emphasizes that "Nationalism is a religion that has come from God . . . "[22] He calls Nationalists to faith, selfless surrender as instruments of the working of the Divine in the movement.

> Have you got a real faith? Or is it merely a political aspiration? Is it merely a larger kind of selfishness? Or is it merely that you wish to be free to oppress others, as you are being oppressed? Do you hold your political creed from a higher source? Is it God that is born in you? Have you realised that you are merely the instruments of God, that your bodies are not your own? You are merely instruments of God for the work of the Almighty.[23]

The theme of surrender to the divine work continues throughout the Bombay speech and recurs in subsequent articles of *Bande Mataram* until Aurobindo's arrest on May 5, 1908.

> Misled by egoism, we believe that we are working, that the results of what we do are our creation, and when anything has to be done we ask ourselves whether we have the strength, the means, the requisite qualities, but in reality all work is done by the will of God and when faith in Him is the mainspring of our actions, success is inevitable.[24]

Though references to the *Gita* might have fit well in such articles, which speak of the surrender and selflessness one is to have in such work, and though in a later period they would often be found in such discussions, the *Gita* is at this point in the background.

A second theme in which Aurobindo might have been expected to draw on his understanding of the *Gita* is the emphasis, after the experiences with Lele, on the importance of hearing the voice within. The Nationalist work in Bengal, he says, is an example of the primacy of intuition. "The intellect having nothing to offer but despair became quiescent, and when the intellect ceased to work, the heart of Bengal was open and ready to receive the voice of God whenever he should speak."[25] Aurobindo, as Feys points out,[26] made the "inner voice" his guide because he believed its counsels were the leading of the Divine. This too reflected his experiences with lele. As Aurobindo later recalled Lele's instructions, Lele said: "Sit in meditation, . . . but do not think, look only at your mind; you will see thoughts *coming into it;* before they can enter throw these away from your mind till your mind is capable of silence."[27] Intuitive understanding is required in the Nationalist movement as in the understanding of the scriptures. Yet, during this period where one might have expected Aurobindo to refer to the *Gita,* especially in the light of references in these articles to the Krishna of the *Puranas,* [28] references to the *Gita* are absent.

PRACTICING "THE YOGA OF THE GITA"

The absence of references to the *Gita* in Aurobindo's writings changes dramatically with a second major set of religious experiences that Aurobindo later called his "second realisation which was that of the cosmic consciousness and of the Divine as all beings and all that is."[29] No new content is added to Aurobindo's stance by these experiences, but they do result in a reorientation toward the movement for *swarāj.* No longer is the push toward Indian independence at a level of ultimacy. Aurobindo instead seeks to promote his religious stance, the *sanātana dharma,* the "eternal religion," which will, in turn, promote India. In his famous Uttarpara Speech, delivered May 30, 1909, about three weeks after his release from a year's confinement in the Alipore jail during a trial in a bombing case in which he was innocent, Aurobindo concludes that as a result of his experiences:

> I say no longer that nationalism is a creed, a religion, a faith; I say that it is the Sanatan Dharma which for us is nationalism. This Hindu nation was born with the Sanatan Dharma, with it it moves and with it it grows. When the Sanatan Dharma declines, then the nation declines, and if the Sanatan Dharma were capable of perishing, with the Sanatan Dharma it would perish.[30]

In the same speech Aurobindo spoke of his experiences in the Alipore jail. The arrest had shaken his faith in the purpose of the Divine. Believing he had surrendered to the work of the Divine, he had anticipated its protection at least until he had completed his mission. He reports that a voice "from within" responded, "Wait and see." In response he felt guided to practice what he calls "the Yoga of the *Gita*" and to meditate with the help of the *Upanishads.* In the Uttarpara Speech it is the *Gitā* which provides much of the material describing his experiences in jail.

> Then He placed the Gita in my hands. His strength entered into me and I was able to do the Sadhana of the Gita. I was not only to understand intellectually but to realise what Sri Krishna demanded of Arjuna and what He demands of those who aspire to do His work, to be free from repulsion and desire, to do work for Him without the demand for fruit, to renounce self-will and become a passive and faithful instrument in His hands, to have an equal heart for high and low, friend and opponent, success and failure, yet not to do His work negligently.[31]

For Aurobindo the *Gita* provided the solution to his crisis, and he began practicing the "yoga of the *Gītā*" while in jail.[32] Believing he was given the *Gita,* by the Divine Within, he was convinced of its call to action. Yet, the content of this action, "the yoga of the *Gita*" or the "sadhana of the *Gitá,*" described in the above quotation, was known to him before this experience. It is action without self-centered attachment to the results, but selfless and done "for Krishna," through which one becomes an instrument in the hands of the Divine. Now identified with the *Gitá,* this teaching became "real" to Aurobindo, and was valued as "what the Hindu religion meant."[33] In other words, Aurobindo identified the *Gitá* with the essential teachings of his own position.

Through these experiences the *Gita* was raised to central importance among the religious texts to which Aurobindo related. Though in Baroda he wrote most about the *Upanishads* and spoke of the *Gita* as part of his literary studies of the *Mahabharata,* and though in *Bande Mataram* the *Gita* was all but absent, it would dominate the two new journals he began in 1909, and its centrality would culminate in a major study, *Essays on the Gita,* in 1916-1920 and in expanded form in *The Synthesis of Yoga.*

The Alipore jail experiences provided Aurobindo with more than a realization of the importance of the *Gita* and its teachings of non-attached action and surrender to the divine work. Aurobindo also believed that he had seen visions similar to that of the universal form of Krishna given to Arjuna in chapter eleven. What he describes in the Uttarpara speech are visions that all is in fact Krishna, all beings, things, and events. When confronted by the enemies in his own struggle, his own Kurukshetra, the criminals in prison, the judge and prosecuting attorney in the courtroom, and the very prison itself, he saw that all of it was Krishna, no matter how evil, disgusting, or personally destructive. Through these visions, Aurobindo says, Krishna "made me realize the central truth of the Hindu religion."

> I looked at the jail that secluded me from men and it was no longer by its high walls that I was imprisoned; no, it was Vasudeva who surrounded me. I walked under the branches of the tree in front of my cell but it was not the tree, I knew it was Vasudeva, it was Sri Krishna whom I saw standing there and holding over me his shade. I looked at the bars of my cell, the very grating that did duty for a door and again I saw Vasudeva. It was Narayana who was guarding and standing sentry over me. Or I lay on the coarse blankets that were given me for a couch and felt the arms of Sri Krishna around me, the arms of my Friend and Lover . . . I looked at the prisoners in the jail, the thieves, the murderers, the swindlers, and as I looked at them I saw Vasudeva, it was Narayana whom I found in these darkened souls and misused bodies . . .[34].

In the courtroom, the vision was the same:

> I looked and it was not the Magistrate whom I saw, it was Vasudeva, it was Narayana who was sitting there on the bench. I looked at the Prosecuting Counsel and it was not the Counsel for the prosecution that I saw; it was Sri Krishna who sat there, it was my Lover and Friend who sat there and smiled. "Now do you fear?" He said, "I am in all men and I overrule their actions and their words. My protection is still with you and you shall not fear."[35]

Aurobindo's experience confirmed Arjuna's in chapter eleven. He believed he had seen that all is Krishna and, like the vision of the *Gīta* that all is the work of Krishna. Though he does not emphasize the destructive element of the Divine as does the vision of the Gita's eleventh chapter, Aurobindo realized that all, good or evil, is Krishna's work, and all fulfills his purpose. "I am Time," Krishna says in *Gita* 11.32 and this calls for the response Aurobindo has previously anticipated: "Be the mere instrument." (*Gita* 11.33) So Aurobindo quotes a similar message to him in the Uttarpara Speech:

> I am working in everybody and whatever men may think or do they can do nothing but help in my purpose. They also are doing my work, they are not my enemies but my instruments. In all your actions you are moving forward without knowing which way you move . . . Since long ago I have been preparing this uprising and now the time has come and it is I who will lead it to its fulfilment [sic].[36]

This, then, adds no new content to Aurobindo's metaphysical position or yogic ideals, but is what he calls a realization of his understanding of the path to the Divine, "the yoga of the *Gita*," a realization of the content previously emphasized at Baroda. One result of that realization was the centrality of the *Gita* in his writings after Alipore.

In the light of these experiences and the devaluation of nationalism, Aurobindo began two new weekly journals. On June 19, 1909 the *Karmayogin* was first published and on August 23, 1909 its counterpart in Bengali, the *Dharma*, appeared. Aurobindo wrote most of the articles in these journals until his withdrawal to Chandernagore in February, 1910 in response to the "inner voice." Though much space was still given to continued political comment, the journals' purposes can best be summarized as the promotion of spirituality or *brahmatejas*. Aurobindo explained this purpose in the first issue of the *Karmayogin*:

> We have said that *brahmateja* is the thing we need most of all and first of all. In one sense, that means the pre-eminence of religion; but after all, what Europeans mean by religion is not *brahmateja;* which is rather spirituality, the force and energy of thought and action arising from communion with or self-surrender to that within us which rules the world.[37]

Brahmatejas traditionally referred to the glory or power radiating from an accomplished brahman sage which could affect affairs around him. Aurobindo's use of the idea for the journals summarizes his intended purpose. When Aurobindo retired to Chandernagore in 1910 and finally to Pondicherry, he believed that his yogic attainments there would also produce such a *brahmatejas,* that his work would not be a renunciation of life but would actually affect the world about him to bring about more permanent and basic change, the evolution of the earth-consciousness to perfection. His withdrawal, counter to his critics, would not be, in his view, a renunciation of action, but the movement of the active life to another plane of activity. Direct political activity, he believed, would accomplish little of permanent value without *brahmatejas.*[38]

Before his withdrawal, Aurobindo attempted to promote this spirituality in the *Dharma* and the *Karmayogin,* exalting "the yoga of the *Gitā,*" in the *Karmayogin* to the state of "our chief national heritage, our hope for the future, our great force for the purification of the moral weaknesses that stain and hamper our people."[39] Likewise in the *Dharma* he declared that "the *Gītā* will become the universally acknowledged Scripture of the future religion."[40] Besides regular allusions to and quotations from the *Gita,* Aurobindo devoted specific articles in both journals as well as speeches given during 1909–1910 to the *Gita* and its topics. In the *Dharma* he began a series of articles entitled "An Introduction to the *Gītā,*" which he intended to complete as a commentary on the *Gita,* but which remained unfinished when he left British India in 1910.[41]

Aurobindo described the purpose of *Dharma* as spreading the "eternal religion (*sanātana dharma*)" of which he had spoken in the Uttarpara speech, and which he identified with the *Gitā.* To him, this meant education in the three-fold path of the *Gita* leading to union with the Divine: "Knowledge, devotion and non-attached activity are the root of an Aryan education . . ."[42] The *Dharma* carried Krishna's statement of descent (*avatāra*) in *Gita* 4.7 on its front cover: "For whenever a languishing of the *dharma* appears, son of Bharata, a rising of *adharma,* then I send Myself forth. For protection of the good and destruction of evil doers, to firmly establish the *dharma,* I come into being age after age."

The cover of the *Karmayogin* also included a verse from the *Gita.* Under a drawing of Krishna as Arjuna's charioteer teaching the *Gita* to Arjuna, with the army lined up in the background ready for the battle to commence, *Gita* 3.30, which expressed Aurobindo's ideal in the way of action, appeared in Sanskrit: "On Me all actions renouncing, with mind on that which pertains to the self, being free from longing and selfishness, fight, casting off this fever."

In the *Dharma,* the *Karmayogin,* and in a speech given by Aurobindo at Khulna, June 25, 1909, one finds the basic interpretive principles Aurobindo used in understanding the *Gita. Essays on the Gita,* written later at Pondicherry, actually adds little that is new to the source material from 1909–1910, and a number of the ideas in the *Essays* also go back as far as the Baroda materials.

From 1909–10 Aurobindo reaffirmed the importance of one's inner experience as the basic interpretive principle for understanding any scripture, summarized here in in terms of the *Gita*'s threefold path:

> This *sanātana dharma* has many scriptures, Veda, Vedanta, Gita, Upanishad, Darshana, Furana, Tantra, nor could it reject the Bible or the Koran; but its real, most authoritative scripture is in the heart in which the Eternal has His dwelling. It is in our inner spiritual experiences that we shall find the proof and source of the world's Scriptures, the law of knowledge, love and conduct, the basis and inspiration of Karmayoga.[43]

Aurobindo's second interpretive principle continues to be the stress on an active spirituality as opposed to renunciation of actions and societal concerns. In addition to the quotation of *Gita* 3.30 on the cover of *Karmayogin,* the centrality of action is emphasized throughout the pages of the two journals. "The characteristic doctrines of the *Gita* are nothing if they are not a law of life, a *dharma,* and even the most transcendental aspirations of the Vedanta presuppose a preparation in life, for it is only through life that one can reach immortality."[44] This, he says, must be emphasized against traditional understandings affected by "Buddhism" and Shankara. One must return to the Vedanta of the text itself, remembering that Shankara's comments, particularly his "peculiar theory of *māyā,*" which devalues activity in the world, are merely commentary on the text.[45]

He now explicitly uses the *Gita* to comment upon the Indian political scene and its solution. India's weakness is diagnosed by means of a passage upholding caste duties, *Gita* 3.35. India has attempted to do a duty other than her own.

> The nineteenth century in India was imitative, self-forgetful, artificial. It aimed at a successful reproduction of Europe in India, forgetting the deep saying of the Gita, "Better the law of one's own being though it be badly done than an alien *dharma* well-followed; death in one's own *dharma* is better, it is a dangerous thing to follow the law of another's nature."[46]

Likewise, the solution to India's predicament is "the Yoga of the *Gita.*" Quoting *Gita* 18.58, he affirms:

> We have faith and we believe in the great rule of life in the Gita, "Remember me and fight." We believe in the mighty word of assurance to the Bhakta, *maccittaḥ sarvadurgāṇi matprasādāt tariṣyasi,* "If thou reposest thy heart and mind in Me by My grace thou shalt pass safe through all difficulties and dangers." We believe that the Yoga of the Gita will play a large part in the uplifting of the nation, and this attitude is the first condition of the Yoga of the Gita.[47]

Still a nationalist, then, Aurobindo explicitly cites the *Gita* to support nationalism in 1909–10. Likewise, he says, the *Gita* has a political purpose which must not be negated by symbolic, psychological, or allegorical interpretations. Its setting, in fact, anticipates that of the British period in India.[48]

Aurobindo's discussion of the active life is now more consciously called a "yoga" and the three elements of the path of the *Gita* define it: "Yoga is communion with God for knowledge, for love or for work."[49] Specifically, the yoga of the *Gita* involves surrender of oneself to the Divine, working as the instrument of the Divine. This central emphasis, which Aurobindo proclaimed after the experiences with Lele in 1907 and which was briefly touched upon at Baroda, is now identical with the "Yoga of the Gita." The quotation of *Gita* 3.30 on the cover of *Karmayogin,* also testifies to this understanding. Aurobindo's teaching that behind everything is the movement of the Divine, even behind apparant setbacks in one's life and in the nation's life, is a call for surrender to the work the Divine is doing. In "The Greatness of the Individual" Aurobindo quotes *Gitā* 11.32–33, Krishna's explanation of the great vision of chapter eleven. There Krishna is portrayed in his Universal Form as "Time." and there he calls for

Arjuna's surrender: act merely as Krishna's instrument. "For these, they were slain even before and it is I who have slain them; be the occasion only, O Savyasachin."[50] The inevitability of this movement is emphasized in the article by requoting *Gita* 11.32: "Even without thee all they shall not be, the men of war who stand arrayed in the opposing squadrons." Then to reinforce his point he quotes *Gita* 18.59 which speaks of the inevitability of the divine action through Arjuna, even against his resolve not to fight.[51] The *Karmayogin* article concludes: "Those who are swept forward by Kali within them and make no terms with Fate, they alone survive. The greatness of individuals is the greatness of the etermal Energy within."[52]

That the evolution of all as the Becoming of the Absolute is inevitable is a theory found as early as Baroda but most completely developed after Aurobindo's withdrawal to Pondicherry. The Universe is in actuality the Absolute as eternal Becoming. "This is the Zeitgeist, this is the purpose that runs through the process of the centuries, the changes of the suns, this is that which makes evolution possible and provides it with a way, means and a goal."[53] And this evolution involves destruction, apparant setbacks, and pain as well. "That which was true of the great slaying at Kurukshetra is true of all things that are done in this world, of all the creation, destruction and preservation that make up the *līlā* ['sport' of the Divine]."[54]

In Aurobindo's speech at Khulna the "Yoga of the Gita" is further elucidated. It involves *samatā,* "sameness," looking indiscriminately upon all that comes to pass: "happiness and misfortune, praise and blame, honour and dishonour, and success and failure."[55] This attitude arises from the realization that "God is all," all is that Unity, the Divine; there is nothing else. It involves freedom from *dvaṁdva,* the consequent freedom from bondage to the "dualities" of pleasure and pain, attachment and hatred. But in sum this is merely a further elucidation of surrender of one's actions to the Divine within and without. "If you wish to be happy, you must give up all your works to God. You must do all your work for His sake, and therefore sin does not touch you."[56]

Though mentioned in the manuscripts from Baroda, the *Gita* is more clearly defined as a synthesis of Vedanta, Yoga and Sankhya. "In the Gita we find that Sri Krishna unites the Vedanta philosophy with the philosophy of Sankhya."[57] Aurobindo's understanding, however, devalues both positions as discrete systems. According to Aurobindo the Sankhya element is the distinction the *Gitā* makes between an active nature, *prakṛti,* by which all actions take place, and an unattached, inactive soul, *puruṣa*. However, the Vedantic element emphasizes the identity of the soul and the Absolute Brahman; the Self is a part of the Absolute.[58] There is at times a lack of clarity concerning his understanding of the term "part," which he finds in *Gita* 15.7: "just a part (*aṁśa*) of me in the world of the living becomes the individual soul, the eternal . . . " Yet, Aurobindo does not wish to limit the Absolute to either the individual soul or to a universal inactive Self. This ambiguity is clarified by another interpretive principle, the "three purushas."

The concept of the "three purushas," another major interpretive principle in Aurobindo's *Essays on the Gita,*[59] is found first in a *Karmayogin* article, "The Three Purushas." Aurobindo extolls this concept as the solution to "[t]he greatest of all the philosophical problems which human thought has struggled to solve," the nature of the relationship between consciousness and esternal reality. For Aurobindo it solves the problem of the existence of the One without the denial of the Many.[60] By it, he affirms, "The One is for ever, and the Many are for ever because the One is for ever."[61] The Many, therefore, are not merely temporary or the result of a lower level of consciousness. The plurality is as real, as permanent, as the One. Central to this "solution" is *Gita* 15.16–17, a passage which will continue to figure prominently in *Essays on the Gita*. In the *Karmayogin,* Aurobindo translates the passage as follows:

> There are two Purushas in the world, the *akṣara* ["imperishable"] and the *kṣara* ["perishable"],—the *kṣara* is all creatures, the *akṣara* is called *kuṭastha,* the one on the summit. There is another Purusha, the highest (*uttama*), called also *paramātmā* or Supreme Spirit, who enters into the three worlds (the worlds of *suṣupti, svapna, jāgrat,* otherwise the causal, mental and physical planes of existence), and sustains them as their imperishable lord.[62]

He identifies these three purushas with the two birds of the *Upanishads,* one of which is eating the fruit of a tree while the second looks on.[63] He adds a third to these two, the third purusha.

> These are the two Purushas, the *akṣara* or immutable spirit, and the *kṣara* or apparently mutable, and the tree or woman is Prakriti, universal Energy which the Europeans call Nature. The *kṣara* Purusha is the soul in Nature and enjoying Nature, the *akṣara* Purusha is the soul above Nature and watching her. But there is One who is not seated on the tree but occu-

> pies and possesses it, who is not only lord of Himself, but lord of all that is; He is higher than the *kṣara,* higher than the *akṣara,* He is Purushottama, the Soul one with God, with the All.[64]

Thus, the same "person" embraces three existences, what he will call in the *Essays* a triple status or three poises; in other writings he will speak of the three poises of the Supermind consciousness.[65] The first is the person as individual in activity, involved with and evolving in nature and its movements; the second is the inactive *ātman,* eternally untouched, immutable: but the third embraces and transcends them both, the *Purushottama* which transcends the distinctions between Being and Becoming, Unity and Multiplicity by affirming both. "He is all things at once."[66]

Aurobindo can affirm such logically contradictory concepts of the Absolute because he believes that logic is limited in its knowing. It divides and seperates the opposites, while intuitive understanding, his first interpretive principle, transcends them, affirming them both. This explanation will remain incomplete until *The Life Divine* as well as *Essays on the Gita,* but what is important to note here is that the concept of the "three purushas" has already become an interpretive principle in Aurobindo's understanding of the *Gita* and a major metaphysical clue to his thought, while the *Gita* itself is the center of Aurobindo's yoga.

THE GITA AT PONDICHERRY: ITS EARLY IMPORTANCE

With the threat of another arrest and in response to another command from within, Aurobindo turned his journal responsibilities over to others and fled British India for Chandernagore in French territory and finally to Pondicherry, where he would remain until his death on December 5, 1950. Aurobindo withdrew from political activity to perfect his yoga and to thereby affect through *brahmatejas* the evolution of the Universe toward a more permanent good. He expected to return following perfection of his yoga, but he never did, for his yoga was incomplete at his death.[67]

Based on Aurobindo's emphasis in 1909–10 and his early Pondicherry works, we assume that he began his isolated yogic practice with what he called the "Yoga of the *Gita.*" His earliest materials in the Pondicherry period continue to closely identify with the *Gita.* These culminate in his *Essays on the Gita,* published from 1916–1920 in a new journal, the *Arya*. It was in the *Arya,* which was published from August, 1914 to January, 1921, that most of his writings were first published.

This close identification of Aurobindo's yoga with the *Gita* is found in his earliest piece from Pondicherry, published first in book form in 1921 but dating back probably to 1914–15, and entitled, "The Yoga and Its Objects." Though the *Upanishads* and the *Mahabharata* are quoted to support this early study, it is the *Gita* that holds pride of place, being quoted on almost every one of its twenty pages and more than once on many pages. In "The Yoga and Its Objects" Aurobindo now calls his yoga "Purna yoga" ("complete yoga") in the same sense that he will call it "Integral Yoga" in his later systematic writings.[68] He also calls his yoga "Adhyatmayoga," using the term *adhyātma* ("That which pertains to the *ātman*") from *Gìtá* 7.29; 8.3; 11.1. The emphasis of "The Yoga and its Objects" is upon surrender of one's activities and oneself to the Divine because all activity is of the Atman, and thus all is Divine.

> The principle of Adhyatmayoga is, in knowledge, the realisation of all things that we do not see but are aware of—men, things, ourselves, events, gods, titans, angels,—as one divine Brahman, and in action and attitude, an absolute self-surrender to the Paratpara Purusha, the transcendent infinite and universal Personality who is at once personal and impersonal, finite and infinite, self-limiting and illimitable, one and many, and informs with his being not only the Gods above, but man and the worm and the clod below. The surrender must be complete.[69]

The Paratpara ("Superior to the Superior") Purusha is, of course, the third of three purushas of the Karmoyogin period and the Purushottama of the *Essays on the Gita.*

In "the Yoga and its Objects" Aurobindo first explicitly relates the "three purushas" to yogic experiences and, more particularly, to his own experiences as Feys has argued for the *Essays*. In his valuable study, Feys maintains Aurobindo's two earlier experiences, that with Lele and that in the Alipore jail, correspond to the *aksara* purusha and the *ksara* purusha of the *Gita*. The experiences from 1909 to 1920 corresponds to the Purushottama.[70] Feys' argument relies heavily upon Aurobindo's recollections of these experiences from letters written in the 1930's. He does not argue against the possibility that Aurobindo's recollections could be an interpretation of his experiences in the light of the *Gita* (rather than evidence of reading the *Gita* in light of past experiences). The evidence is limited. Yet the language of these past recollections is not the language of the *Gita*. It is the language of Supermind, Overmind, or Higher Mind, the levels of consciousness Aurobindo believed he had experienced later. Feys points to the similarity of Aurobindo's descriptions of the purushas and his own experiences, but presents no evidence of Aurobindo's having consciously attempted to read his experiences in terms of the *Gita*. Indeed, as we have noted, Aurobindo had always clearly stated that experience is superior to scripture. It would not be surprising for him to read the *Gita* in terms of his experiences.

A portion of Feys' argument is strengthened, however, by consideration of "The Yoga and its Objects," which preceeded the *Essays*. He discusses the practice of Purna Yoga or Adhyatmayoga in terms of three "processes": first, complete surrender to the Divine; second, observing the working of the divine power in oneself; and third, perceiving all as the Divine like the vision of *Gita* chapter eleven. Aurobindo speaks of his experiences of the "three purushas" as three chronological experiences in the "third process." His discussion of this process is interspersed with references to the *Gita*.

The first experience in that third process, of perceiving all as the divine and impersonal Absolute and of perceiving phenomena as form without substance, corresponds to his experiences with Lele. Aurobindo says:

> First, as a rule, in the process of knowledge one comes to see pervading all space and time one divine impersonal existence, *sad-ātman,* without movement, distinction or feature, *śāntam alakṣaṇam,* in which all names and forms seem to stand with a very doubtful or a very minor reality. In this realisation the One may seem to be the only reality and everything else *māyā,* a purposeless and inexplicable illusion.[71]

Compare this with description later of the experiences with Lele: ". . . they made me see with a stupendous intensity the world as a cinematographic play of vacant forms in the impersonal universality of the Absolute Brahman."[72] In terms of the three purushas, this corresponds to an experience of the *akṣara* purusha.

Aurobindo's second experience of the third process—seeing all things as God—corresponds to his experience in the Alipore jail, namely his experience of the *kṣara* purusha of the *Gita*. Aurobindo writes:

> But afterwards, if you do not stop short and limit yourself by the impersonal realisation, you will come to see the same *ātman* not only containing and supporting all created things, but informing and filling them, and eventually you will be able to understand that even the names and forms are Brahman. You will then be able to live more and more in the knowledge which the Upanishads and the Gita hold up as the rule of life; you will see the Self in all existing things and all existing things in the Self, *ātmānam sarvabhūteṣu sarvabhūtāni cātmani* (*Gita* 6.29); you will be aware of all things as Brahman, *sarvam khalvidam brahma.*[73]

Just as Aurobindo described seeing all as Krishna in the Uttarpara speech after emerging from the Alipore jail, and just as he did not accept his yogic experiences with Lele as definitive because they did not affirm the reality of the phenomenal world, so too, the experience of the *kṣara* purusha affirms not only the inactive Absolute and the unreality of the phenomenal, but an Absolute active in phenomena.

Feys' difficulty is in identifying the third experience (of the third process), the Purushottama of the *Essays,* the Supermind of the *Live Divine,* and the third experience of "The Yoga and its Objects." He claims it was a protracted experience, spread over the decade from 1909–1920, based on Aurobindo's 1932 statement: ". . . and it took me ten more years of intense Yoga under a supreme inner guidance to trace it out and that was because I had my past and the world's past to assimilate and overpass before I could find and found the future."[74] Aurobindo does speak of a "third realisation" in his later letters: ". . . that of the supreme Reality with the static and dynamic Brahman as its two aspects."[75] But unlike the other three "realisations," this one is difficult to identify, and if Feys' suggestion is correct, it is the only one of the four that is not a specific experience or datable set of experiences.[76]

"The Yoga and its Objects" describes the chronologically third experience of "all things as God," as that of the Purushottama of the *Essays* and the Supermind of the *Life Divine:*

> But the crowning realisation of this yoga is when you become aware of the whole world as the expression, play or Lila of an infinite divine personality, when you see in all, not the impersonal *sad-ātman* which is the basis of manifest existence,—although you do not lose that knowledge,—but Sri Krishna who at once is, bases and transcends all manifest and unmanifest existence, *avyakto vyaktāt paraḥ.*[77]

Yet Aurobindo never claimed to have experienced the highest consciousness of the evolutionary sequence, the Supermind. Even his "fourth realisation" on his "Day of Siddhi," November 14, 1926, is described as a descent of the lower Overmind consciousness in preparation for the descent of the higher Supermind consciousness. In Aurobindo's later description of the "Day of Siddhi" he described it succinctly: an experience "of the higher planes of consciousness leading to the Supermind."[78] And once, in response to a disciple's question as to whether Aurobindo had ever experienced Krishna, he identified Krishna with Overmind: "Krishna is not the supramental Light. The descent of Krishna would mean the descent of the Overmind Godhead preparing, though not itself actually, the descent of the Supermind and Ananda."[79] He distinguished this Krishna "who was incarnate at Brindavan and Dwarka and Kurukshetra and who was the guide of my Yoga and with whom I realised identity" from "the Krishna of the Gita who is the transcendent Godhead, Paramatma, Parabrahma, Purushottama . . ."[80]

Most likely, then, the experience of the third purusha, the Purushottama, the highest experience in the perceiving of all things as Divine, was for Aurobindo a future and final attainment. Since he died with his yoga incomplete, never experiencing this, but instead realizing new intermediate stages between Mind and Supermind, Feys' identification is problematic. The Purushottama of the *Essays* and the third experience of "The Yoga and its Objects," was an experience to which Aurobindo looked forward but which may have never arrived.

ESSAYS ON THE GITA

The first issue of the monthly *Arya* began publication on August 15, 1914. Its third year began with the articles which would make up Aurobindo's *Essays on the Gita*. The "First Series" of the *Essays* appeared from August, 1916 to July, 1918 and the "Second Series" from August, 1918 to July, 1920. Each series was published separately in book form until they were both published together in one volume in 1959, nine years after Aurobindo's death. One might have expected great revisions of the *Essays*, given the development of Aurobindo's specialized vocabulary for the stages of consciousness-evolution he believed he had experienced from the writing of the *Essays* until 1950. Yet, the *Essays* appear to have undergone only minor stylistic changes, none substantial, and no change in vocabulary. As Aurobindo's vocabulary moved further from the *Gita,* and his experiences, he believed, moved beyond the *Gita,* it is as if he left the text behind.

Simultaneously with publication of the *Essays,* the *Arya* also published from August, 1914 through January, 1921 Aurobindo's series amplifying the yoga of the *Gita* and providing a bridge between it and his later understandings. These articles were later published together as *The Synthesis of Yoga.* Aurobindo later revised and enlarged the first twelve chapters of Part One, "The Yoga of Works," but not the remainder. The structure of *The Synthesis of Yoga* reflects the threefold path of the *Gita.* "Synthesis" is the key term in the Introduction, "The Conditions of Synthesis." Part One is "The Yoga of Divine Works"; Part Two, "The Yoga of Integral Knowledge"; Part Three, "The Yoga of Divine Love"; and Part Four, "The Yoga of Self-perfection."[81] Its language is much like that of the first edition of the *Life Divine,* and Aurobindo's works of the mid-twenties. Later editions of these works, however, reflect his "fourth realisation" of his "Day of Siddhi" as well as what he believed were his experiences of further states of consciousness. These required him to revise the *Life Divine* in 1939–40 and even add four chapters to Part Two of Book Two of that work.[82]

As one might expect, Aurobindo's interpretation of the *Gita* in the *Essays* continues to deny that any text is "the eternal Word of God," or that Truth is found in its entirety in any scripture.[83] Every scripture contains an historically conditioned element along with its eternal message. Thus, Aurobindo seeks "the actual living truths it contains, apart from their metaphysical form. . . ." The *Essays* attempt to extract the nontemporal, universal teachings from the *Gita* on the basis of the authority of Aurobindo's experience. "What is entirely of permanent value is that which besides being universal has been experienced, lived and seen with a higher than the intellectual vision."[84] He believes these experiences are not private; they are open to all. Yet his own attainments were matched or surpassed he believed only by those of "the Mother," a French woman, Mira Richard, who met Aurobindo in 1914 and supervised the Sri Aurobindo Ashram from Aurobindo's "Day of Siddhi" until her death in 1973. He believed she incarnated the Supermind.[85]

In spite of these disclaimers, and in spite of his discussions about departing from the limitations of the *Gita* in letters from the 1930s and 1940s, one does not find any examples in the *Essays* of his rejecting the *Gita*'s teachings. Even what appears in the *Gita* to be limited by time transcends that condition if properly understood.

> In the Gita there is very little that is merely local or temporal and its spirit is so large, profound and universal that even this little can easily be universalised without the sense of the teaching suffering any diminution or violation; rather by giving an ampler scope to it than belonged to the country and epoch, the teaching gains in depth, truth and power. Often indeed the Gita itself suggests the wider scope that can in this way be given to an idea in itself local or limited.[86]

Thus, Aurobindo rejects nothing from the *Gita,* as he understands it, in spite of his disclaimers. The *Gita,* he clearly believed at this point taught his own yoga.

The *Gita* continued to be for Aurobindo a yoga, a *sādhana,* a discipline to follow, rather than a metaphysical system and Aurobindo reiterated this in the Essays. "It is in fact primarily a practical system of Yoga that it teaches and it brings in metaphysical ideas only as explanatory of its practical system. . . ."[87] It is practical, universal and living. Yet the *Gita*'s emphasis upon action has been misunderstood by those Indian Nationalists who have tried to turn it into a document teaching disinterested performance of duties with the good of the nation as its goal. Contrary to B.C. Chatterji and Tilak, he believed it is not exclusively a *karmayoga,* a yoga of action, in which knowledge and devotion are subordinated.[88] The denial that the *Gita* is solely a gospel of social action is not, as Feys argues, due to Aurobindo's own withdrawal from Nationalist activity (which for Aurobindo was *not* a renunciation of action),[89] but reflects his concern that such interpretations miss the deeper, spiritual, synthesis of the *Gita* which includes action, as well as devotion and knowledge.

> It is not the rule of a large moral and intellectual altruism which is here announced, but that of a spiritual unity with God and with this world of beings who dwell in him and in whom he dwells. It is not an injunction to subordinate the individual to society and humanity or immolate egoism on the altar of the human collectivity, but to fulfil the individual in God and to sacrifice the ego on the one true altar of the all-embracing Divinity.[90]

In the *Essays,* Aurobindo adds another interpretive principle: the *Gita*'s teaching must be seen as progressive, the whole teaching must be used to interpret each individual part and the complete teaching is clear at the *Gita*'s end. There are, then, three great steps in the *Gita*'s argument, based on the ideas of right action, *karman,* knowledge, *jñāna,* and devotion, *bhakti.* The first step is that of selfless sacrifice of works: "by the renunciation of desire and a perfect equality works have to be done as a sacrifice by man as the doer, a sacrifice to a deity who is the supreme and only Self though by him not yet realised in his own being." The second step is the yoga of knowledge, *jñāna,* which links *karmayoga* to a realization of the true nature of the Self and the world. Thus, action takes place with a new consciousness: "not only the desire of the fruit, but the claim to be the doer of works has to be renounced in the realisation of the Self as the equal, the inactive, the immutable principle and of all works as simply the operation of universal Force, of the Nature-Soul, Prakitti, the unequal, active, mutable power." The third step, Aurobindo argues, is the addition of devotion; *bhakti.* This is not devotion to a deity separate from oneself, but a seeking of the Self as divine: "Lastly, the supreme Self has to be seen as the supreme Purusha governing this Prakriti, of whom the soul in Nature is a partial manifestation, by whom all works are directed, in a perfect transcendence, through Nature."[91] Thus, one never ends one's actions. Instead one sees the activity of Nature as the willful, directed activity of the Divine and the Divine as identical with one's Self. The human soul realizes that it shares in the transcendence as well as in the works, that the works are the works of the Supreme active/inactive Self. Nature's works are one's own when seen universally, and not in terms of the limited ego. One becomes free to do the will of God, acting "in a perfect spiritual liberty."[92]

The three steps of the yoga of the *Gita* surprisingly are not reflective of the key interpretive principle used by Aurobindo to understand the *Gita*'s metaphysics, the "three purushas." Aurobindo uses *Gita* 15.16-18 regularly throughout the *Essays,* either directly quoting the passage or alluding again and again to his understanding of its teaching. Though the later chapters present the *Gita*'s full teaching, the passage from chapter fifteen is first brought in as early as Aurobindo's discussion of *sāṃkhya* and *yoga* in *Gita* 2.39.[93] It is considered the *Gita*'s main contribution to Indian thought.

> This idea of the Purushottama, though continually implied in the Upanishads, is disengaged and definitely brought out by the Gita and has exercised a powerful influence on the later develoments of the Indian religious conscousness. It is the

> foundation of the highest Bhaktiyoga which claims to exceed the rigid definitions of monistic philosophy; it is at the back of the philosophy of the devotional Puranas.[94]

One might add, as well, that it is also the foundation of Aurobindo's own religious stance, for the Purushottama, as the Supermind, embodies his conviction that the Absolute is not just beyond distinctions of Being and Becoming, Inactivity and Activity, and Unity and Multiplicity, but embraces them all in Itself. In the *Life Divine,* Saccidananda is described as being beyond such distinctions but it also contains them; it is a state not merely of *neti....neti,* "not this, not this," but also *iti....iti,* "this, this." Negations limit the Absolute as well.[95] Similarly, in the *Essays* the Purushottama embraces these dualities.

> The Uttama is the Lord, the supreme Brahman, the supreme Self, who possesses both the immutable unity and the mobile multiplicity. It is by a large mobility and action of His nature, His energy, His will and power, that He manifests Himself in the world and by a greater stillness and immobility of His being that He is aloof from it; yet is He as Purushottama above both the aloofness form Nature and the attachment to Nature.[96]

Aurobindo, therefore, rejects the interpretations of the non-dualists, such as the ninth century thinker Shankara, who believed the highest Reality of Vedanta was Brahman, a state of pure consciousness. At the *Gita*'s time, Aurobindo writes, Vedanta was "pantheistic at the basis, monistic at the summit."[97] It did not take seriously Upanishadic references to the Absolute in personal terms. In affirming the Purushottama, the *Gita* restores the significance of such terms: "the Gita is going to represent the Ishwara, the Purushottama, as higher even than the still and immutable Brahman, and the loss of ego in the impersonal comes in at the beginning as only a great initial and necessary step towards union with the Purushottama."[98] The principle of progressive teaching interprets earlier chapters that, out of their context, may appear monistic in terms of the Purushottama explicity set forth later. This approach departs from "the general contemporary mind of Indian thought," for it presents a more synthetic affirmation of reality.[99]

Yet, the Purushottama does not represent common theism either. "It is something greater than the Ishtadeva [chosen god of the devotee] that receives the surrender."[100] Though there are passages in the

Gita in which Krishna, as a theistic deity, appears to claim highest status for himself as god among gods,[101] Aurobindo interprets these as references not merely to Krishna the *avatāra* or highest god, but to the Purushottama. For example, Aurobindo translates *Gita* 5.29 as: "When a man has known Me as the Enjoyer of sacrifice and Tapasya (of all askesis and energisms), the mighty lord of all the worlds, the friend of all creatures, he comes by the peace." Then he comments, using the Purushottama as the interpretive principle: "We get back to the great idea of the Gita, the idea of the Purushottama—though that name is not given till close upon the end, it is always that which Krishna means by his 'I' and 'Me'. . . ."[102]

Finally, the concept of the Purushottama prevents the Yogin's acquiesence in a belief in the mechanical determinism of Nature. "It makes it clear that is is not in the end Nature which mechanically determines its own action; it is the will of the Supreme which inspires her. . . ."[103] The Highest embraces the personal and, thus, the concept of will, as well as the impersonal and the idea of determinism.

Auobindo's theory of the evolution of consciousness holds these contradictory concepts together. Mind, the level of logic, is on a lower level in that process and has only a limited power of knowing. It therefore needs illumination from higher levels of consciousness, and Aurobindo believes he has experienced that above Mind are more synthetic, more intuitive levels of consciousness, just as below Mind are the more divisive levels of Matter, Psyche and Life.[104] Though the *Essays* speak little of this evolution, one finds it behind its interpretations, and the final chapter of the *Essays* begins with "Existence is not merely a machinery of Nature, a wheel of law in which the soul is entangled for a moment or for ages; it is a constant manifestation of the Spirit."[105]

Likewise, the setting of the *Gita* on the battlefield of great destruction, Aurobindo believes, is not meant as an allegory as pacifists would have it. Rather than symbolical, the setting is typical. Arjuna is the representative human being: ". . . in the Gita he typifies the human soul of action brought face to face through that action in its highest and most violent crisis with the problem of human life and its apparent incompatibility with the spiritual state or even with a purely ethical ideal of perfection."[106]

Kurukshetra itself represents the fact that life as the activity of the Divine is a battle, a field of death: "God the Terrible, this is the vision that Arjuna sees on that field of massacre."[107] Aurobindo thus takes the setting and the vision of destruction in relationship to

Krishna's universal form in chapter eleven quite literally. The importance of destruction in the evolutionary process must be recognized, he believes, for that too is Divine. To "look existence in the face," is to "look God in the face," to "acknowledge Kurukshetra," to surrender to the Divine "law of Life by Death."[108] The *Essays* were written with World War I as part of their background, but Aruobindo the yogin was no pacifist. He supported the Allies in World War II and even made a small contribution to the Viceroy's War Purposes Fund while in withdrawal at Pondicherry. He was convinced that Hitler was either possessed by an *asura,* demon, or incarnated one.[109] Kurukshetra, then, represents a step forward in the evolution of the Divine: "a meeting and wrestling of forces which progress by mutual destruction towards a continually changing adjustment expressive of a progressive harmonising and hopeful of a perfect harmony based upon some yet ungrasped potentiality of oneness."[110] This calls for surrender to the Purushottama of the *Gita* and integration, thereby, of the living truths of the vision of chapter eleven. The Purushottama of the "triple status of the purusha" is the central principle of *Gita* interpretation for Aurobindo.

BEYOND THE GITA

With the completion of the *Essays* and *The Synthesis of Yoga,* the *Gita* moved off center stage in Aurobindo's work. There intervenes the experiences of his "Day of Siddhi" on November 24, 1926, which convinced him of the existence of further levels of consciousness. It is not that he abandoned the *Gita* in his last two and one-half decades. Sixteen of the fifty-six chapters of the revised *Life Divine* carry superscriptions from the *Gita.* But Aurobindo's letters to his disciples from the 1930s and 1940s indicate that he believed his consciousness had moved beyond what the *Gita* teaches. He continued to identify his message with the *Gita* but raised objections not raised before. Unlike the *Gita,* he now says, his aim in "Integral Yoga" is not the cessation of rebirth but perfection of Self and world within the Becoming of the Absolute. More important, however, the *Gita,* "does not bring forward the idea of a spiritual evolution or the idea of the higher planes and the supramental Truth-Consciousness and the bringing down of that consciousness as the means of the complete transformation of earthly life."[111] His critique that the *Gita* does not emphasize the evolution is of interest because he did not make this criticism in the *Essays.* Instead, as noted above, one finds the evolutionary theory behind his interpretations of the verses, though not in the *Gita* itself. That the concept of the higher planes of consciousness is not in the *Gita,* argues that his experiences have further subordinated the *Gita.* Finally, he disagrees with the *Gita* because it "seems to admit the cessation of birth in the world as the ultimate aim or at least the ultimate culmination of Yoga. . ."[112] Again, this criticism was not found in the *Essays;* though it is clearly the *Gita*'s aim, Aurobindo's goal was to affirm the eternal Becoming of the Absolute and, thus, rebirth as Absolute.[113] In fact, the elements brought forward in Aurobindo's critique are not only what Aurobino says "constitute the novelty of Sri Aurobindo's message as compared to the Hindu tradition," but are the major emphases of Aurobindo's integral yoga.

Thus, as Aurobindo believed that experience is the authority to be used to interpret a scripture, he now believed that his experience had taken him beyond the teachings of the *Gita,* not to reject it but to surpass it. What began in the Baroda period as an interest in the *Gita* as the synthesis of knowledge, devotion and works, what remained quietly behind the scenes during his Nationalist days, but burst forth as a central text following his incarceration at Alipore, what was the center of his yoga at Pondicherry, culminating in a commentary and another major work, had now moved into the background. The experiential authority asserted itself beyond all other authorities. The *Gita*-yogin had transcended the *Gita;* so he believed.

CHAPTER FIVE

Gandhi and the Bhagavadgita

J. T. F. JORDENS

No book was more central to Gandhi's life and thought than the *Bhagavadgita*. He constantly referred to it as his "spiritual dictionary," "the mother who never let him down," or his *kāmadhenū*, "the cow that grants all wishes." In the thousands of letters of spiritual advice he wrote, references to the *Gita* abound, and also encouragement for regular reading of the text. Communal recitation of the *Gita* was a regular feature of life in his ashrams; in fact it was the principal religious ritual. Gandhi's main work on the *Gita (Discourses on the Gita)* was originally given as talks during morning prayers in the Satyagraham Ashram at Ahmedabad over a period of nine months in 1926, when Mahadev Desai and Punjabhai took notes which were later edited and published.[1] During his stay in Yeravda jail in 1929, Gandhi wrote a Gujarati translation of the *Gita*, with an introduction and commentary, which was entitled *Anasaktiyoga*. This was later translated into English by Mahadev Desai, and published as *The Gita according to Gandhi*.[2] While in the same jail in 1930 and 1932, Gandhi sent weekly letters about the *Gita* to be read out at Ashram prayer meetings; they are collectively known as his 'Letters on the *Gītā*'.[3] Altogether, Gandhi wrote some 360 pages about his favourite scripture, more than he wrote on any one other topic.

In his autobiography, Gandhi recalled his first meaningful encounter with the work when in 1889, at the end of his second year in England, two Theosophists invited him to read with them the *Gita* in Sir Edwin Arnold's translation.[4] Although he was greatly impressed by the work at first reading, he did not start studying it more closely until 1903, ten years after his arrival in South Africa. Again it was close contact with Theosophists that spurred him to consider his own Hindu tradition. He commenced regular reading of the *Gita* and devoted some time to learning Sanskrit.[5] However, there is no evidence that the *Gita* at that time played an important part in his life. Occasionally he expressed some interest in publishing his own edition of it,[6] but textual references to it are very rare in his writings of the South African period, and at no stage do they suggest any attempt at interpreting the meaning of the work or reflecting on the basis of its authority.

Gandhi's first clear statement on the meaning of the *Gita* appeared in his "Satyagraha Leaflet No. 18" of 8 May, 1919. He had called for a hartal on Sunday, May 11, and had suggested that people should observe a fast and read the *Gita*. This immediately led some Hindus to question the appropriateness of that work for such an occasion, since they felt it promoted violence. Gandhi replied that the *Gita* was not a work of history, but a religious text that seized on the 'occasion' of the *Mahabharata* war in order to draw attention to "the war going on in our own bodies between the forces of Good (Pandavas) and the forces of Evil (Kauravas)".[7] In a letter to Sakarlal Dave written shortly afterwards, on 19 May, he referred as follows to what he saw as his personal qualification for interpreting the *Gita:* "I have something far more powerful than argument, namely, experience. . . ."[8]

By 1919, therefore, Gandhi had clearly conceived what became two basic principles of his interpretation: the allegorical character of the *Gita* as a whole, and the primacy of "experience" among the qualifications of the interpreter. During his period in Yeravda jail in 1922, Gandhi read voraciously,[9] and he also spent a lot of time on a close study of the *Gita*. In fact, he compiled a glossary of terms used in the work, the *Gītākosh,* which was later revised to incorporate meanings given in his *Anasaktiyoga.*[10] On October, 11, 1925, he published in *Navajivan* a six-page article entitled "Meaning of the Gita."[11] This too was written in answer to questions put to him by Hindus about the validity of his interpretations. This document summarizes the fully-developed Gandhian approach to the *Gita* which is the subject of this chapter.

It is evident that by 1925 Gandhi had fully worked out his approach to, and explanation of, the text, and his later writings do not add anything significantly new. Such development as did occur after 1925 was only the practical elaboration and concrete application of the principles he had already formulated: he produced a translation with commentary and compiled a glossary; his own reading of the *Gita* intensified; *Gita*-recitation became an essential feature of the routine of his ashrams; and his correspondence continually referred to his favorite text. When spinning became a vital part of his routine, he justified it by reference to the *Gita,* and he did the same in his justification of non-cooperation and in his fight against the blight of untouchability. Increasingly he stressed that schools should incorporate the study of the *Gita* in their curriculums.

In short, Gandhi's effort at formulating his own interpretation of the *Gita* started only after his return to India in 1919, and was fully and definitively articulated by 1925. Whereas the interpretation of the *Gita* by Aurobindo, for example, went through significant changes during his lifetime, that of Gandhi did not. Discussion of the various aspects of his interpretation is facilitated because there is no need for a developmental treatment. Because of the unchanging nature of Gandhi's interpretation, we can treat his writings as one internally coherent body of evidence, and seek answers to a logical sequence of questions. First the question is asked as to how Gandhi viewed the concept of the authority of 'scripture' in general. This leads to a description of the precise place of the *Gita* among the *Shastras,* which is followed by an analysis of Gandhi's credentials as an interpreter. The next section looks at the basic tenets of Gandhi's interpretation of the context of the work as a whole, and at his specific interpretation of particular key concepts. The conclusion tries to link Gandhi's interpretation to other aspects of his total view of life, and suggests some of the major formative influences on his interpretation.

THE AUTHORITY OF THE SCRIPTURES

During the first part of his stay in South Africa, Gandhi was in very close contact with ardent Christians who tried their best to win him over to their beliefs.[12] The resultant interchange raised in Gandhi's mind a large number of questions around scriptural authority, specifically of the Bible and of the *Vedas.* He found a lot of arguments to counter his Evangelical friends in the books of Edward Maitland, founder of the Esoteric Christian Union, which presented allegorical interpretations of the Gospels and proclaimed the fundamental identity of all great religions.[13] In his difficulties and doubts he turned to his friend and mentor, Rajchandra Rajivbhai, with some of his questions, and later he recalled that a long letter from his friend had eased his mind.[14] The anxious doubts about scriptural authority seem to have receded because he no longer considered Christianity a personal challenge that threatened his adherence to Hinduism. It was only after his final return to India that questions about the nature of scriptural authority started to return to the fore; this time they were prompted by Hindus who disagreed with his doctrines, with his interpretations of scripture, or with what they saw as his rejection of clear *shastric* injunctions. These new pressures made Gandhi formulate and clarify his own ideas.

The basis of Gandhi's interpretation of the authority of the *shastras* was his conviction of their historical character—that no scriptures are eternal in themselves, but that they are all the limited products of a particular time: "Vedas, Upanishads, Smritis, Puranas and Itihasas . . . do not enunciate anew the eternal truths, but show how these were practised at the time to which the books belong".[15] Consequently, he believed, it was not surprising that they abound in contradictions,[16] and, even worse, that "there is hardly an immoral practice for which it would be difficult to find Shastric sanction".[17] Moreover, there is such a profusion of books called 'shastras', that even listing them would seem an impossible task.[18] Even if one accepted, as Gandhi did, that some works, such as the *Saṃhitā*,[19] are of primary importance, these works too suffered from what he called "a process of double distillation": "First they come through a human prophet, and then through the commentaries of interpreters. None of them comes from God directly."[20] Elsewhere he stressed the same idea in the context of a discussion about the Gospels: "Only God is changeless and as His message is received through the imperfect human medium, it is always liable to suffer distortion in proportion as the medium is pure or otherwise."[21]

On the one hand therefore, Gandhi accepted that the *shastras* suffered from severe historical limitations, but on the other he stood by their authority, which he repeatedly affirmed: "I do accept the Shastras as authoritative";[22] "the sum total of these books is certainly inspired";[23] "I believe in the Puranas as sacred books. . . ."[24] But what exactly was that authoritative core of truth, and how did one proceed to peel off the misleading layers of historicity? In this respect he indicated the broad criteria for rejecting shastric statements thus: "That which is opposed to trained reason, cannot be claimed as Shastra no matter how ancient it may be."[25] Gandhi mentioned the test of reason, but questions of 'rationality' did not often preoccupy him, except for the occasional affirmation of his disbelief in miracles,[26] and his objection to logical inconsistencies. This is not surprising given the fact that Gandhi had no interest whatsoever in the 'dogmatic' or 'theological' superstructures of religion. He expressed that attitude very forcefully as follows: "It is a misuse of our intellectual energy and a waste of time to go on reading what we cannot put into practice."[27]

The crucial, final test of the validity of a scriptural text lies elsewhere: "From my youth upwards, I learnt the art of estimating the value of scriptures on the basis of their ethical teaching."[28] Here we touch the central nerve of the Gandhian approach: religion is about action, and "what cannot be followed out in day-to-day practice cannot be called religion".[29] No wonder that morality was for Gandhi the infallible touchstone of the truth of the *shastras.* He affirmed this conviction over and over again: "Nothing that is inconsistent with the universally accepted first principles of morality has for me the authority of the Shastras";[30] and ". . . any conduct that is contrary to truth and ahimsa is to be eschewed and any book that violates these principles is not a shastra",[31] etc. Gandhi referred to difficulties he experienced in coming to grips with the most sacred and ancient of Hindu scriptures, the *Saṃhitā;* these difficulties were not problems of intellectual grasp of their meaning, but difficulties "in applying them to daily conduct."[32] The crucial acid test of ethics made him "refuse to accept the authority of a shastra which supports untouchability."[33] He most emphatically affirmed that supremacy of ethics when he stated:

> If I discovered that those scriptures, which are known as Vedas, Upanishads, Bhagavad Gita, Smritis, etc., clearly showed that they claimed divine authority for untouchability . . ., then nothing on this earth would hold me to Hinduism.[34]

If it is through that supreme test of ethics that one is enabled to peel away the unacceptable and historic layers from the essential core of the *shastras,* then it must follow that the essential truth of the *shastras* consists of an ethical message:

> Learned men may please themselves and draw seemingly profound meanings from the Shastras, but what they offer is not the real sense of these. Only those who have experience in the practice of their truths can explain the real meaning of the Shastras.[35]

The *Gita* itself, in stanza 16.23, says "Let the *Shastra* be thy authority". Gandhi's interpretation is of considerable interest when he explains the meaning of the *Gita*'s injunction: "We should be guided by the authority of the Shastras. That Shastra means *shistāchāra,* that is we should follow the example of those forefathers of ours who were holy and fearless".[36] According to him that is what scriptures are about, right conduct, and that is where the scripture speaks with authority—the authority of the saints of yore who have successfully put the ethical principles they proclaim into practice in their own lives. It is successful practice, no passive reception of "revealed" truths, that lends authority to their precepts.

The Gita among the Shastras

From the multitude of available texts, Gandhi chose the *Gita* as his personal guide, and as the touchstone of all *shastras:* "nothing that is inconsistent with the main theme of the *Gita* is Shastra, no matter where it is found printed."[37] This firm assertion is often repeated in different words: the *Gita* is "the essence of dharma,"[38] "a synthesis of the Hindu religion"[39] and "the key to a knowledge of the Shastras."[40] He has stated: "whatever is contrary to its main theme I reject as un-Hindu,"[41] and "if all the other scriptures were reduced to ashes, the seven hundred verses of this imperishable booklet are quite enough to tell me what Hinduism is and how one can live up to it."[42]

One of the reasons for this preeminence of the *Gita* is its pan-Hindu universality: "It is accepted by all Hindu sects as authoritative."[43] As such it is distinct from the many sectarian scriptures that find favor with only a section of Hindus. Although other texts, and particular the *Saṃhitās,* do have that same pan-Hindu quality, what makes the *Gita* more effectively universal is that it is an easy text, cast in "incredibly simple Sanskrit,"[44] and accessible in the original to anyone with even a rudimentary knowledge of that language. The difficult language of the *Vedas,* for example, puts them out of reach of all except a few specialists. The *Gita* differs from many other texts in yet another way: according to Gandhi it is free from dogma,[45] and as such is accessible, acceptable and applicable to everybody, because, it "excludes no Faith and no teacher."[46]

However these reasons for the pre-eminent place of the *Gita* were only peripheral to Gandhi; the cardinal reason was that "in a short compass it gives a complete reasoned moral code,"[47] and it provides "in a nutshell the secret art of living."[48] In other Hindu texts the ethical core is dispersed and hidden in an abundance of embellishments, obscurities, dogmatic elaborations, mythical cycles, and ritualistic discourses; it requires scholarship, effort and endless time to sift the pure gold from the dross. But the *Gita* "is a pure religious discourse without any embellishment. It simply describes the progress of the pilgrim soul towards the Supreme Goal. Therefore there is no question of selection."[49] The *Gita* is supreme among the *shastras* because, in a clear, direct and succinct fashion, "it enunciates the principles on which all conduct must be based."[50]

Since for Gandhi the essence of religion lay in ethical action, it is quite logical that for him the *Gita* occupied the highest place among the *shastras.* Moreover, he did not look upon the *Gita* as being just a book of theory, a handbook with rules for religious living; to him the knowledge it contained was "the fruit of experience."[51] The author of the *Gita* was not just an inspired theoretician: he summarized the basic principles of perfect living after having put them into practice, and the knowledge that resulted was the fruit of that test. Gandhi heard the echo of that truth reverberate in the very text: "I have felt that the *Gita* teaches that what cannot be followed out in day-to-day practice cannot be called religion."[52]

There is no doubt that much of the text of the *Gītā* deals with principles of action. However, it also contains, especially in later chapters, a significant number of statements of a different kind, dealing with questions of a theoretical and theological nature. To Gandhi these were of a secondary significance, and he made this quite clear by unequivocally indicating what he considered to be the "core" of the *Gita:* "the theme of the Gita is contained in the second chapter";[53] "From the last verse of Chapter II, it would seem that Sri Krishna had nothing further to add";[54] and, "with Chapter II the Gita ends. It need not have been followed by anything more."[55] In fact, Gandhi was prepared to go even further, and he repeatedly declared that the last nineteen stanzas of Chapter II constituted the essence of the *Gita,* and that all the rest was no more than an explanation and elaboration of that basic message. "These stanzas are the key to the understanding of the *Gita.* I would even go so far as to advise people to reject statements in the poem which bear a meaning contrary to that of these nineteen stanzas".[56] These assertions by Gandhi about the crucial importance of the second chapter are confirmed by his writings on the *Gita:* nearly half of his commentary, (120 pages), is devoted to chapters two, three, and four. The remaining fourteen chapters get very short shrift; they average less than ten pages each. A rough count of Gandhi's quotations from the *Gita* confirms that pattern: about two-thirds of his quotations (approximately 110) come from chapters two and three (as opposed to up to only ten, or none at all, found in each of the remaining chapters.

Gandhi's Credentials as Interpreter

Since Gandhi put forward his own interpretation with confidence and a show of authority, it needs to be asked what qualifications he claimed to have as an interpreter. With regard to the general question of whether the task of the interpreter is limited to discovering the exact meaning of the text itself, Gandhi's rejection is categorical: "a literal interpretation lands one in a sea of contradictions. The letter killeth, the spirit giveth life."[57] When trying to determine the meaning of a text, "one should not stick to its letter, but try to understand its spirit, its meaning in the total context."[58] In other words, interpretation is not a process of establishing the literal meaning of the text, although we should take note of the rules of grammar[59]—but interpretation by its very nature means 'new' interpretation, expansion of the literal meaning, application to new circumstances.

In fact, the author of *Gita* had himself, according to Gandhi, given an example "by extending the meaning of words."[60] The *Gita*

> has given a new meaning to karma, sannyasa, yajna, etc. It has breathed new life into Hinduism. It has given an original rule of conduct. Not that what the *Gita* has given was not implied in the previous writings but the *Gita* put these implications in a concrete shape.[61]

Since the author of the *Gita* himself has thus expanded the meanings of the concepts he inherited,

> There is no harm in our expanding the meaning of the word "yajna", even if the new meaning we attach to the term was never in Vyasa's mind. We shall do no injustice to Vyasa by expanding the meaning of his words. Sons should enrich the legacy of their fathers.[62]

Text interpretation, therefore, is not a matter of discovering the literal meaning, but more importantly of expanding the meaning of the text and applying it to new circumstances of life. Since religious questions are for Gandhi not about ideology, but about action, the "new" interpretation referred to is not a function of discovering a speculative framework, but is concerned with ethical principles and their practical implementation.

What are the necessary qualifications for such a task? Naturally, one must be sufficiently versed in Sanskrit to understand the text; but that requires no scholarship: "The *Gītā* was not composed as a learned treatise".[63] Great scholars have written extensive commentaries on the work, and Gandhi read them and evaluated them as follows:

> I have read Lokamanya Tilak's and Shankaracharya's commentaries and tried to understand them as well as I could. I am not qualified to pronounce judgement on their learning. If we accept the point of view I have suggested, the question of expressing an opinion on their learning does not arise.[64]

In other words, their scholarship, however profound, is irrelevant to the real task of interpretation as Gandhi conceived it. He readily admitted that "from the point of view of scholarship, my qualifications for attempting the translation would seem to be nil."[65] But, on the other hand, he was "sure that learned commentaries are of much less value than the experience of one limited intelligence".[66]

This brings us to what Gandhi felt were the positive qualifications required of the interpreter:

> For understanding the meaning of the Shastras, one must have a well-cultivated moral sensibility and experience in the practice of their rules. . . . Hence anyone who offers to interpret the Shastras must have observed the prescribed disciplines in his life . . . only those who have experience in the practice of their truths can explain the real meaning of the Shastras.[67]

Only he can interpret the *Gita* correctly "who tries to follow its teaching in practice, and the correctness of the interpretation will be in proportion to his success in living according to the teaching".[68] In other words, since religion is about action, the interpretation of scripture acquires validity in so far as it can suggest putting the principles of religious action into practice. The message contained in the *Gita* is itself "the fruit of experience",[69] and that message can only be properly understood by making it yet again the fruit of experience.

That is the qualification which Gandhi claimed as his own. He accepted that others had offered different renderings, which had "their own place." But he added:

> I am not aware of the claims made by the translators of enforcing the meaning of the *Gītā* in their own lives. At the back of my reading there is the claim of an endeavour to enforce the meaning in my own conduct for an unbroken period of forty years.[70]

Therefore, even if his qualifications for scholarship were nil, Gandhi asserted: ". . . as one following its teaching I may be considered to be fairly well qualified."[71] In fact, Gandhi considered himself to be so well qualified that he boldly preferred his own versions to that of Vyasa:

> Let it be granted, that according to the letter of the *Gita* it is possible to say that warfare is consistent with renunciation of fruit. But after 40 years' unremitting endeavour fully to enforce the teaching of the *Gita* in my own life, I have, in all humility, felt that perfect renunciation is impossible without perfect observance of ahimsa in every shape and form.[72]

He repeated that idea elsewhere even more strongly: "I believe that the teaching of the *Gita* does not justify war, even if the author of the *Gita* had intended otherwise."[73] Gandhi's right to interpretation stemmed from his "moral sensibility" and was vindicated by his unrelenting practice; his interpretations had changed his own life, and had brought about "marvellous concrete results. It changes men's lives."[74] It is no wonder that he remained convinced that, as he put it:

> my philosophy represents the true meaning of the *Gita*. I may be mistaken. Such a mistake can do no harm either to me or to anybody. For the source of my inspiration is of no consequence if what I stand for be unadulterated truth.[75]

It is in this context that one should understand the "inner voice" Gandhi often referred to when announcing important decisions. This "inner voice" was the response of his own moral sensitivity, sharpened and finely tuned by long practice. This response always concerned decisions about a particular course of action, which sometimes was disapproved by and completely baffled his closest collaborators. The decision could often not be rationally justified, but in Gandhi's mind, it did not need that kind of justification. His finely tuned moral sense had spoken, and to him its supreme authority overrode all other considerations.

GANDHI'S INTERPRETATION

Our consideration of the content of Gandhi's interpretation of the *Gita* falls into two sections. The first describes his basic conception of the work as a whole and his explanation of its essential message. The second section explores the way in which Gandhi deals with those aspects of the *Gita* that to many other interpreters constitute the very core of its meaning, namely the doctrine of *bhakti* and the progressive self-revelation of Krishna.

During the entire South African period, Gandhi used the *Gita* merely as a collection of religiously useful "texts"; he drew attention to particular verses and their special message, much in the same way as he used to refer to texts from the Gospels or the Koran. The first time he wrote down his view of the meaning of the *Gita* as a whole was in 1919, in his "Satyagraha Leaflet No. 18." This was elicited by Hindus challenging his call for reading of the *Gita* during the coming hartal: they claimed that the text was inappropriate because it recommended killing of enemies, and therefore was not relevant to the *satyāgraha* context. Gandhi answered as follows:

> Now the *Bhagavad Gītā* is not a historical work, it is a great religious book, summing up the teaching of all religions. The poet has seized the occasion of the war between the Pandavas and the Kauravas on the field of Kurukshetra for drawing attention to the war going on in our bodies between the forces of Good (Pandavas) and the forces of Evil (Kauravas) and has shown that the latter would be destroyed and there should be no remissness in carrying on the battle against the forces of Evil, mistaking them through ignorance for forces of Good.[76]

This idea was occasionally reiterated in the succeeding years: "The *Gītā* speaks of the war between the divine and the demoniac,"[77] or "it deals with the ceaseless spiritual war going on in the human Kurukshetra."[78] A new development occurred in 1922 during Gandhi's spell in Yeravda jail, where he read the *Mahabharata* through for the first time: "The Mahabharata I had never read except in scraps. I was even prejudiced against it."[79] The reading took him four months, at the end of which he formulated his interpretation of the whole epic thus:

> The Mahabharata is not to me a historical record. It is hopeless as a history. But it deals with eternal verities in an alle-

gorical fashion. It takes up historical personages and events and transforms them into angels or devils as it suits the purpose of the poet whose theme is the external duel between good and evil, spirit and matter, God and Satan. It is like a mighty river which in its progress absorbs many streams, some even muddy.[80]

Gandhi considered that its "magnificent ending demonstrated the utter nothingness of earthly power . . . [and the] inexorable law of cause and effect," by which he meant the law of karma.[81]

In his article "Meaning of the Gita," published in *Navajivan* on November 11, 1925, Gandhi answered a correspondent's denial that the *Gita* taught non-violence by situating the *Gita* in the context of the *Mahabharata*. Previously he had argued that the author of the *Gita* only used the battle as an "occasion" for its teaching, and that he used it in such a way "because he did not look upon war as morally wrong." However, that was no longer acceptable because his interpretation of the *Mahabharata* had advanced another step:

Vyasa wrote his supremely beautiful epic to depict the futility of war. What did the Kauravas' defeat and the Pandavas' victory avail? How many among the victors survived? What was their fate? What was the end of Kunti, mother of the Pandavas? What trace is left today of the Yadava race?[82]

In other words, the *Mahabharata* epic had now become to Gandhi the epic *against* war because it described the utter futility of a pyrrhic victory in which both victors and vanquished lose their all. Henceforth Gandhi's main argument for holding that the *Gita* was a treatise on non-violence was the assertion that it constituted a central episode in the great anti-war epic.

Gandhi never tired of repeating that the essence of the *Gita* was expressed in the last twenty stanzas of Chapter two. What is the objective context of these stanzas, and why did Gandhi elevate them in this way? These lines basically constitute Krishna's answer to Arjuna's specific request for a description of the person whom Krishna calls a *sthitaprajñā,* one whose mentality is stabilized, one who has achieved perfect control over his inner self. These twenty verses abound in words signifying 'control', and also in terms referring to the senses, and to feelings of attachment, love, and lust. They describe the person who has achieved complete mastery over his inner and outer senses, and over his desires and dislikes, and who has reached an attitude of total indifference to all that may please or displease him. Such a person is at peace with himself, and his attitude to the outside world is one of equanimity and indifference.

Most commentators would consider the passage in question very important since it sketches the basic principles and sets the tone for the following two chapters. However, it seems quite clear, and most commentators would agree, that the state of mind described in that passage is not presented as the final aim of perfection, but rather as an important step on the spiritual path. Whoever achieves that state of mind is well prepared, first, for devoting his life to selfless performance of duty, and second for the *bhakti* that dedicates all action to Krishna. In other words, self-control, non-attachment, and mental equalibrium prepare the mind for total devotion to Krishna, the highest, secret doctrine of the *Gita*.[83] For Gandhi, however, control and non-attachment as described in the passage are not just mental and moral preparations for the fullness of religious life; he considers them to be the very essence of religion, and consequently the very essence of the message of the *Gita*.

The passage in question does not at any stage even mention the word *bhakti,* nor does it refer to Krishna. Yet Gandhi holds that after these verses Krishna really had no more to say, and that the rest of the *Gita* was only an elaboration of the principles clearly stated in this passage, which he felt express the very essence of Hinduism and of all religion. To Gandhi religion essentially refers to the mental attitude of the individual, religion is a 'state of mind'. It consists of the individual's complete control over his senses, desires and attachments; it is the total mastery of the spirit over the flesh, bringing about inner peace, total self-sufficiency and perfect equanimity. "Self-realisation is the subject of the *Gītā,* as it is of all scriptures."[84] This concept of religion is supremely individualistic and moralistic. If the *Gita* is, as it is in the eyes of many, "a song about the Lord," that Lord does not appear even once in the passage which Gandhi considered to be the essence of the *Gita*.

This brings us to the question of how Gandhi conceived the figure of Krishna, and how he interpreted those passages of the *Gita* which have very specific things to say about Krishna. A letter to Jamnadas Gandhi written in 1900 shows that Gandhi had already formed his basic opinions on the doctrine of *avatāra* before his final return to India. The essential ideas stated in that letter are the following. Every *ātman* about to attain *mokṣa* is an avatar or divine incarnation. Once it has reached *mokṣa,* it naturally becomes one with the absolute, and as such, perfect. But while alive on earth, avatars cannot be perfect, as they are striving for perfection. As historical persons they are necessarily imperfect beings; but they are invested with perfection when looked upon as 'ideal.'[85]

From those early days onward Gandhi often referred to the imperfections of the historical Krishna, for example: "Krishna, Rama and others were divine incarnations . . . but we need not believe in their perfection while yet alive";[86] "nor do I regard Rama and Krishna as portrayed in the two poems as infallible beings."[87] The historical Krishna was a man, an embodied *ātman* just like every other human being. Krishna brought to fruition through his own efforts his own potential of achieving *mokṣa:* as such he became an avatar. But this potentiality is part of everyone's being: "We too can be like them when immense punya [merit] has accrued to us".[88] In this sense, therefore, there is nothing 'ontologically' different about Krishna in relation to his birth or concerning his relationship with the Absolute: he is an *ātman* who has realized that full potential which is equally possible for any other *ātman.*

But that is not how Hindus generally look upon Krishna as *avatāra:* to many he is the perfect ideal, the ground of all being, the Lord of the universe. Gandhi knew that "For the faithful Hindu, his incarnation is without blemish. Krishna of the Hindu devotee is a perfect being,"[89] and accepted that view himself, but he added his own twist to it. To him, this ideal, divine Krishna was "an imaginary figure,"[90] "an imaginary incarnation."[91] In his commentary on the *Gita,* he succinctly explained it thus:

> Krishna of the *Gītā* is perfection and right knowledge personified; but the picture is imaginary. This does not mean that Krishna, the adored of his people, never lived. But perfection is imagined. The idea of a perfect incarnation is an after-growth.[92]

Gandhi referred to this aspect of avatar as *sampūrnāvatāra,*[93] "full incarnation," and distinguished it from the other concept of the 'partial' avatar, a condition accessible to all:

> Whatever qualities are attributed to God, are also attributed to the *atman.* Just as God is unborn, unageing and undying, so is the *atman.* The *atman* is an eternal part of God, and that is why it possesses the attributes of God. The *atman* is birthless and yet is born in a body and therefore it must be considered as a partial incarnation of God. Full incarnation can-

> not be understood through the intellect. This is a matter of imagination as well as of faith.[94]

How, then, does Gandhi interpret the famous verses of the *Gita* at the beginning of Chapter Four: "Though unborn, though Myself is eternal, though Lord of Beings, resorting to My own material nature, I come into being by My own mysterious power".[95] According to Gandhi, this verse does not in any special way refer to Krishna, but it indicates the essential nature of the *ātman,* and proclaims that in the final instance all *ātmans* are only expressions of the One. He warns us not to take this text too literally:

> When Krishna says that He incarnates Himself as a human being, he only uses the idiom of common speech. God never incarnates Himself as an *ātman* and is never born as a human being. He is ever the same. When, from our human point of view, we see special excellence in some individual, we look upon him as an avatar. In God's language there is no such avatar; it exists only in the language of human beings'.[96]

In view of the above, it is not surprising that Gandhi was never interested in a careful consideration of those passages of the *Gita* which to the mind of many other commentators, try to communicate some 'ontological' aspects of the special nature of Krishna. Those who are convinced that the purpose of the *Gita* is the presentation of a progressive self-revelation of Krishna, view with special interest all texts that mention the relationship of Krishna to other fundamental entities like Brahman, Bhagavat, *prakṛti,* Purushottama, and Ishvara. Since Gandhi did not believe that such was the purpose of the *Gita,* he lightly skipped over texts of that kind. Important passages such as 7.4ff., 8.20 ff., and the final verses of Chapter fifteen are either translated without a word of comment or completely omitted. To Gandhi the *Gita* does not offer a self-revelation of Krishna. Moreover, his own concept of Krishna as *avatāra* is not the result of his own study of the *Gita;* as we have seen, it was firmly established many years before he engaged in a thorough study of the work.

Another aspect of the content of the *Gita* that is important and has occupied the mind of many commentators, is the exact relationship between the three main 'disciplines' advocated, namely desireless action, knowledge, and *bhakti.* Many would agree that historically the *Gita* offered the Hindu a new method, a new way, of achieving the ultimate goal of *mokṣa,* which until then could be reached only by those who totally renounced the world of action and attained special knowledge. The *Gita's* message was the message of *bhakti: mokṣa* is accessible to all those who, having purified action by the renunciation of desire and illuminated their minds with knowledge, suffused their action with love of Krishna; this was the new way of devotional love. Gandhi's approach to *bhakti* was no less than a Copernican revolution: "Renunciation is the central sun, round which devotion, knowledge and the rest revolve like planets."[97] To him renunciation is the primary value of the *Gita,* ". . . right knowledge is necessary for attaining [it],"[98] and ". . . in order that knowledge may not run riot, the author of the *Gītā* has insisted on devotion accompanying it."[99] In other words, *bhakti* is useful for keeping knowledge in balance, and knowledge is necessary to show the way, but both of them are only means by which to achieve the real goal, to reach that sun around which they revolve, namely renunciation.

Gandhi was always suspicious about the Hindu conception of *bhakti,* which is not surprising in one who hailed from a province where the Vallabhacharya sect was very prominent, a sect that had become notorious for the excesses of its *bhakti* rituals.[100] *Bhakti,* Gandhi wrote, "is no soft-hearted effusiveness"; and "rosaries, forehead marks, offerings . . . are no test [of it]."[101] He went on to elaborate his own definition of a *bhakta* in a long paragraph which stressed the virtues of self control, indifference and renunciation, which included a single reference to "a mind and soul dedicated to God," but which managed to avoid mentioning Krishna's name. It concluded: "to be a real devotee is to realize oneself."[102]

Elsewhere Gandhi acknowledged that the twelfth chapter of the *Gita* described the characteristics of a *bhakta.* He went on to point out that these were essentially the same as those of the *sthitaprajña,* "the man of self-control," described in the second chapter. Gandhi remarked that whereas the description of the second chapter was "rigorous," that of the twelfth was cast "in ordinary language" with a touch of poetry.[103] Wherever one turns in Gandhi's writings, *bhakti* is always downgraded. In fact, this too was an attitude that can be found expressed in the South African period: "The true meaning of *bhakti* is search for the *ātman.* When the *ātman* realises itself, *bhakti* is transformed into *jñāna.*"[104]

A discussion of the Hindu concept of *bhakti* usually involves some account of *prasāda,* or "grace," the free and 'undeserved' bestowing of spiritual advancement by the Lord. Gandhi mostly ignored this side of *bhakti,* but when he was specifically asked, "If a person following the path of devotion does not or cannot believe in Divine grace, what else can sustain his faith?" he answered as follows: "The word 'grace' is a poetic term. Bhakti itself is poetry." He went on to explain that, speaking logically, "all that happens is the effect of karma." However, because karma is so mysterious and unfathomable, we tend to say 'loosely' that everything happens 'through the grace of God'. The latter is only a poetic expression affirming that the law of karma is itself identical with God.[105] This explanation of *prasāda* completely empties it of meaning: the "grace" of the Lord is not divine intervention to spiritually uplift a deserving individual, but merely a poetical way of describing the inexorable law of karmic retribution, directed by God because it is identical with him.

THE THREAD OF LOGIC

All the questions we have asked so far about Gandhi's approach to scripture and scriptural authority in general, and about his conception of the authority and the message of the *Gita* in particular, have furnished a long list of answers. But they happen to constitute much more than just a list: there runs through these answers a strong thread of internal logic, and together they throw considerable light on Gandhi's concept of religion. The central pivot of Gandhi's conception is that religion's fundamental aim is self-realization. This is to be achieved by ethical action controlling senses, mind, and ego, that is, by conquering matter by spirit. The ultimate goal of that self-realization is *mokṣa,* cessation of the cycle of transmigration and absorption into the absolute. However, Gandhi's focus of attention is never eschatological: his constant concern is with self-realization in this life, or rather with self-control in every action here and now. Religion is a state of mind, it is "the quality of one's soul."[106]

Viewed from this standpoint, Gandhi's conception of scripture is perfectly logical. The scriptures of all religions are historical documents which illustrate how, throughout the centuries, great saints have achieved self-realization in their own lives. The essence of the scriptures is not that they reveal dogmatic truths, profound myths, or rituals necessary for salvation; nor is it that they show new ways to *mokṣa,* such as *bhakti,* or announce a redeemer or an avatar whose very birth or action offers liberation to humanity. The parts of the scriptures that deal with these themes are only secondary, as they describe mere superstructures determined by historical and cultural circumstance, products of what Gandhi calls "imagination".

They may be, and often are, most useful to help individuals along in their struggle for self-realization, but they do not offer ontological truth. Gandhi himself had no interest in these aspects of scripture, because he was concerned with what for him was its essence: the illustration of actual methods of self-control that have guided great saints towards realizing the supreme goal of self realization.

It is no wonder that Gandhi chose the *Gita* as his favorite *shastra.* So many other religious texts are so rich in their elaboration of the paraphernalia of dogma, myth, and ritual, that this core message of self-control is very difficult to distill from them. The *Gita,* on the other hand, concentrates on that very core of ethical action with very little embellishment; it is a text that "lends itself to social moralizing."[107] It is also understandable that Gandhi chose the last section of the second chapter as the central text of the *Gita,* because it describes succinctly and in detail the *sthitaprajñā,* the one who has achieved total self-control. According to Gandhi, the author of the *Gita* was himself such an individual, and the text describes how he achieved his self-realization.

To Gandhi's mind the *Gita* is not a self-revelation of Krishna. Krishna as 'full avatar' is a magnificent product of the Hindu imagination, and such an 'imagined ideal' can be of considerable help to the Hindu in his attempts at self-control—just as the "ideal Christ" may stimulate the efforts of a Christian. The polarity *bhakti-prasāda,* love and grace, does not offer a magical short cut to salvation; it is only an imaginative way of expressing the idea that the law of karma is in the final instance identical with the Absolute. If, as Gandhi asserts, religion is about self-realization and the *Gita* is about self-control, then interpretations of a historical, academic or theological type only skim the surface. The real task of the interpreter becomes self-evident: it is to put the ethical code of the *Gita* into effect in his own life. That is exactly what Gandhi claimed to have done, and what entitled him to the rank of 'real' interpreter.

Sources of the Gandhian Interpretation

How did Gandhi arrive at his very individual interpretation of the *Gita*? His own sustained study of the text started in earnest only in 1925. However, the basic principles of his interpretation were not a consequence of that study, but a guide; they were firmly established as part of the conception of religion and of Hinduism he had developed long before he concentrated on the *Gita.* We have noted that Gandhi's first readings of the *Gita* came about through contact with Theosophists. Another chapter in this volume shows that the Theosophist interpreters of the *Gita* stressed the allegorical aspect. However, I have not found any evidence that this was actually discussed between Gandhi and his friends, or that Gandhi at that stage was at all concerned with questions of interpretation.

It was during his South African period that he first gave serious thought to the meaning of the scriptures and the essence of religion. This reflection was stimulated by close Christian contacts whose claims about Christianity raised doubts in his mind about Hinduism. He wrote to Edward Maitland, founder of the Esoteric Christian Union, who sent him two of his books, which Gandhi "greatly liked." In fact he became a propagandist of Esoteric Christian Union Literature, and mentioned the organization on his letterhead. He corresponded regularly with Maitland till his death in 1897, ordered multiple copies of his books, and defended the author in the *Natal Advertiser.*[108] The connection, therefore, was not simply a casual one, and it is worthwhile to investigate what ideas on scripture Maitland propounded.

The Christians who tried to convert Gandhi to Christianity were mostly 'evangelicals,' who believed that humanity had fallen into sin and that only the atonement of Christ could save; faith in Christ was the door to heaven. They held that proof of their beliefs lay in the unique and final revelation of the Bible, which they interpreted in a fundamentalist way. Many of Maitland's ideas provided Gandhi with an answer to the questions and anxieties he experienced when assailed by the arguments of profoundly convinced Christians whom he admired and loved. First of all he believed in the universality of revelation: specific sacred books were only the constant re-revealing of a universal revelation.[109] Second, Maitland rejected historic and fundamentalist interpretations. To him the Gospel narrative does not deal primarily "with material things or persons, but with spiritual signification,"[110] and its purpose is "to exhibit and illustrate processes and principles which are purely spiritual."[111] It is most interesting to note the way in which Maitland interpreted the figure of Christ: "Christ Jesus, then, is no other than the hidden and true man of the Spirit, the Perfect Humanity, the Express Image of the Divine Glory."[112] In fact, "between the man who becomes a Christ, and other men, there is no difference whatever in kind. The difference . . . consists in difference of unfoldment of the spiritual nature possessed by all in virtue of their common derivation."[113]

Maitland's ideas must have helped Gandhi cope with the claims of some Christian friends, but he remained unclear about the position and validity of Hinduism and its scriptures. In 1894 he wrote to his Jain friend, Rajchandra Rajivbhai, whom he called Raychand, listing a number of pertinent questions. Raychand's answers "pacified" him.[114] It is in these answers that we find fundamental ideas that are very similar to those we found to be the basic principles of Gandhi's concept of scripture and religion, and of *Gita*-interpretation.

In answer to questions about *ātman* and *mokṣa,* Raychand offered the following ideas. The *ātman* is fundamentally different from all else that exists, and is the author *(kartā)* of its own *mokṣa*. In the state of bondage, the *ātman* commits deeds of anger, love, attachment, greed, etc. *Mokṣa* is freedom from such attachment, from all bondage of passions and the body; it is the state of self-realization in which the spirit fully realizes its own pure nature and its freedom from all connection with matter. The word God, or *īśvara,* does not signify a unique being of great power, or a creator of the universe; it is a term describing the perfect state of the *ātman* in *mokṣa.*[115]

Raychand made it quite clear that in his opinion scriptures, and specifically the *Vedas* and the *Gita,* were historical works composed by human beings. To say that they were "revealed by God" really meant that they were composed by persons who had attained the illumination of *mokṣa.* In answer to the question as to how one should go about assessing the claim of superiority by any particular religion, Raychand pointed to the "test of proof:" that "that religion alone is the best and is truly strong, which is most helpful in destroying the bondage of worldly life and can establish us in the state which is our essence."[116] In other words, the real test of the validity of a religion and its scripture consists in the practical application of its precepts. Raychand reaffirmed this when he wrote about the *Puranas* that he thought that Brahma, Vishnu and Shiva had to be understood "allegorically," and that it would be better "to try to profit from the instruction they [the *Puranas*] contain, rather than attempt in vain to ascertain the principles embodied in the personification of Brahma, and so on."[117]

In answer to Gandhi's questions about Christ and Krishna, Raychand asserted that "incarnations" or avatars were logically impossible. Calling Krishna "God" only meant expressing the belief that Krishna's *ātman* had attained *mokṣa*. Interestingly, Gandhi also asked explicit questions about *bhakti:* "Can an illiterate person attain *moksa* through *bhakti* alone?" and "Can we attain salvation through faith in them [Krishna and Rama as avatars]?" Raychand's answers are revealing: *bhakti* has the power of purifying knowledge, but knowledge is the cause of *mokṣa,* whereas *bhakti* only plays a subsidiary role. Faith in Krishna and devotional worship cannot cause *mokṣa* but they can help us to gain the means for attaining *mokṣa,* if they help us follow Krishna's teaching and example and thus free ourselves from all forms of attachment.[118]

The parallelism between Raychand's ideas as expressed in that letter of 1894 and those of Gandhi described in the earlier part of this essay, is so persistent and striking that one has to conclude that Raychand's influence on Gandhi's ideas was decisive. Gandhi's admiration for his friend has been conclusively shown, but it is of interest to draw attention to the exact terms in which Gandhi expressed his praise:

> His writings are the quintessence of his experiences. . . . One rare feature of his writings is that he always set down what he had felt in his own experience. . . . He was a man of self-control, . . . the state of freedom from attachment was spontaneous to him, . . . his devotion to dharma was evident in every action of his.[119]

Gandhi admired Raychand because of his self-control and his freedom from attachment: he was like the *sthitaprajñā* of the *Gita.* He admired his writings on religion because of their pragmatic and experimental nature. Raychand obviously was a man very much after Gandhi's own heart.

While Raychand undoubtedly had great influence on Gandhi during a crucial period of his personal development, this seed did not fall on virgin soil. From his youth Gandhi had been disenchanted with ritualism and myth, and irritated by the exclusive and contradictory claims of various religions. Moreover by temperament and inclination, he had always been a moral practitioner and a stubborn individualist; during his South African period he was constantly experimenting with various forms of self-control. Raychand's general principles struck a chord in him. They provided a logical framework that not only supported his moralistic and individualistic approach to religion, but also allowed him to judge other religions and accept their positive aspects without having to reject Hinduism. That framework in the final instance determined most aspects of Gandhi's interpretation of the *Gita.*

This does not mean that Gandhi inherited Jainism from Raychand; he always considered himself thoroughly Hindu. However, one should remember that for Gandhi all religions were in essence the same. When he was very pointedly asked the question "What is the difference between the *Gita's* theism and the Jain doctrine that there is no God?" he answered, "I have never seen any difference between the Jain doctrine and the general Vedic doctrine. The difference is only one of point of view." He then went on to explain how the point of view was different. The *Gita,* he wrote, "is a poem," and "the conversation between Lord Krishna and Arjuna is imaginary"; this imaginative way of writing was not "inappropriate or untruthful," however. Jainism, on the other hand "stated the truth logically and unpoetically" in declaring there was no God. When one went to the root of things, Jainism and the *Gita* both expressed the same truth, that religion is the individual's effort to achieve freedom from attachment; only the medium for expressing that truth was different.[120]

Gandhi's approach to the *Gita* differs markedly from the method of many traditional interpreters who expend great effort on textual interpretation and on establishing the internal logic of the various theoretical statements and practical directives of the text. But in one important way Gandhi's approach is in close conformity with a major traditional rule of interpretation. He identifies the central, the key passage in the text: the *mahāvákya,* "the great statement" that gives the central message, in terms of which all the rest of the text must be explained. For Gandhi the last twenty stanzas of Chapter two constitute the *Gita's mahāvākya* in the description of the *sthitaprajñā.* This passage in fact expresses most succinctly, without any mythical, ritual, or dogmatic paraphernalia, without "imagination," the essence of religion as he saw it. His concept of the nature of the scripture was largely inherited from Raychandra. Jainism, moreover, gave Gandhi the basic theoretical structure that best fitted his own deepest nature, that of a "religious activist," with its dualism of *jīva-ajīva,* spirit and matter, its inexorable law of karma, and its conception of the gradual purification of the *ātman* necessary on the highroad to self-realization.[121]

CHAPTER SIX

Vinoba Bhave's Talks on the Gita

BOYD H. WILSON

Vinoba Bhave was born Vinayak Narhari Bhave on August 11, 1895, at Gagoda in the Kolaba district of Bombay Presidency to a brahmin family.[1] He attended Baroda High School and Baroda College from 1906–1916. Here his primary interest was mathematics, although he showed a predilection for Sanskrit.

He left college in 1916, however, with a sense of a higher calling. Shortly after leaving, Vinoba read the inauguration address delivered by Gandhi at Benares Hindu University. He immediately began corresponding with Gandhi, broaching questions about religion and politics especially. After the exchange of many letters, he finally went to Kochrab Ashram in June, 1916, to meet Gandhi. Reflecting later on this day, Vinoba said

> Providence took me to Gandhiji and I found in him not only the peace of the Himalayas but also the burning fervor of revolution for freedom. I said to myself that both of my desires had been fulfilled.[2]

While at the ashram with Gandhi, Vinoba pursued his interest in Sanskrit and Indian literature. He studied the *Upanishads,* the *Bhagavadgita,* the *Brahma Sutras,* Shankara's *Bhashya* on the *Sutras, Manusmriti,* Patanjali's *Yoga Sutras,* Nyaya and Vaisheshika *Sutras* and *Yajnavalkya Smriti.* In addition to this broad range of study, he also taught classes in Sanskrit, the *Gita* and the *Upanishads.*[3] But his activities at the ashram were more than just academic; Vinoba immersed himself in Gandhi's 'Constructive Programme.' Among other things, this included the advancement of khadi and village industries, education, sanitation, and hygiene. He did, however, bring his academic penchant to these tasks; he wrote books on educational theory as well as a book on spinning. His principal duty in the Constructive Program focused on implementation of Gandhi's goal of *sarvodaya*—the welfare of all.

Vinoba was an active participant in many *satyāgraha* campaigns and was arrested six times in conjunction with these campaigns. Two of his most popular works are the product of imprisonment. *Talks on the Gita* is a compilation of eighteen lectures delivered while in Dhula jail: Vinoba spoke on one chapter of the *Gita* every Sunday for eighteen successive weeks from February 21 to June 19, 1932.[4] *The Steadfast Wisdom* is also a collection of eighteen talks on the last eighteen verses of chapter two of the *Gita* (2.55–72), which Vinoba delivered while in Seoni jail in 1944. These two works give Vinoba's most direct understanding and interpretation of the *Gita.*

Vinoba stayed in Gandhi's shadow until the Mahatma's untimely death cast him into the light. Many looked to him as Gandhi's logical and legitimate spiritual heir. Vinoba recalls:

> After the death of Mahātma Gandhi, I had to come out of my *Ashram* life to seek the power of non-violence. This was my second exit . . . [5]

At first, this "second exit" was spent working with refugees from Pakistan. He also worked on a movement he termed *karchan-mukti,* 'freedom from gold.' In this movement, Vinoba hoped to " . . . rid man of the slavery to money and investigate economic, social, intellectual, and moral potentialities of productive physical labor performed intelligently."[6]

The real focus of Vinoba's career, however, came about almost by accident in April, 1951. He had attended a Sarvodaya Samaj meeting and on the way home passed through the Telanga district of Andhra, where he was approached by Harijans who requested his help in procuring eighty acres of land. He took it up at a public meeting and a rich farmer donated one hundred of his five hundred acres of land. This act of generosity inspired Vinoba; he marks this as the beginning of Bhoodan.[7] Bhoodan Yajna (the sacrifice of the gift of land) marks, then, the center of Vinoba's concerns for the rest of his career. All later movements such as Gramdan (donation of villages), Sampattidan (donation of money, etc.), even Shanti Sena (Peace Brigade) revolve around this center.

Vinoba founded five ashrams and published a number of magazines and journals.[8] All of his efforts were directed toward the improvement of the social status of the powerless and helpless. In 1969 he retired from active public work to what he called *kṣetra sanya* (older field), although he continued as the inspiration of the Sarvodaya movement. He served as the voice of conscience for the government as well as the popular movements.

On November 5, 1982, Vinoba suffered a mild heart attack. Although doctors were certain that with proper treatment and medication he could recover, Vinoba began preparation for this *prayopasan* (a Jain tradition of starving to death). He abandoned not only medication, but food and water as well. The nation watched as its "walking saint" slowly slipped away. Indira Gandhi tried to persuade Vinoba to eat, but he was convinced his time had come to enter the five elements.[9] On November 15, 1982, Vinoba Bhave died.

Although much of Vinoba's career was spent in the shadow of Gandhi, he is far more than a dim echo of Gandhian concerns. He was more devoted to scholarship and philosophical study of the Indian past than Gandhi. Therefore, although he learned much from Gandhi, although he continued developing and building on the base established while he worked with and under him, Vinoba did not spend the rest of his life rehearsing slogans that he had learned from the Mahatma. As will be shown, there is a congruence and cohesion with Gandhi, but Vinoba continued to elaborate rather than reiterate.

Gandhi met him when Vinoba was twenty-one years old and recognized the dedication and potential in this young man. Gandhi entrusted to him many responsibilities in his constructive program, proving his confidence in Vinoba's abilities. Gandhi's opinion of Vinoba was so high that he chose him as the first *satyāgrahi* in the individual *satyāgraha* campaign of 1940. Yet even at this late date, Gandhi had to write an article entitled "Who is Vinoba Bhave" for the *Harijan* in order to introduce his most trusted disciple.[10] Gandhi explained that he chose Vinoba because he suspected that this would be the last *satyāgraha* campaign and he wanted it to be flawless.[11]

Much of Vinoba's influence can be measured tangibly by citing the extent of the success of the Bhoodan program. Although exact figures are difficult to obtain, it seems safe to conclude that over four million acres of land were donated to the poor, with nearly 1.3 million acres already distributed.[12] His Gramdan, the donation of all property in a village to the public good, had totalled over 170,000 villages in 1971.[13]

At his death, Vinoba was awarded the honor of national recognition; the national flag was lowered to half-mast throughout the Indian sub-continent. Many states declared one to three days of official mourning. Indira Gandhi returned to India early from Leonid Brezhnev's funeral in the Soviet Union in order to attend Vinoba's funeral. In a eulogy broadcast throughout India, she referred to him as the "spiritual heir of Mahatma Gandhi," adding that Vinoba was "deeply immersed in the ancient wisdom but was not a revivalist." President Zail Singh described Vinoba as a "saint" and a "stalwart from the generation of freedom fighters."[14]

Many of Vinoba's socio-political concerns had their inception with Gandhi. *Sarvodaya,* the movement for the "welfare of all," became almost synonymous with Vinoba Bhave. He iterated the words of Gandhi when he explained that *sarvodaya* means "the good of all is in the good of one."[15] He coined the battle cry "*sarvobhuthite ratah*" (the good and welfare of all).[16] He went on to organize the Sarvodaya Samaj and the Serv Seva Sangh (the executive body of Sarvodaya), thereby giving organizational structure to a movement which received inspiration from Gandhi.

Vinoba learned the principles of *swarāj* (self-rule) from Gandhi and he elaborated this concern as well. He translated *swarāj* into *gramrāj* (village rule) in which he envisioned a nation of self-ruled villages held together in a loose coalition of common concerns.[17] He sought *lokśakti* (power of the people), construing a conflict between *lokniti* (politics of the people) and *rajniti* (politics of the king, or power politics).[18] He attempted to implement this goal by encouraging the powerful to become *gramsevaks* (servants of the village) and establishing the *Gram Sabha* (village council) and the *Gram Seva Mandal* (village service association).[19] All of this was an attempt to bring to fruition Gandhi's seminal idea of *swarāj.*

Vinoba continued to develop and elaborate Gandhian themes throughout his career. The focal theme of Bhoodan certainly had its roots in *sarvodaya,* but it was primarily the product of Vinoba's inspiration. The purpose of Bhoodan, he says, is to "rouse people to an awareness of their own strength, to get them to stand on their own feet."[20] To Vinoba the ultimate aim of Bhoodan is to free people from attachments and bring about a union of hearts.[21] He characterizes Bhoodan Yajna as a three-fold revolution in which first hearts are changed, then lives, and then the entire social structure of the nation.[22]

Bhoodan Yajna inspired Vinoba with regard to the concept of *dāna*—"giving" or "charity." *Dāna* became his rallying cry, his call to arms. To Vinoba, *dāna* was more than just giving or gift, it was *yajña* (sacrifice), *samvibhoga* (equitable distribution), *dharma* (duty toward society).[23] He developed the idea of *dāna* to include almost every sphere of life, touching every person. One could not avoid giving, regardless of his/her lack of means. For those who had no land for Bhoodan, there was Sampattidan, the gift of money or other tangible goods.[24] For those without tangible goods there was opportunity for *dāna* in Shramdan, the gift of physical labor, Premdan, the gift of friendship or love, or Buddhidan, the gift of knowledge or teaching.[25]

Vinoba extended the concept of *dāna* to include everything. *Sutranjali* is the gift of hand-spun yarn, given in the spirit of sacrifice by the poorest person. *Annadan* is the gift of the pen, given by journalists, etc., in support of a good cause. The ultimate gift is *samagradan,* the gift of all or *jivadan,* the gift of one's life. In these gifts, one has given all, including life itself, for the good of others.[26]

It is this spirit of giving all which informs his concept of *yajña*—which is the inspiration of an individual causing him/her to give all for the good of another. *Yajña* is the heart of Vinoba's mission: starting with sarvodaya and ending in jivadan.[27]

VINOBA'S ATTITUDES TOWARDS THE GITA

Vinoba studied the sacred texts of many religions; he even learned Arabic in order to read the *Qur'an* in its original language. But for him, nothing surpassed the *Bhagavadgita* in wisdom and practicality. It was the "King of Scriptures."[28] The very enunciation of the words of the *Gita* was for him an act of worship equivalent to Rāmanāma.[29] Vinoba considered the *Gita* a work of art (*kala*) and as such it was a gift to all humankind, not just India.[30]

Vinoba expressed his attitude toward the *Gita* most clearly in the introduction to his *Talks on the Gita.*

> The bond between the *Gita* and me transcends reason. My heart and mind have both received more nourishment from the *Gita* than my body has from my mother's milk . . . I live and move in the atmosphere of the *Gita.* The *Gita* is my life's breath.[31]

Vinoba feels that the power of the *Gita* lies in the fact that it is a suitable handbook for anyone's life. It is a description of life which is based on direct, personal, spiritual experience. This description is clear and understandable to the ordinary person. Although there may be deeper hidden meanings mined only by *sadhaks,* there is a personal message for every individual in the words of the *Gita.* No matter what one's need may be, the *Gita* addresses that need and presents a solution to any problem. It is mystical in its ability to adapt to any person and situation.[32]

Inasmuch as the *Gita* is a handbook for life, Vinoba is confident when he calls it a textbook of Hindu *dharma* (*dharma śāstra*). It is a *śāstra* in that it teaches a science, and the science it teaches is *dharma.*[33] But the *Gita* teaches *dharma* by example and by word, so that the reader is led patiently yet directly along the path of *dharma.*[34] In questions of *dharma,* Vinoba is willing to contrast the *Gita* with the lawbook of Manu, asserting that the *Gita*'s path is more attainable.[35]

This means that the *Gita* is for Vinoba the authoritative religious text. It is the "Upanishad of Upanishads," containing the essence, the core of Upanishadic teachings,[36] the essence of Vedic *dharma,* in fact, the very essence of the *Vedas.* The *Gita* is the King of Scriptures.[37]

As noted above, Vinoba refers to the *Gita* as a *śāstra,* meaning that it is a textbook which teaches a science (in this case, the science of *dharma*). A *śāstra* is meant to be read and understood by everyone. In another context, Vinoba refers to the *Gita* as a *sūtra,* which implies a great deal more.[38] A *sūtra* is arcane and mystical, requiring an adept interpreter. Yet couched within the terse recondite words of a *sūtra* is much wisdom. This juxtaposition of *śāstra* and *sūtra* in reference to the *Gita* tells much about Vinoba's view of the nature of the *Gita.* It is a textbook, a *śāstra,* which is easily approached and understood. It tells about life and how to live it. But at the same time the *Gita* is a philosophical text, a *sūtra,* which teaches the mysteries of the universe. These teachings are deeper and must be mined by the sages and *sadhaks.* It is these scholars who are able to discern the essence of the *Vedas* and *Upanishads* in the pages of the *Gita.* Yet, at the same time, a child can read the *Gita* and be blessed. This is the nature of the *Gita.*

Vinoba contrasts the purpose of the *Ramayana* with the purpose of the *Mahabharata;* the *Ramayana* is an ethical poem, the *Mahabharata* is a treatise on the science of society.[39] Since the *Gita* lies in the center of the *Mahabharata* and contains the essence of its teachings, the purpose of the *Gita* is to show how one functions in society. The key to this function is *dharma,* particularly *swadharma.* The purpose of the *Gita* is to remove the illusions caused by desire and confusion and to lead one in the path of his own duty in society.[40]

The *Gita* teaches principles of life which are meant to be tested and implemented in the context of society.[41]

There is a personal, individual purpose to the *Gita* as well. It teaches the path to purity of life; it teaches the way of *bhakti*. The *Gita* teaches how to synthesize the apparently divergent paths of *saṃnyāsa* and *karma*. This synthesis is the path of *bhakti*. But *bhakti* involves more than worship of a heavenly god; it includes dedication and sacrifice. These characteristics, once acquired, are best demonstrated in society. So even the personal message of the *Gita* has, for Vinoba, societal implications.[42] The key to the Gita's teachings in this regard is *sthita prajñā*—the steadfast wisdom. *Sthita prajñā* is the knowledge of the integration of religious and spiritual truth with the life in society.[43]

The *Gita* is the most valuable component of the *Mahabharata*, which is a mine of pure gold.[44] The words of the *Gita* offer help to one no matter what the problem. The daily reading of the *Gita* leads one directly to the Lord. For this reason, the *Gita* is a formula for spiritual power and success. The principles inculcated by the *Gita* lead to the perfection of life, *sacchidānanda*. These principles are the practical application of the truths of all of *śruti* and *smṛti*.[45]

The value of the *Gita* to Vinoba, then, is that it serves as the most convenient path to goals which seem unattainable. It is a handbook of doctrine and practice which both teaches and leads. It can be used by anyone, anywhere, at any time, for any purpose. Clearly, for him it is the most valuable book in the world.

VINOBA'S INTERPRETATION OF THE GITA

Vinoba's two works devoted entirely to the *Gita*, *Talks on the Gita* and *The Steadfast Wisdom*, are not verse-by-verse interpretations; rather in both works the ideas of the *Gita* serve as a kind of springboard for the development and expression of his own concerns. Nevertheless, in both works care has been taken in the analysis, interpretation, and exegesis of the text. Although there is not a section of either work in which Vinoba carefully and specifically sets forth his hermeneutic, it is possible to extrapolate from his interpretations and handling of the text the rules under which he is implicitly operating.[46] These rules can be seen to fall under four rubrics: grammatical or lexical, textual or contextual, structural, and comparative.

Under the category of grammatical or lexical analysis, the primary rule employed is to note the word used in a passage.[47] Vinoba often bases his interpretation of a passage on the specific word employed in the text. From the full meaning of the word, he is able to construct a meaning to the passage. This full meaning may entail a study of the etymology or derivation of the word.[48] It may follow from the dissolution of the compound in which the word is found.[49] It may also involve a study of the context of the word,[50] the same word's meaning in other contexts,[51] or the meaning given to the word by other interpreters.[52]

Also under the category of grammatical or lexical analysis, Vinoba analyzes the grammatical structure and usage of particular passages to derive his interpretation.[53] He cites not only etymologies and compound dissolutions, but he also analyzes synonyms in order to interpret a text. He is conscious, too, when attempting to exegete a passage of figures of speech, verbal pictures, comparisons, and examples employed in the text.[55] Furthermore, he is sensitive to the symbolic usages of language as well as allegorical references.[56]

Finally, Vinoba is conscious of the special nature of technical terms, terms which cannot be understood in their normal meaning because they are infused with new and particular meaning and significance in the *Gita*.[57] In order to discover the special meaning of these terms, Vinoba compares other usages of them in the *Gita* and analyzes the specific context of their use.[58]

This leads to the second category of interpretive rules employed by Vinoba, textual or contextual analysis. Here, Vinoba studies not only words, but teachings, concepts, and images in relation to the surrounding text. He is informed of the meaning of a specific text by the context in which it is found.

He operates with several rules which pertain to the specific context, i.e., section, chapter, or teaching, in which a passage is found. For example, he feels that the broader subject of a section (chapter, etc.) determines what a specific passage within that section means.[59] If a passage is unclear by itself, it is possible to determine its meaning by citing the general context of meaning in which it is encountered. Similarly, the citation and study of the introduction of a section (chapter, etc.) can explain or determine the meaning or significance of the rest of that section.[60] If the introduction is unclear, then Vinoba looks to the other end, to the conclusion, for his interpretive guide.[61]

Finally, if the specific context of a passage does not give any lucid direction, Vinoba looks to other similar contexts. He seeks a context in which the same teaching is found and hopes that this second or third context is more helpful.[62] The citation of this other context helps interpret not only the specific text or passage involved, but also helps to elucidate the entire context of the passage. This interpretation of the obscure by the less obscure forms another category to be discussed below.

The next hermeneutical category employed by Vinoba is structural analysis, or the interpretation of the particular by the general. He discerns a development of teaching in the *Gita,* so he interprets in light of this developmental structure. The structure and progressive development of a teaching is instrumental in his interpretation. A subject is often continued or completed in another text or pericope and Vinoba must cite both places in order to derive the complete teaching.[63] Although sometimes the first statement of a teaching is the most complete,[64] it is more often the case that an idea is developed slowly in the *Gita.* So Vinoba tries to discern the structure of this developing idea in order to interpret the *Gita* in general and specific passages in particular.[65]

Part of Vinoba's interpretation based on structure and development derives from his perception of the *Gita* as a unified whole. Due to this belief, he can interpret specific passages in the light of the general meaning of the *Gita.*[66] Similarly, he is able to interpret passages based on his knowledge of the general purpose of a passage itself and its internal structure.[67] The smaller structure is known and analyzed in light of the greater structure. This device is best demonstrated when Vinoba interprets a pericope on the basis of the "essence of the *Gita.*"[68] Knowing the essence enables him to discern the basic, essential teaching within the specific verses.

The final category of interpretation that is apparently operative in Vinoba's methodology is comparative analysis. In this case, he compares the obscure with the clear in order to understand the meaning of passages and verses. The most general rule here is that the basic or essential teaching, established in one context, serves as an interpretive spectrum for other subordinate or abstruse teachings.[69] In this regard, Vinoba compares teachings in one section or chapter with clearer and more lucid teachings in other contexts.[70]

Vinoba is also willing to step out of the confines of the *Gita* for his interpretive guides. He compares the teachings of the *Gita* with other *śruti* and *smṛti,* and he compares examples from the *Gita* with similar examples in other *śruti* and *smṛti.*[71] He also refers to other commentators to compare his understanding of a pericope with what others have said, either about the passage under question or about its theme.[72] These comparisons both inform and undergird his interpretation.

Beyond the rules which are implicitly operative in Vinoba's interpretation, there are also specific methods which are discernible. Methods are distinct from the rules insofar as they are means of interpretation based upon the rules but extending beyond them. Vinoba's rules of interpretation take him to the text; his methods of interpretation lead him to his philosophical position.

A study of Vinoba's methods of interpretation indicates that there is a subtle search for the 'real meaning' of the *Bhagavadgita.* It is found in the text, perhaps, but it is not necessarily evident to the average reader. The real meaning is that level of understanding which is, it seems, informed by Vinoba's philosophy and also instrumental in the formation of that philosophy.[73]

Vinoba's first method which bespeaks a search for "real meaning" is found in his altering of the text. Before interpreting a passage, Vinoba often changes the reading of the text at hand. The changed reading may help to make his point, or it may help him to make sense of the passage.[74] He corrects the reading of an entire passage or just a word in the passage in order to correlate with his understanding of the passage. Or, he alters the translation to match an idea he has about the text.[75] He adds words to the text to make the meaning clearer and he reads words into a verse to make a point.[76] He also reconstrues a text, renames sections, and restructures portions of the text to abet his understanding of the passage or the text as a whole.[77] In each of these instances, Vinoba's preunderstanding of the text, or his perception of what the *Gita* really means, direct him.

Likewise, it is such knowledge or preunderstanding which enables him to disagree with other commentators and interpreters.[78] He seems to know, perhaps intuitively, what the *Gita* really means and is thereby able to dispute with those who have missed this meaning. In a similar manner, Vinoba disagrees with normal and approved understanding of texts and words within these texts. He seems to know what these texts and words really mean.[79]

That Vinoba is seeking, or has already found, the real meaning of the *Gita* is discerned in his desire to find—and his penchant for finding—the essence of things.[80] He frequently refers to the essence of the *Gita* from a brief discussion of a passage.[81] He also seems to know the essence of the *Upanishads* and all the *Vedas.*[82] This knowledge and determination of the essence of the *Gita* (as well as the *Vedas*) indicates a level of preunderstanding on Vinoba's part. He could not declare the essence of the *Gita* without already knowing the entire content and message of the *Gita*.

This knowledge and preknowledge is also demonstrated in Vinoba's ability to state the purpose of specific portions of the *Gita* as well as the *Gita* as a whole. He is able to determine the significance of passages, the reason that certain verses are taught, and even the aim or specific purpose of a text.[83] Such determination requires knowledge brought to the text rather than knowledge gained from the text.

Likewise, Vinoba feels confident in stating the intention of a passage. He finds, beyond the direct statement of the passage, a latent intention that is the real reason for the teaching in the passage. Often, the ordinary meanings of the words in a passage do not sufficiently reflect the intention or the real meaning of the verse. So Vinoba finds the words which best express this intention,[84] and even feels that he can state the intention behind the words of Krishna in certain passages.[85] Vinoba actually does seem to know more than the text says; he somehow knows the real meaning, and thus the purpose, aim, and intention of each passage.

While seeking—and finding—the deeper, symbolic teachings of the Gita, Vinoba is able to expound the deeper and symbolic meanings of specific teachings of the text[86] and is able to disclose the deeper, hidden meanings of words used in these specific teachings.[87] He uncovers the esoteric teachings of the *Gita*.

Finally, though, what Vinoba is clearly looking for in his interpretation of the *Gita* is the real meaning for *him*. That is, he hopes to find a personal message in the *Gita* that is pertinent to his life experience. He does, however, intermingle his search for personal meaning in the *Gita* with the imposition of his personal ideas on the *Gita*. Like Gandhi he considers experience to be the touchstone of an authoritative text.[88] That means that he is able to base his interpretations on life experience as well as on knowledge of the text.[89] Or, he can give his personal feelings about the value of a text from his experiences with it. He also justifies his interpretations of a passage by his personal beliefs.[90] In each of these instances, Vinoba is simultaneously looking for a message from the *Gita* that speaks directly to him while at the same time using his personal knowledge and experience to determine what the *Gita* really has to say.

All of these methods—changing a passage, disagreeing with other commentators, finding the essence, knowing the purpose or intention, discovering the deep symbolic meaning, and searching for a personal message—are both a search for 'real meaning' and a testimony to the fact that Vinoba already perceives this meaning. It is difficult to determine if Vinoba is informed by the *Gita* as he develops his understanding of the meaning of the text or if his preunderstanding imposes itself on his interpretation. The significance of this difficulty will be seen below as we try to discover the influence of the *Gita* on the thought of Vinoba.

THE MESSAGE OF THE GITA

Vinoba's interpretation of the message of the *Gita* follows, in part, from his understanding of its structure and development. The following sets Vinoba's perception of the work's structure and development. First are general statements about the structural development, and then there are more specific statements regarding his analyses of individual chapters.

Vinoba sees the *Gita* falling into four sections. Chapters one through five teach the science of life; in it the whole scheme of life and the means of achieving life's purposes are set out. Chapters six through eleven give a vision of *bhakti,* expounding the philosophy of devotion.[91] Chapter twelve is a transitional chapter which teaches the qualities of the *bhakta* and introduces the concept of knowledge (*jñāna*). Chapters thirteen through fifteen describe the principle of *jñāna*—how to separate the Self from the body, how to master the three *guṇas,* how to see God everywhere. These chapters are devoted to the elaboration of the ineffable aspect of God. Chapter fifteen gives the complete science of life; after this nothing else remains. All the ideas of the *Gita* find their fulfillment in chapter fifteen.[92] Chapters sixteen and seventeen are supplements and chapter eighteen is the conclusion.[93]

Vinoba analyzes the development of the *Gita* chapter by chapter in the following manner:

Chapter one—primarily introduction; teaches the futile illusion of mine and not mine; aims to destroy delusion and lead to *svadharma.*

Chapter two—begins the teaching of the *Gita;* sketches the whole philosophy of life; removes the illusion introduced in chapter one; teaches the basic principles of life; in eighteen verses (2.55–72) contains the essence of the eighteen chapters: *sthitaprajñā.*

Chapter three—explains more completely the philosophy of life found in chapter two; teaches the way of action (karma).

Chapter four—teaches *vikarma* (inward action).

Chapter five—teaches two ways of *saṃnyāsa;* explains two aspects of *vikarma* and *akarma.*

Chapter six—teaches *dhyanayoga,* the way of meditation; introduces methods of *vikarma* and means of attaining *akarma;* shows importance of one-pointedness (*ekagrata*).

Chapter seven—teaches means of *bhakti: ekagrata* (toward the Lord) which is *prapatti* or surrender; means for knowing the Lord.

Chapter eight—shows the way on constancy, the *yoga* of *satatya.*

Chapter nine—teaches *rājayoga,* the way of dedication of all to Krishna; shows the way of perfect dedication and service.

Chapter ten—the successive steps of God-realization are enumerated.

Chapter eleven—teaches cosmic awareness; teaches how to see God in all creation.

Chapter twelve—compares *nirguṇa* and *saguṇa* forms of worship; gives the qualities of the *bhakta;* concludes the treatment of the philosophy of bhakti; teaches non-attachment.

Chapter thirteen—shows the need for separating the Self from the body.

Chapter fourteen—analyzes the whole of nature and diagnoses its maladies; describes the effort necessary for separating the self from the body.

Chapter fifteen—gives the complete science of life; teaches how to see God in everything.

Chapter sixteen—serves as a supplement; teaches acquisition of divine qualities.

Chapter seventeen—second supplement, teaches yoga of *karyakarma,* regularity in action.

Chapter eighteen—conclusion.[94]

Vinoba conceives of the general message of the *Gita* revolving around five interrelated foci: duty, *bhakti,* desirelessness, dedication, and sacrifice. These teachings function as the basis of his interpretation of the *Gita* as well as the foundation of his philosophy.

He says that the start of the *Gita* is

> based on the principle that anyone can be worthy of Moksha if he performs his duty with love, devotion, and singleness of purpose.[95]

The gate to *mokṣa* is open to all if duty is performed well. The *Gita* teaches the duty that is necessary, and that duty includes love (of fellow humankind and creation) and devotion (to God).[96] For Vinoba, love of humankind and devotion to God are really the same thing. This he derives from the *Gita*.

The inculcation of *bhakti* is a principal teaching of the *Gita*. The *Gita* wants every action filled with *bhakti*.[97] *Bhakti* is worship of God, but the *Gita* teaches that one is to see God in all of creation.[98] Worship of God takes on a broader meaning, including, therefore, the service of all.

Bhakti also involves desirelessness. The *Gita* teaches action without attachment: to act without desire and without hatred. This involves renouncing the fruit of one's actions without actually ceasing to act. Desire attached to action produces bad results; without desire, actions become pure.[99] Giving up desire involves the control of the senses: first the outer senses and then the inner senses. The mind is calmed, the body is calmed, the senses are calmed.[100] From this results the elimination of desire and the attainment of pure *bhakti*.

Such *bhakti* is manifested in the dedication of everything to the Lord. The *Gita* teaches the transformation of karma into *akarma*, and this is realized through abandoning the fruit of one's action and dedicating the fruit and the action to God. This yoga of dedication the *Gita* calls *rājayoga;* it is a combination of *karmayoga* and *bhaktiyoga*. It is, in fact, the combination of karma and *bhakti* based on *jñāna*. The knowledge necessary for their combination is the fact that God is present in all creation, in all action. So *bhakti* must culminate in dedication.[101]

The *bhakti* of dedication is known in sacrifice (*yajña*). The *Gita* teaches harmonious living of the individual and society through sacrifice (*yajña*), charity (dāna) and austerity (*tapas*). Sacrifice is the key. The *Gita* teaches the combination of service to humanity (*dāna*) and spiritual growth (*tapas*). The result is *yajña,* sacrifice.[102] This spirit of sacrifice is demonstrated in the yoga of dedication, the cessation of all desires and dedication of all actions and their fruits to the Lord.

As seen above, Vinoba finds the teachings of the *Gita* to have broader implications than those for the devotee alone. The *Gita*'s teachings spread out to include human society, in fact all of creation. Whereas *bhakti* may be the principal teaching, its ramifications subsume desirelessness, dedication and sacrifice. These all combine, in Vinoba's perception, to constitute the duty of everyone.

Vinoba sees all of the concerns mentioned above coming to full fruition in the *Gita*. He cites with approval Shankara's commentary on 11.55, which Shankara calls *sarvārthasara,* the heart of the meaning of the whole *Gita:*

> He who bears enmity toward none, he who stands impartial and is free from attachment and serves me selflessly, he who dedicates to me all that he does, he who is filled with devotion to me, all-enduring; free of passion and desire, full of love, such a devotee becomes an instrument in the hand of the Lord.[103]

This, Vinoba says, is "the essence of the Gita's teaching." It strings together all the teachings of the *Gita* and places them at the center of one's duty.

This, however, is not the only context in which Vinoba enounces the essence of the *Gita*. As noted above, he finds the description of the man of steadfast wisdom (*sthita prajñā*) in 2.55–72 to be the essence of the *Gita.*[104] He summarizes the essential message of the *Gita* in these words:

> Establish yourself in God and do not become infatuated with objects of the senses. That is enough. All your desires will be washed away.[105]

Again, Vinoba finds the entire message of the *Gita* to be found in the simple injunction, "Do not renounce action; renounce the fruit of action."[106]

In another context, Vinoba claims that the essence of the *Gita* is the same as that of the *Vedas*. We should build our lives on the foundation of service, love, and knowledge (karma, *bhakti, jñāna*). This is the highest human goal, the *paramartha,* the *puruṣottama*. The *Gita* teaches the path that leads to the oneness (*advaita*) of these paths of *bhakti,* karma, *jñāna*. That path is the essence of the *Gita*'s teaching.[107]

In each of these various declarations there is both a distinction and a congruence. The distinction is articulated but the congruence is found in their analysis. The focus of the *Gita,* according to Vinoba, seems to be the service to humanity (karma) that results from the understanding (*jñāna*) that worship of God (*bhakti*) entails the recognition of the Lord in all creation. This *bhakti* finds its greatest manifestation in the dedication of such service to the glory of God. This focuses attention on the strands of concerns brought together in the passage cited from Shankara's commentary.

THE MESSAGE OF VINOBA AND THE MESSAGE OF THE GITA

When the context of Vinoba's two works on the *Gita* is considered, namely that he delivered these talks while in prison in conjunction with *satyāgraha* campaigns, one is not surprised so much by the marriage of *Gita* and Gandhi as by the scarcity of explicit connection.[108] To be sure, Vinoba made frequent references to Gandhi's programs in these talks, but for the most part these references were as an aside rather than linked directly to the topic under consideration. However, there is sufficient integration of Gandhian ideas in his exposition to detect their influence in his interpretation.

The primary concern, as would be expected, is *satyāgraha*. Vinoba uses his exposition of the *Gita* to undergird his commitment to the campaign. He sees *satyāgraha* validated in the *Gita* several times. Illustrating the teaching in Chapter 13, which discriminates between the body and the Self, he says:

> This too is the lesson we learn from satyagraha. The body and the Self are two different things. The day a man discovers this secret, his real education, his real growth begins. It is only then that satyagraha will succeed.[109]

Satyāgraha is the admixture of two necessary components: *satya* (truth) and *ahimsā* (non-violence). Vinoba finds these truths interwoven through the truths of the *Gita,* for as his guru Gandhi taught him, he considers truth and non-violence to be the heart of the Hindu *dharma.* Vinoba says that throughout the *Gita* several meanings of *ahiṃsa* are taught, both negative and positive. Truth and non-violence are equated by Vinoba in his interpretations of several passages in the *Gita.* In fact, he finds these two principles to be the key to understanding much of the advice that Lord Krishna delivers to Arjuna on the field of Kuru. *Ahiṃsā* (and its sister, *satya*) is the yoga of the ultimate goal of humankind (*puruṣottama yoga*) taught by the *Gita.*[110]

Gandhi taught that in a struggle for a righteous cause the means and the ends must be identical. Vinoba finds this truth taught in many places in the *Gita.* In fact, this is the discipline of *karmayoga:* in *karmayoga,* the path and the goal (means and end) are known to be the same. Gandhi also taught that *brahmacārya* (sense control) must be followed as part of the means or the end would be tainted. Vinoba finds support for this admonition in the *Gita.*[111]

Vinoba also finds confirmation for many other concerns of Gandhi in the *Gita*. The concept of *svadeśa* (support of one's own country) is in the *Gita*. The *Gita* teaches that *saguṇa* worship is known to be *svadeśa*. Furthermore, part of everyone's *svadharma* (individual duty) is *svadeśa*. Support for Gandhi's ideas about *varṇa-aśrama dharma* as well as Hindu-Muslim unity are found in the *Gita*.[112]

In each of these instances, Vinoba is seen to introduce ideas that he learned from his encounters with Gandhi into his exposition of the *Gita*. But there is clearly a bi-lateral relationship. His Gandhian ideas help him understand the *Gita* and the *Gita* enriches and completes his ideas. It does not seem that he is superimposing ideas upon the *Gita*, but rather allowing the *Gita* to inform much of the philosophy he acquired from Gandhi.

Naturally, *sarvodaya* (the welfare of all) is a concept that Vinoba learned from Gandhi. But he was very instrumental in its development and later his name became synonymous with *sarvodaya*, so it is here considered as part of Vinoba's own message. And this messsage of *sarvodaya* is found by Vinoba to permeate the *Gita*. The goal of service to others is a primary message of the *Gita*.

> "I" and "mine" are swept away and then whatever remains is for the sake of the Lord. Life is lived entirely for the good of others. There is nothing else. This is what the *Gita* teaches again and again.[114]

This conflation of "the sake of the Lord" and "the good of others" is a theme that runs throughout Vinoba's works, and therefore is found in his expositions of the *Gita*, where he finds the idea that love of God is synonymous with service to humanity. Vinoba says, "the old concept of *bhakti* should be reiterated as *sarvodaya*."[115] *Sarvodaya* is to "see all beings with equal eye" and it is the *parabhakti*, the highest type of devotion described in the *Gita*.[116] This is the *samyayoga* (the discipline of equality) taught in the *Gita*.[117]

Vinoba finds the many paths (yogas) taught in the *Gita* to coalesce in *sarvodaya*, service to society and humanity. *Dhyanayoga* (path of meditation) involves the detachment that comes from thinking in terms of the whole world rather than just the self. *Karmayoga* (path of action) leads to desireless action manifested in working for the welfare of society. The *karma yogi* helps society maintain order, prosperity and goodwill while serving as an example for society. The *jñāna yogi* (follower of the path of knowledge) naturally serves others, for he does not discriminate between the self, others, and the Lord.

This is the knowledge of *advaita,* that the self and society are the same.[118]

Bhaktiyoga (path of worship) demonstrates this same truth, for the devotee learns to see that the Lord is known and worshipped only in his creation. So love and service become synonymouns. It is the *nirguṇa bhakta* or *advaita bhakta* who recognizes this best, and knows that devotion to God is expressed in serving the good of all and seeking the welfare of all beings. This is because service to the world is known to be the same as spiritual development.[119]

Vinoba, therefore, is able to discover the foundations of the spirit of *sarvodaya* in all the teachings, all the yogas of the *Gita,* a discovery which is derived primarily from the identification of creator with creation. It also comes from the perception of *bhakti* as worship of the unmanifest God through service to the manifest creation. So the *Gita,* in inculcating *bhakti,* is found to be calling one to the welfare of all—*sarvodaya.*

Vinoba does not discover his message of Bhoodan explicitly taught in the *Gita,* although its spirit is certainly present. Bhoodan (the gift of land) is a specific application of *sarvodaya.* It is the recognition of the Lord as one's neighbor and the living of one's life for this Lord. This message Vinoba learns from the *Gita.* Likewise, the *Gita* teaches that in giving anything to one's neighbor, the important question to ask is not how much was given but if it was given in love and in the spirit of dedication to God.[120] Vinoba later translates this spirit into the impetus of his Bhoodan Yajna.

Vinoba finds his message of *dāna* (charity or giving) given articulation in the *Gita. Dāna* is considered a means of purification; giving in the proper spirit purifies the giver, the gift, and the recipient. Inasmuch as Vinoba finds the presence of God in all creation, giving to the poor, like service to the poor, is giving to God. The *Gita* encourages one to recognize God as *Daridranarayan*—God in the form of the poor. Vinoba equates *dāna* with service, so that anything the *Gita* teaches regarding service is pertinent to giving.[121]

Vinoba equates service with *yajña* (sacrifice) as well. Anything done in the spirit of service is considered *yajña.* The *Gita* teaches that *yajña,* too, is a means of purification; it purifies the things of creation that we use. The *Gita* also teaches, according to Vinoba, that all of life is a continual *yajña-karma,* a sacrificial performance. Furthermore, *yajña* is not complete, the *Gita* teaches, until all of one's life and actions are dedicated to the Lord. Without this dedication, service is not sacrifice; it is merely activity.[122]

That Vinoba finds the message of the *Gita* to be congruent with his message is most clearly seen in his coalescence of three *Gita* teachings into one concern. *Yajña, dāna,* and *tapas* are seen by the *Gita* as the methods of fulfilling duties to the three orders into which one is born: the universe, society, and the body. *Yajña* discharges the debt to the universe for partaking of creation; *dāna* discharges the debt to society; *tapas* pays the debt to the body. Vinoba then collapses all these methods into service.[123]

In Vinoba's message, then, service becomes the focus of all his concerns. True devotion (*bhakti*) is known only through service; giving (*dāna*) is best realized as service; sacrifice (*yajña*) is fully performed as service; spiritual discipline (*tapas*) is found in service.[124] Service to humanity and to creation is the cornerstone of Vinoba's program. All else, *sarvodaya, bhoodan, dāna,* etc., is built upon this concept of service. This message he discovered in the *Gita.*

CONCLUSION

As has been shown above, the *Gita* was instrumental in shaping some of the basic concerns that Vinoba pursued throughout his career. Perhaps its most significant influence was to reveal to Vinoba the identification of service with worship. But in order to fully evaluate the role of the *Gita* in his thought, his later works need to be investigated.

Some of Vinoba's works have no direct references to the *Gita* at all.[125] Although this does not mean that the *Gita* played no role in their development, it does imply that Vinoba felt no need to draw specific support from the *Gita.* Vinoba obviously considers the *Gita* to be a touchstone of truth; in a work on the *Japji* (a Sikh prayer; a portion of the *Adi Granth*), he cites the *Gita* for confirmation of teachings found in the *Japji.*[126]

A survey of Vinoba's works reveals that he considers the practical teachings of the *Gita,* which link philosophy with action, to be the most formative in his thought. These practical teachings include a program of constructive work for everyday practice. This program is based on the *Gita's* teachings of non-attachment and desirelessness, the way to total dedication, which is worship of God. Since God is found in every living being, worship of God is service to creation.[127] Vinoba summarizes by saying what seems to be the main message of the *Gita* for him: "The *Gita* shows that what one does is more important than what he says."[128] This emphasis on action rather than words certainly summarizes the career of Vinoba himself.

Although the influence of the *Gita,* may not be easily documented, it may be more easily deduced. A study of his *Talks on the Gita* and *The Steadfast Wisdom* leads one to the conclusion that certain teachings in the *Gita* impressed him greatly, teachings that can be traced throughout Vinoba's career.

One in particular is the meaning of *bhakti* in this world. The message of the *Gita* that seems to have influenced him the most is that of *bhakti* as service-worship of the Lord in service to creation. This spirit serves as the spirit impelling his Bhoodan Yajna, as well as all his other *dānas* (Sampatti dāna, Premadsdāna, etc.), his concept of sacrifice (*yajña*), and his growing understanding of *sarvodaya.* If work in the world is service and worship of the Lord, if God appears most clearly as one's neighbor, then there is nothing to be done other than to immerse oneself entirely in the pursuit of the welfare of all.[129] So Vinoba reasoned, and so he lived.

The message of desirelessness and the abandonment of fruits equally inspired Vinoba. Desirelessness generates the spirit that Vinoba inculcates in the various aspects of *dāna* (giving). One should not hold to his/her property, money, talents, gifts, etc., jealously and with desire for reward. Likewise, one should not act nobly in service to humanity and all creation in expectation of some personal benefit or prestige. Things are given and actions must be performed in the spirit of desirelessness, not counting the reward, renouncing their fruits.[130]

Similarly, this spirit lies behind Vinoba's understanding of "dedication," an understanding acquired from the *Gita.* True desirelessness is manifested in the dedication of all actions to the Lord. First renounce the fruits or your actions and then dedicate them to the Lord. This infuses them with purity and holiness. Vinoba believed that his actions could become beautiful and divine if dedicated to the Lord; he claims to have lived his life with that as his goal.[131]

Finally, Vinoba's concept of *yajña* (sacrifice), which informed so many of the activities and ideas in his career, is derived from the *Gita. Yajña,* the attitude of service to others and surrender to the Lord, is the culmination of *bhakti,* desirelessness, dedication, and *dāna.* Its spirit is the inspiration of Vinoba's Bhoodan Yajna and all the concomitant "gifts" (*dāna*). The *Gita* teaches practical lessons for life's experiences; what he learns in the *Gita,* he puts to work in the field.[132]

It is difficult to assess the influence Vinoba's philosophy had upon his interpretation of the *Gita*. His two works on the *Gita* are among the earliest of his recorded ideas. On the one hand, it may appear that he has introduced ideas into the *Gita* in order to support his own position. On the other, it can be argued that the seeds of his later thoughts are found in Vinoba's reading of the *Gita* and thus, the *Gita* influenced his philosophy. Such speculation is rather idle, for without specific documentation regarding the source of his ideas, conclusions are unfounded and unconvincing.

However, it is clear when he introduces ideas in his exposition of the *Gita,* like Hindu-Muslim unity, khadi, spinning and the *charkha, swadeśa,* or *satyāgraha,* that he has brought them to the text rather than deriving them from the text.[133] Yet closer study reveals that Vinoba is not claiming these matters are taught in the *Gita,* he uses them primarily as examples of teachings that are found in the *Gita*.

Later, Vinoba began to propound a philosophy called *Samyayoga*. This philosophy taught the necessity for seeing all things with an equal eye. This led to seeing the Lord in all creation; it led to *bhakti* as service; it led to *yajña, dāna,* and dedication. Vinoba claims that this *Samyayoga* is the main teaching of the *Gita*.[134] *Samyayoga,* is an attempt to systematize his ideas about the *Gita* and his ideas about social action and social programs, rather than a way of justifying or undergirding his ideas with the authority of the *Gita*.

It is difficult to make an assessment of any creative, active thinker in terms of the influence on him or his influences on someone or something else. A review of Vinoba's attitude toward the *Gita,* his interpretation of the *Gita,* his perception of the message of the *Gita,* and his own message, leads to the conclusion that Vinoba Bhave was, probably, deeply influenced by the teachings of the *Gita*. His life and career demonstrated an attempt to live the life he saw demanded by this text.

CHAPTER SEVEN

Swami Vivekananda's Use of the Bhagavadgita

HAROLD W. FRENCH

The title requested of me for this study is extremely apt. Vivekananda can be described as utilitarian in his approach to the *Gita,* employing it to reinforce his message both to the West and within India. Yet this is not a casual functionalism.[1] He wrote no commentaries or translations, and his only systematic treatises on the *Gita* are contained in three addresses in California in 1895 and one in Bengal about three years later. Nevertheless, his eight volumes of *Collected Works* are replete with references to it. Lectures, formal addresses, interviews, even his personal correspondence are laced with quotations from the *Gita.* If his method be deemed utilitarian, then any assessment of its worth must depend on the value we give to his objectives, and, scholastically, our judgment as to whether his references to the *Gita* derive from a superficial or deeper understanding of its content. This study will attempt to discuss, then, the uses for which he employed the *Gita* and the manner in which it was used. Is the *Gita* enhanced by his usage of it? Does it acquire more stature in the minds of the various publics that he addressed, including literary and philosophic scholars of the *Gita* itself?

VIVEKANANDA'S LIFE, ENCAPSULATED

A noted Indian educator, and fellow student in the early 1880s comments on what he saw happening to his friend, Narendanath Dutt, later known as Vivekananda:

> I watched with intense interest the transformation that went on under my eyes. The attitude of a young rampant Vedantist—cum Hegelian—cum revolutionary like myself towards

> the cult of religious ecstasy and Kali-worship may be easily imagined; and the spectacle of a born iconoclast and free-thinker like Vivekananda, a creative and dominating intelligence, a tamer of souls, himself caught in the meshes of what appeared to me an uncouth, supernatural mysticism, was a riddle which my philosophy of the pure reason could scarcely read at the time.[2]

Vivekananda was receiving a thoroughly Western education at Scottish Presbyterian College in Calcutta, founded by Alexander Duff, when he began to be acquainted with the motherlode of Hinduism through Ramakrishna. Alternating with a superficial skepticism, the mind of the young Naren was also engaged in a religious quest of some depth, as might be inferred from the question which he asked Ramakrishna on their first visit. It was a brash question, one which he had asked of other reputed sages: "Sir, have you seen God?" Instead of the usual evasions or qualified responses, Ramakrishna's was amazingly direct: "Yes, my son, I have seen God, just as I see you before me, only much more intensely." A powerful dynamic surfaced in subsequent encounters between the two, each recognizing an intense spiritual magnetism, but each giving time for testing. Naren soon discovered that Ramakrishna possessed a great intellect underneath the emotional nature that initially seemed so overpowering. "Outwardly he was all Bhakta but inwardly all Jñanin. I am the exact opposite."[3] The combination of paths of which the *Gita* speaks seems to have been experienced personally by the young Vivekananda, as his relationship with Ramakrishna unfolded.

Although bereft by Ramakrishna's death in 1886, the group of monastic disciples began to pledge themselves to a common life that would give each the range to explore his own spiritual path. Naren, who had become, in effect, their recognized leader, was tempted by the reclusive life of the hermetic monk, sealed from the world in the vastnesses of the Himalayas. But word came to him that his sister, back in Calcutta, had taken her life, and so he returned, apparently to re-define his vocational goal. He was not to leave the monastic calling, but to make it responsive to human need.

After visiting renowned centers of pilgrimage, he turned to an intensive, probing look at modern India. His long and patient tour to the north of India, then down its western side, culminated in 1893 in his first out-of-the-body experience, which occurred at the tip of the sub-continent's Cape Comorin peninsula on a rock some two hundred yards out subsequently to be known as Vivekananda

Rock, to which he swam through shark-infested waters. In this moment of geographical and psychological outsideness, looking back on *Bharat Mata,* Mother India, a sense of mission began to focus for him. He returned to Madras, rather than Bengal, where some friends helped him to sharpen that focus. A Parliament of Religions, with delegates from the world's nations and faiths, was gathering later that year in Chicago, as part of the Columbian Exposition or World's Fair. No matter that India's delegates had been determined some two years earlier. In recognition of Naren's natural gifts, and because of some economic gifts from the Maharajah of Khetri, it was determined that Naren, who now took the name of Vivekananda, should go to Chicago as India's best champion.

His arrival in Chicago, a month early, allowed him to indulge in the various exhibits and attractions of the fair. Intoxicated by its circus atmosphere, and by his vastly intensified initial exposure to the West, Vivekananda soon found that his money was being rapidly depleted. A fortuitous trip to Boston, and the acquaintance and hospitality of some well-positioned friends there, assisted him greatly. Sanskrit Professor J.H. Wright invited him to speak at Harvard, and, on learning of his not having credentials to speak at the Parliament, is quoted as having said, "To ask for your credentials is like asking the sun to state its right to shine in the heavens." Wright then addressed a letter to the Chairman in charge of delegates, saying, again extravagantly, "Here is a man who is more learned than all of our learned professors put together."[4] Armed with this letter, but with no formal presentation, Vivekananda nevertheless rose late in the first day's proceedings and gave his first brief address, which began with his stirring words, "Sisters and brothers of America!" It seemed to strike an authentic keynote, and responding to his ringing words and regal bearing, the press reports that the audience rose to applaud for several minutes before he could continue.

The Parliament was far from a one-man show, but the "cyclonic monk from India," as the media dubbed him, made a most impressive appearance, speaking several more times, and afterwards going on a lecture tour. Tiring of speeches, he began to work more intimately with small groups of persons on the West Coast, in New York, and in Europe, institutionalizing the Ramakrishna Movement in New York in 1895 as perhaps the first such Eastern religious movement to come to the West in modern times. He had a message for the West, distilled from the ancient wisdom of India's spiritual sages. Initially, he conceived of gaining some material help from the West for India in return. This, however, evolved into a different mission. To raise funds, perhaps, would involve him in the acknowledgement of shortcomings of Indian society; the missionaries were making great capital of these already, and he was extolling the greatness of India's spiritual wisdom. While it is difficult to trace the details of this change of strategy,[5] it is clear that his goal for India had become a more personal, spiritual one.

What messages for the West and East did he have, and specifically, what did he have to share from the *Gita,* which he described as "The best authority on Vedanta,"[6] which, he believed, was Hinduism universalized? "The only commentary, the authoritative commentary on the *Vedas,* has been made once and for all by Him who inspired the *Vedas*—Krishna in the Gita."[7]

Returning to India to a hero's welcome late in 1897,[8] he set out to implement his mission of an updated Hinduism, responsive to human needs. The Ramakrishna Mission, the social component of the Math or monastery, began to be engaged in the formation of hospitals, homes, and schools, to gather funds for flood and famine relief, etc. He journeyed once more to the West, in 1899, and, in a much more low-key manner, returned to India the following year. He was consolidating his work; the large lecture hall was largely abandoned. He was fitting others to carry on the work after his departure, which came, rather suddenly, on July 4th, 1902. He was thirty–nine.

VIVEKANANDA'S CRITICAL USE OF THE GITA

It is initially surprising to find that Vivekananda's critical observations on the *Gita* in the West seem more traditionally Indian, and his addresses in India more informed by modern scholarship. We may judge from this that he preceived his Western listeners as being less sophisticated in their understanding of Indian texts, which was undoubtedly true. By contrast, the novice monks whom he addressed in Bengal were treated to a relatively rather heady fare of critical methodology. But in each case, these four formal discourses frustrate our expectations as to scholarly format.[9] We are never told the versions from which he quotes the *Gita;* are the translations his own? We have almost no bibliographical data; footnotes, marginalia, are missing. If there are interpretive sources which he employs, we do not know in what manner he employs them. Only a few are named, let alone quoted. His lecture to the young monks in Bengal, nevertheless, does contain some historical/critical observation. He notes how questions of historicity of the *Gita* could be clarified considerably if the widely reputed commentary by Bodhyana, antedating Shankara, were not so shrouded in darkness. He states that he could not find a copy of it in the whole of his travels in India in the early 1890s. He tells his hearers that historic questions are questions of truth, however difficult of resolution, and not irrelevant if they are to know the substance of the *Gita.*[10]

But his greater concerns are with the cultic Krishna, spawned by whatever shadowy original may have inspired later legends. "It is human nature to build round the real character of a great man all sorts of imaginary superhuman attributes. As regards Krishna the same must have happened, but it seems quite probable that he was a king."[11] A paucity of information on origins, however, inhibits his "quest of the historical Krishna." His method is not 'de-mythologizing,' to get to the essential, earliest core of the teaching, but, if we may coin an alternative term, 'multi-mythologizing,' to focus attention on the varied strands of the tradition and the vivid manner in which mythic and cultic life has been stimulated by the figure of Krishna. Thus he remarks, satirically, "Many of our people think that Krishna as the lover of the Gopis is something rather uncanny, and the Europeans do not like it much. Dr. So-and-so does not like it. Certainly, then, the Gopis have to go! Without the sanction of Europeans how can Krishna live? He cannot!"[12] Again, he specifically counsels, "If you want to be a Bhakta, it is not at all necessary for you to know whether Krishna was born in Mathurā or in Vraja, what he was doing, or just the exact date on which he pronounced the teachings of the Gita. You only require to *feel* the craving for the beautiful lessons of duty and love in the Gita."[13] While, his primary counsel from the *Gita* for India is in the direction of karma and *jñāna* yogic strategies, as we shall see, here he also validates the more characteristically devotional response. Perhaps, in this relativization of the critical approach, he also indicates his own lack of interest in formal research of that character.

For western readers, however, who were more historically minded, he could oblige with at least some superficial conclusions concerning origins. Every religion, he suggests, must have some economic value to succeed. With the *Upanishads,* however (and here he is treating the *Gita* as an *Upanishad*), there is very little economic value, but tremendous altruism. There is very little kingdom in them, yet they were discovered by kings who held royal power in their hands. "The seed of Buddhism is here, in the ordinary struggle between the king and the priest."[14] Krishna is the reconciler of this struggle, as Buddhism later was. Vivekananda seems intent in the West, earlier, to establish the priority of the *Gita* and the earlier *Upanishads,* which he dates at about 5000 and 6000 B.C., over Buddhism.[15] Back in India, he would appear to have developed a greater feeling for Buddhism, so that his interest in speculation concerning origins, fades.

VIVEKANANDA'S USES OF THE GITA IN THE WEST

Vivekananda once suggested that the two special characteristics of the *Gita* are reconciliation of paths and work without desire.[16] These seem clearly to have been the most common lessons which he drew from the *Gita* for his western audience. There are several facets to the first, beginning with his first two-minute oration at the Parliament of Religions, where he is quoted as saying, "The present convention, which is one of the most august assemblies ever held, is in itself a vindication: a declaration to the world of the wonderful doctrine preached in the *Gita:* 'Whosoever comes to Me, through whatsoever form, I reach him; all men are struggling through paths which in the end lead to Me.' . . . I fervently hope that the bell that tolled this morning in honor of this convention may be the death-knell of all fanaticism, of all persecutions with the sword or with the pen, and of all uncharitable feelings between persons wending their way to the same goal."[17] This hope, however, was destined to last but briefly, for even in the Parliament exclusivist claims were made which he felt compelled to refute. Joseph Cook, a non-sectarian minister from Boston, had at various times sought to dismiss liberal religious persuasions. "Boston, under Channing, Parker and Emerson, has three times tried to found a new religion," he observed, "but each attempt is now a last year's bird's nest."[18] Surprisingly he had met Keshub Chander Sen in 1882 in India, and Ramakrishna also, briefly, but these contacts had little liberalizing influence on him apart from generating a personal warmth towards Keshub. "The Brahmos are in the vestibule of Christianity, with their faces turned toward the inner doors; while radical Unitarians in the Occident are in the same vestibule, but often with their faces turned toward the outer doors."[19] In the Parliament, Cook asked rhetorically, "What religion can wash Lady Macbeth's right hand?" and he affirmed, "It is clear that we cannot escape from conscience and God and our record of sin. It is a certainty and a strategic certainty that, except Christianity, there is no religion under heaven or among men that effectively provides for the peace of the soul by its harmonization with itself, its God, and its record of sin."[20]

We cannot be certain, as some interpreters contend, that a part of Vivekananda's address on Hinduism, given five days after Cook's, was in direct response to Cook's. But the contrasting emphasis is clear. Vivekananda exhorted:

> Allow me to call you, brethren, by that sweet name, heirs of immortal bliss—yea, the Hindu refuses to call you sinners. Ye are the children of God, the sharers of immortal bliss, holy and perfect beings, ye are divinities on earth. Sinners? It is a sin to call a man so; it is a standing libel on human nature. Come up, O lions and shake off the delusion that you are sheep.[21]

There were thus areas which he discovered did not allow for facile harmonization. Differing views of human nature and exclusivist claims were two of these. "It does not matter," he states, following the insight of the ninth chapter of the *Gita* cited above, "whether one approaches the destination in a carriage with four horses, in an electric car, or rolling on the ground. The goal is the same."[22] The theory of incarnation gives Hinduism a basis for toleration of alternate paths; we see in them the workings of various avatars and the human responses to their power. He quotes *Gita* 4:18, "Whenever virtue subsides and irreligion prevails, I come down. Again and again I come. Therefore, whenever thou seest a great soul struggling to uplift mankind, know that I am come, and worship." "At the same time," Vivekananda asks, "if He comes as Jesus or as Buddha, why is there so much schism?"[23] If, he would appear to be saying, we find in one of these great persons what we regard as truth, we ought to expect to find echoes of that truth in other such persons, to look for it, and not to demean it or explain it away when it occurs. "You say Uncle Sam is everybody's uncle. If there is a god, you ought to be able to see him. [And, by implication, so should everyone else, in whatever guise.] If not, let him go."[24] It is the Upanishadic insight, that Truth is One.

In support of this, he cites several similarities between Jesus of Nazareth and Krishna. Krishna was of royal birth. King Kamsa, hearing that a child who would be king would be born in such and such a family, ordered a massacre of male infants. Krishna's parents were in prison when he was born. A light suddenly shone in the prison and Krishna spoke, saying, "I am the light of the world, born for the good of the world." Sages affirmed that God Himself was born, and they went to pay Him homage.[25] Just as he sought to make Krishna familiar by comparison with known circumstances in the life of Jesus, Vivekananda pointed to the *Gita* as the inspiration of some of America's richest literary figures. In a lecture to the Shakespeare Club in Pasadena in 1900, he claimed that the *Gita* was the source of Emerson's inspiration. Visiting Carlyle, Emerson had been presented by him with a copy of the *Gita*. "That little book is responsible for the Concord Movement," Vivekananda claimed.[26]

The practical problem with the harmonization of religions, lay for Vivekananda in the definitions by most of them of religion as doctrine, with assent to dogma as the mark of belonging. By contrast, he says, religion in India does not consist in doctrine, but in realization, by whatever path. He quotes *Gita* 3:35 as follows, "Better die in your own path than attempt the path of another."[27] This may not carry the full weight of the meaning of *dharma* in the original, but he is speaking to Americans. "What do you mean by 'saving people' and all believing in the same doctrine?" he asks. "It cannot be. . . . We start a religion and make a set of dogmas and betray the goal of mankind and treat everyone as having the same nature. . . . If you want to be religious," he counsels, "enter not the gate of any organized religion. They do a hundred times more evil than good, because they stop the growth of each one's religious development."[28]

The answer, for Vivekananda, would appear to be personal confidence in your own insight and strength, and restraint in assuming that your path is better than that of another. In refuting the doctrine that says human beings are sinners because Adam sinned, and are saved because Christ died, Vivekananda states, "No man's seeing God can help you the least bit except it may excite you and urge you to do the same thing. That is the whole value of the ancient's examples. Nothing more. Just signposts along the way. No man's eating can satisfy another man. No man's seeing God can save another man."[29] Again, in underscoring his Parliament appeal that we recognize our identity as lions and not sheep, Vivekananda refers to the *Gita*, 6:5, saying, "It is a tremendous error to feel helpless. Do not seek help from anyone. We are our own help. If we cannot help ourselves, there is none to help us."[30] He nears the conclusion of his California lectures on the *Gita* with the following words:

> There is only one sin. That is weakness. When I was a boy I read Milton's *Paradise Lost.* The only good man I had any respect for was Satan. The only saint is that soul that never weakens, faces everything, and determines to die game.
>
> Stand up and die game! . . . Do not add one lunacy to another, Do not add your weakness to the evil that is going to come. That is all I have to say to the world. Be strong![31]

To the other side of the coin, personal strength which does not seek to overpower others, Vivekananda counsels: "Each one thinks his method is best. Very good! But remember, it may be good for *you.*"[32] Citing *Gita,* chapter 3, verses 26 and 29, he observes; "Even if you have knowledge, do not disturb the childlike faith of the ignorant. On the other hand, go down to their level and gradually bring them up."[33] It is in these various ways that Vivekananda sought to effect, through the *Gita's* message, a tolerance of paths among westerners. They must believe in the validity of the insights of various great teachers. They must have confidence in their own insights, as well. And they must not be so presumptuous as to believe that what has worked for them will be easily tailored for another's spiritual garb.

The other message for the West from the *Gita,* as Vivekananda sought to teach it, was the lesson of non-attachment to work, calmness in the midst of strife. It was not an exhortation to work; that message was reserved for India, as we shall see. The western work ethic was visible enough to the outsider, but he could critique, in the spirit of the *Gita,* the manner in which it was done, and the anxiety which it produced. Krishna, here, is the example. With Krishna, "non-attachment is the central idea. He does not need anything. He does not want anything. He works for work's sake."[34] Similarly, Buddha is the ideal karma yogin, who did not work for any reward.[35] Yet, Vivekananda prefers Krishna as the more representative human example. While Buddha and other spiritual leaders were monastics, with no sympathetic understanding for householders, Krishna fulfilled his roles as a son, a king, and a father.[36] For Americans, the symbolism is that Krishna lived the truth in the midst of the battlefield of life. *Gita* 4:18 is quoted as follows: "He who in the midst of intense activity finds himself in the greatest calmness, and in the greatest peace finds intense activity, that is the greatest Yogi as well as the wisest man."[37]

The battlefield of Kurukshetra had abundant parallels to the American scene for Vivekananda, who was alternately attracted and repelled by its materialism. In Boston once he had planned to speak on the subject of his master, Ramakrishna, but at the sight of a crowd composed of persons of wealth and position and of a civilization represented by foxes and wolves he was so repelled that he lashed out furiously. Hundreds noisily left the hall and the press was furious. Nikhilananda records the remorse Vivekananda felt after reflecting on what he had done. "His Master had never uttered a word of condemnation against anybody, even the most wicked person; yet he, while talking about Ramakrishna, had criticized these good-hearted people who were eager to learn about the Master. He felt that he was unworthy of Sri Ramakrishna and resolved not to discuss him in public or even to write about him again."[38]

A natural affection for the freshness, brashness, and energy of the American spirit also impressed him. Anticipating his first return to India, after several years in the West, he could write to a friend, "It is to Amerique—there is where the heart is. I love the Yankee land. I like to see new things. I do not care a fig about old ruins and mope a life out about old histories and keep sighing about the ancients. I have too much vigour in my blood for that. In America is the place, the people, the opportunity for everything. I have become horribly radical. I am just going to India to see what I can do in that awful mess of conservative jellyfish."[39]

Yet the conservative jellyfish perhaps could teach America something about tranquility. Vivekananda reminded his San Francisco hearers of the message in *Gita* 2:45 and elsewhere concerning the giving up of all desires. "When he has become perfectly satisfied, he has no more cravings."[40] Such a man lives by different rhythms from the herd. "Where it is dark night for the sense bound world, the self-controlled man is awake. It is daylight for him. . . . And where the world is awake, the sage sleeps."[41] It is this alternative gyroscope of *Gita* 2.65 which the western world needs for balance. The question which Vivekananda seeks to address, then, is how to channel the West's abundant energy in such a manner as to bring spiritual freedom and not material bondage to its citizens. If non-attachment to work is the central message of the *Gita,* as Vivekananda asserts variously, then America was peculiarly in need of this work.

VIVEKANANDA'S USES OF THE GITA IN INDIA

If work without desire was a hallmark of the *Gita's* message for the West, Vivekananda's prescription for India was simpler still:

"WORK." There is more, but this is the karma yogic core of his teaching, the one which he judged that his people most needed to hear from the sacred pages. How to awaken the slumbering giant? Vivekananda interpreted the Western spirit of power and energy as natural to the Yavana or Greek temperament; the Arya, by contrast, tends toward quietness and meditation. The former is characterized by enjoyment, the latter by renunciation. But then he makes the judgment, "Europe and America are the advanced children of the Yavanas, a glory to their forefathers; but the modern inhabitants of the land of Bharata are not the glory of the ancient Aryas."[42] Although he feels that the ancestral fire will once more manifest itself, it is presently buried latent beneath ashes. These ashes are the delusion of India, who believes that she is pursuing *sattva,* or truth, when she is actually drowning in a sea of *tamas.* His indictment continues:

> Where the most dull want to hide their stupidity by covering it with a false desire for the highest knowledge which is beyond all activities, either psychological or mental; where one, born and bred in lifelong laziness, wants to throw the veil of renunciation over his unfitness for work; where the most diabolical try to make their cruelty appear, under the cloak of austerity, as a part of religion; . . . where knowledge consists only in getting some books by heart, genius consists in chewing the cud of others' thoughts . . . ; do we require any other proof to show that that country is being day by day drowned in Tamas?[43]

He then goes on to say that the nation and each person must pass from *tamas* through *rajas* to *sattva.* Where he feels that the West was almost wholly lacking in *sattva,* it is *rajas,* the spirit of energy, which was practically absent in India. His oratorical portrait of what India needs is eloquent; these three energy modes of expressions of *prakṛti* found in the *Gita,* are the categories by which he expresses it:

> What we should have is what we have not, perhaps, what our forefathers even had not—that which the Yavanas had; that, impelled by the life-vibration of which, is issuing forth in rapid succession from the great dynamo of Europe. The electric flow of that tremendous power vivifying the whole world. We want that. We want that energy, that love of independence, that spirit of self-reliance, that immovable fortitude, that dexterity in action, that bond of unity of purpose, that thirst for improvement . . . we want—that intense spirit of

activity (Rajas) which will flow through our every vein, from head to foot.[44]

He addressed a Madras gathering shortly after his 1897 return to India, urging them, "First of all, our young men must be strong. Religion will come afterwards. Be strong, my young friends; that is my advice to you. You will be nearer to Heaven through football than through the study of the Gita. These are bold words, but I have to say them, for I love you . . . You will understand the Gita better with your biceps, your muscles, a little stronger. You will understand the mighty genius and the mighty strength of Krishna better with a little of strong blood in you."[45] "Yield not to unmanliness, O Son of Pritha."[46] This was a keynote for his message on the *Gita* to the young monastics back in Bengal. "Thou art Atman imperishable, beyond all evil. Having forgotten thy real nature, thou hast, by thinking thyself a sinner, as one afflicted with bodily evils and mental grief, thou hast made thyself so—this doth not befit thee!"[47] He had told a California audience earlier that for Indians the problem is how to become what they really are, to regain their lost selfhood;[48] now he draws on those *jñānin* aspects of the *Gita* to reinforce the imperative to strong, karma yogic behavior. A Bengali disciple recorded his instructions in 1898 on several occasions in the monastery in Belur, sometimes linking these two themes from the *Gita,* but invariably emphasizing these strains of *jñāna* and karma. "Shri Krishna spoke the Gita, establishing Himself in the Atman. Those passages of the Gita where He speaks with the word 'I' invariably indicate the Atman: 'Take refuge in Me alone,' means, 'Be established in the Atman.' This knowledge of the Atman is the highest aim of the Gita."[49] Again the disciple observes, "On the lips of Swamiji were very often heard the words of the Gita, 'A doer of good never comes to grief, my son.' "[50] Asked by a disciple how an artist should try to represent the Krishna of the *Gita,* Vivekananda, after discussing and demonstrating possible battlefield scenes and poses, asked him in return, "Now tell me what idea this picture of the Preacher of the Gita conveys to you?" The response was, "Activity combined with firmness and serenity." Vivekananda replied enthusiastically, "Ay, that's it! Intense action in the whole body, and withal a face expressing the profound calmness and serenity of the blue sky."[51]

How is it that the *bhakti* components of the *Gita* are de-emphasized, or slanted towards more Upanishadic, Advaitic interpretations, and that the activist flavor everywhere dominates? ("Work is worship", etc.) Again, it would seem to be that India, in his judgment, had had enough of ceremonials. He addressed his brother monks in 1894 from America, giving them, in one of his first letters back to Bengal, some sense of how he expected them to proceed, and what to avoid, in an eloquent satirical treatise on ceremonials.

> If you want any good to come, just throw your ceremonials overboard and worship the Living God, the Man-God—every being that wears a human form—God in His universal as well as individual aspect. The universal aspect of God means this world, and worshipping it means serving it—this indeed is work, not indulging in ceremonials. Neither is it work to cogitate as to whether the rice plate should be placed in front of the God for ten minutes or for half an hour—that is called lunacy. Millions of rupees have been spent only that the temple doors at Varanasi or Vrindaban may play at opening and shutting all day long! Now the Lord is having his toilet, now He is taking His meals, now He is busy on something else we know not what. . . . And all this, while the Living God is dying for want of food, for want of education! The banias of Bombay are erecting hospitals for bugs—while they would do nothing for men—even if they die! You have not the brain to understand this simple thing—that it is a plague with our country, and lunatic asylums are rife all over. . . ."[52]

Later, in a more temperate mood, he could confess to his *gurubhais,* "I am trying and always trying to keep down the rush of *Bhakti* welling within me. I am trying to bind and bind myself with the iron chains of *Jñāna,* for still my work to my motherland is unfinished, and my message to the world not yet fully delivered. So, as soon as I find that *Bhakti* feelings are trying to come up to sweep me off my feet, I give a hard knock to them and make myself adamant by bringing up austere *Jñāna.*"[53]

Authority questions remained, however, and the example of Ramakrishna was often cited as precedent for alternative directions which the Movement might take. It was an ultimate example which had at times resulted in devotion, Ramakrishna *bhakti,* in the movement, for Vivekananda and most of the other followers interpreted Ramakrishna as an incarnation, an *avatāra.* One of Vivekananda's hymns to Ramakrishna contained these lines: "He who quelled the noise, terrible like that at the time of destruction, arising from the battle (of Kurukshetra), who destroyed the terrible yet natural night of ignorance (of Arjuna) and who roared out the Gita sweet and appeasing; that renowned soul is born now as Shri Ramakrishna."[54] But given the divine authority of Ramakrishna, who best could interpret Ramakrishna? In one heated exchange, Vivekananda railed at his brother monks:

> You think you understand Shri Ramakrishna better than myself! You think *Jñāna* is dry knowledge to be attained by a desert path, killing out the tenderest faculties of the heart. Your *Bhakti* is sentimental nonsense which makes one impotent. You want to preach Ramakrishna as you have understood him which is mighty little. Hands off! Who cares for your Ramakrishna? Who cares for your *Bhakti* and *Mukti*? Who cares what the Scriptures say? I will go to hell cheerfully a thousand times, if I can rouse my countrymen, immersed in *Tamas,* and make them stand on their feet and be Men, inspired with the spirit of *Karma-Yoga.* I am not a follower of Ramakrishna or any one, I am a follower of him only who carries out my plans! I am not a servant of Ramakrishna or any one, but of him only who serves and helps others, without caring for his own *Mukti.*[55]

Despite his disavowals, the priority of *karmayoga* was a lesson which he had learned earlier from Ramakrishna. When he had implored Ramakrishna to show him the way to *nirvakalpa samadhi,* the state of ultimate release, he was given a surprisingly sharp rebuke by his gentle master. "Shame on you!" Ramakrishna exclaimed. "I never thought you to be so mean as to be anxious for your own salvation only whereas you have powers to do so much good to mankind."[56]

The *Gita*'s message authenticated his own deep missionary imperative. It taught a ministry to human need, a ministry activated most vividly by energizing the people of India to claim their own strong, if dormant, identity. Vivekananda noted western objections to Krishna's militant counsel to Arjuna in chapter two of the *Gita,* and responded by suggesting that all of Arjuna's apparently sophisticated arguments against participating in combat stemmed from cowardice.[57] It was not non-resistance from strength, which would have been true renunciation. The sattvic goal of renunciation can only be pursued after one has passed through the inferno of his passions, has engaged the foe in battle, has exercised the karma yogic imperative of resistance to evil. In support of this, he gives an example of a conversation which he had with a young man in India:

> who I had known as a very stupid, dull person, who knew nothing and had not the desire to know anything, and was living the life of a brute. He asked me what he should do to know God, how he was to get free. 'Can you tell a lie?' I asked him. 'No,' he replied. 'Then you must learn to do so. It is better to tell a lie than to be a brute, or a log of wood. You are inactive; you have not certainly reached the highest state, which is beyond all actions, calm and serene; you are too dull even to do something wicked.' That was an extreme case, of course, and I was joking with him; but what I meant was that a man must be active in order to pass through activity to perfect calmness.[58]

This *karma-jñāna* blending from the *Gita* is the model whereby all persons in India may be energized.

> It is there for everyone in every occupation of life. These conceptions of the Vedanta must come out, must remain not only in the forest, not only in the cave, but they must come out to work at the bar and the bench, in the pulpit, and in the cottage of the poor man, with the fishermen that are catching fish, and with the students that are studying. They call to every man, woman and child whatever be their occupation, wherever they may be.[59]

For each, it follows, "if the fisherman thinks that he is the Spirit, he will be a better fisherman," etc. "If you teach Vedanta to a fisherman, he will say, I am as good a man as you; I am a fisherman, you are a philosopher, but I have the same God in me as you have in you."[60] So, for Vivekananda, castes might continue, but not privilege; there is to be equality, but with division of labor. We see in his program, then, a case for social service, but not for social reform. He is impatient, for instance, with questions about what to do with the widow problem and the women question. "Let me answer once and for all - am I a widow that you ask me that nonsense? Am I a woman that you ask me that question again and again? Who are you to solve women's problems? Are you the Lord God that you should rule over every widow and every woman? Hands off!"[61] His point is that you do not help others by presuming to identify with their lot, which is impossible. Your help may actually inhibit their own Self reliance, their experience of the power resident in their own true identity.

In addressing a Madras gathering which would have been composed primarily of brahmins, he stated that the *Gita* advocates true

Brahminhood for all. There is to be no doing away with caste, but there is to be no warfare among the castes. Just as in the *Mahabharata* hie observes, there was only one caste at the beginning of the Satya Yuga, so in the coming Satya Yuga, his vision for India's future, all castes will return to true Brahminhood, the ideal of humanity in India. In the meantime, he states:

> The days of exclusive privileges and exclusive claims are gone, gone for ever from the soil of India, and it is one of the great blessings of British Rule in India. Even to the Mohammedan Rule we owe that great blessing, the destruction of exclusive privilege . . . The Mohammedan conquest of India came as a salvation to the downtrodden, to the poor. That is why one-fifth of our people have become Mohammedans. It was not the sword that did it all. It would be the height of madness to think it was all the work of sword and fire. And one-fifth—one half—of your Madras people will become Christians if you do not take care. Was there ever a sillier thing before in the world than what I saw in Malabar country? The poor Pariah is not allowed to pass through the same street as the high-caste man, but if he changes his name to a hodge-podge English name, it is all right; or to a Mohammedan name, it is all right.[62]

India, after centuries of alien political domination, had become, in Vivekananda's thought, a servile, boot-licking race. The mission which he began to intuit from the rock off Cape Comorin, subsequently to be named in his honor and a temple erected upon it, did have a part in energizing India. The tiny surface of Vivekananda Rock became a place of vision from which the conch shell of Kurukshetra might again be heard to awaken the fearful and slothful to engage in life's battle. Vivekananda's use of the *Gita,* in the West and in the East, and in the insights which ripened from his bridges between them, was active and outward in its intent, and an understanding Vivekananda thought was faithful in spirit to the *Gita*'s own best wisdom.

CHAPTER EIGHT

The Bhagavadgita *in* Radhakrishnan's Apologetics

ROBERT N. MINOR*

Sarvepalli Radhakrishnan (1888–1975) has been eulogized as a "bridge-builder" between East and West. As educator, philosopher and statesman holding positions in both Indian and Western institutions, his "bridge-building" involved the defense and advocacy of what he defined as an ideal 'Hinduism,' a "religion of the spirit" that would solve the human predicaments of the twentieth-century. His writings and speeches were filled with quotations from Indian as well as Western sources. Although he found support for his position almost everywhere he looked, he was convinced that 'the Indian' or 'Hindu' ideal best embodied it.[1]

The *Bhagavadgita* was central to his apologetic interests. It provided support not as a document of orientalist, historical, or scholarly interest, but as a proof-text for his arguments and pleas both to Western critics of Indian religion and to Indians whom he believed had fallen from the ideal which he defended. His translation and commentary, first published in 1947 in London and in 1948 in the United States, continues to be in demand, with regular popular edition reprints making it available in Europe, North America, and India.

Radhakrishnan saw the *Gita* as "an important document of revitalized and renascent India," "a document of Civil Religion for the modern Indian nation-state,"[2] and a document for a Civil Religion for the world community. He believed the *Gita* is a document of which India could be proud. This study, placing it in the context of Radhakrishnan's life and writings, will show that as a text of persuasion and proof for his "religion of the spirit," it bore the weight of his construction of the ideal religious position.

THE GITA AND EARLY ETHICAL APOLOGETICS

Radhakrishnan tells us that it was during his first teaching appointment at Madras Presidency College that he studied "the classics of Hinduism," which included the *Gita*.[3] His prior education had been at Christian mission schools, culminating in a B.A. and M.A. from Madras Christian College with training in Western philosophy. He entered the teaching profession with an apologetic interest: to defend what he first called "Vedanta" and later "Hinduism" against the attacks levelled against "it" by his teachers, Christian missionaries, and other critics.[4] His writings during this early period were intended to show first, that "Vedanta" had an ethical intent, specifically a strong basis for social morality and a concern for human welfare. In this endeavor the *Gita* was a central scripture.

Radhakrishnan also labored to show that "Vedanta, Hinduism," as it should be in contrast to how it has, he believed, deteriorated, is a solid, viable philosophy, able to compete with and even surpass the philosophies prevalent in the twentieth century. Though this latter intention would continue throughout his life, its early apologetic thrust culminated in his 1920 work, *The Reign of Religion in Contemporary Philosophy*.[5] For this goal, the *Upanishads* were central, though he also considered the *Gita* in agreement with the "monistic idealism" he found in the *Upanishads*.

Although in the first two articles he wrote as a student at Madras Christian College, appearing in 1908, he evidenced little knowledge of the *Gita,* in his M.A. thesis under Professor A.G. Hogg, the place of the *Gita* in Radhakrishnan's apologetics was already established. Thus, his later study of the "classics of Hinduism" appears to have only confirmed and deepened his knowledge of the *Gita* but not enlightened his earlier understanding, which was based particularly on Telang's 1852 translation of the text. Radhakrishnan did not know Sanskrit at this time.

The articles written prior to the thesis evidence his apologetic interest in the *Gita*'s significance as a source for "Vedanta, Hindu" ethics. In "Indian Philosophy: The Vedas and the Six Systems." the *Gita* is merely listed as one of the sources for Indian thought, and in "Karma and Free Will," an article on a theme which will in later writings evoke citation of or allusion to the *Gita,* only citation of a reference to *Gita* 3.34 which is found in the work of Shankara, the eights century exponent of the Vedanta with whom Radhakrishnan identified himself, is given. The translation is Telang's: "every sense has its affections and aversions to its objects fixed. One should not become subject to them, for they are one's opponents." He comments on that verse: "Herein is hinted the proper significance of Karma."[6] Here is the beginning of Radhakrishnan's use of the *Gita* for ethical apologetics in "Hinduism."

His Master's thesis, written to defend the ethical basis of Vedanta, shows a familiarity with the *Gita* as an ethical text, but includes only a few references to its metaphysical position. The basis for Vedantic metaphysics is established most often through citations of the *Upanishads* and the use of philosophical arguments from his Western training and from philosophers such as Kant, Aristotle, Hegel, and Bailie. But when he begins the sections entitled "The Gnana Yoga," "The Karma Yoga," and "Criticism," the *Gita* is his major source. Likewise, in the portion of the "Introduction" on "The Opposition between Karma and Free-will," the *Gita* is again central.

Radhakrishnan interprets the predicament dealt with by the *Gita* as the conflict between reason and sense or duty and inclination. Like the Western philosophy he was emulating, the solution is found in the control of the desires of the senses by reason. "It is because he [Arjuna] was dominated by both sensibility and reason and there was perpetual conflict between them that we *have* the Gita."[7] Arjuna stands for the ordinary individual who must control his passions through reason. This emphasis dominates his early writings, but changes to an emphasis upon intuitive, experiential knowledge later.

The *Gita*'s solution is similar to that of Kant, "doing duty for duty's sake without any personal attachment or hope of a reward."[8] Though actions are said to be enjoined in the scriptures, only rules that justify themselves by reason are required. And, in fact, setting a scripture up as an authority for moral action is not only unreasonable but gives rise to "the evils of priestcraft" that result in a high degree of intolerance: "more than half the wars, half the sin, misery and all the religious persecutions, the massacres, burnings, torturings that have occurred in this world are attributable to its baneful influence so that if we accept something to be infallible, we are thereby leading to priestly rule, priestcraft, and spiritual despotism."[9] Radhakrishnan, thus, characterizes "Vedanta ethics" as a "moderate rationalism."[10]

One critic to whom Radhakrishnan responded is S.A. Desai of the Brahmo Samaj, who in lectures to the Samaj argued that the state of mind enjoined by the *Gita* results inevitably in asceticism and that the motiveless action which it preaches is an impossibility. Radhakrishnan responded that the first critique misunderstands that the *Gita* itself declares that actionlessness is impossible and that actions must be performed. To the second, Radhakrishnan responded that the *Gita* does not teach motiveless action but that action must be performed without "the egoistic motives of affection and aversion."[11] There are passages which could support Desai's claim, he says, and the existence of these "apparent contradictions and inconsistencies" has kept the *Gita* from being ranked as a classic work in philosophy. "The properly philosophical positions are often imbedded in extraneous matter which is indifferent to the argument, so that these accretions obscure the general trend and impair the force of the writing. It behoves us to gather together what is valuable and give it its proper setting."[12] Though he takes the *Gita* as a document which in order to "fulfil the desires of its devotees" speaks of the formless Absolute as if it takes up form in incarnations, this interpretive principle remains unused until his *Indian Philosophy.*

Radhakrishnan continues these themes in two major articles for the *International Journal of Ethics* in 1911 and 1914. In "The Ethics of the Bhagavad-gita and Kant," Radhakrishnan's purpose is to discuss the differences between the ethics of the *Gita* (often called Vedanta in the article) and Kant in response to previous discussions of their similarities. His goal, he says: "is to lay bare the practical side of the Vedanta system, or, more accurately, the Bhagavadgita, and to compare its teaching with that of Kant on the fundamental questions of free will, the moral problem, and the law of duty."[13] His intention is explicitly apologetic: "But it may seem to some that the very conception of the ethics of the Bhagavadgita is impossible, since it is incompatible with a belief in the doctrine of karma."[14] The theme of the 1908 "Karma and Free Will" article is here developed within the context of the *Gita.* Specifically, Radhakrishnan quotes Hegel's critique: "No morality, no determination of freedom, no rights, no duties have any place here; so that the people of India are sunk in complete immorality."[15]

The article caught the attention of the Indian Nationalist leader Bal Gangadhar Tilak, who was in Mandalay prison. Tilak responded with marginal notes which indicated his support of Radhakrishnan's "activistic interpretation of the Bhagavadgita," and later included Radhakrishnan's name in his own *Gita Rahasya.*[16] In a 1921 article, Radhakrishnan returned the support Tilak had given him: "Tilak, a born fighter of evil and injustice, did not feel inclined to support the quietistic interpretation of the teaching of the Bhagavad Gita. . . . The scholastic commentators have used the Bhagavad Gita in the interests of their own metaphysical and religious views and twisted out of its shape the true message of the Gita. Tilak attempts to restore the natural sense of the Bhagavad Gita by making Karma Yoga its central secret."[17]

Radhakrishnan's second article in this period that featured the *Gita* was "The Ethics of the Vedanta" of 1914. As was the pattern in his M.A. thesis, here there are three references to the *Upanishads,* while the *Gita* is quoted twelve times. "A system of philosophy is generally tested by its ethical doctrine," Radhakrishnan begins;[18] Vedanta, for him, is essentially a single system of philosophy with the *Gita* as its major ethical text. In setting forth its ethics and their metaphysical roots in Vedanta, Radhakrishnan's concerns are two-fold. First is the apologetic interest, for "advanced thought has its own fashions, and it has become a philosophic fashion of the present day to consider the Vedanta system a non-ethical one."[19] The second concern is a critique of Indians who he believes, are not practicing the ideal set forth in Vedanta, i.e. in the *Gita*: "Unless India recovers from her stupor, there is no chance for her. She must meet death from without. But if she takes to heart the lessons of her great religion and ethics, which bid her neither sit, nor stand, but go, she will have victory from within."[20]

Radhakrishnan's apologetic thrust was a response to three criticisms: (1) that Vedanta is "a mystical flight into other-worldly experience" and not "a rational system of thought deserving the name 'philosophy' and the praise of philosophers"; (2) "that its doctrine of karma taught that people were not responsible for their deeds" and, thus, results in fatalism; and (3) "that Vedanta taught that the world was unreal, illusory."[21] Using the *Gita* in response to the first charge, Radhakrishnan argued that though Vedanta is monistic and its goal is *mokṣa,* liberation, central to Vedanta is a life of active service to humanity and the world.

> Sri Krishna argues in the Bhagvadgita that life and action are deeper than logical processes. He advises Arjuna not to fritter away his life in scruples, tremors, and hesitations, but asks him wholeheartedly to perform his duty. The highest knowledge cannot be got by turning our attention inward, but only by conducting ourselves in our external relations, fully imbued with the spirit of the all-presence of the divine. The Vedanta ethics does not ask us to sit with folded hands or, like the mystic, look down on earth or up to heaven, at nothing in particular. In the world here and now, the individual inspired

> by the vision beatific must do his level best to make his small corner of the world happier, nobler, and better. It is not the mystic in his cell or the philosopher in his retreat who is held up as a model, but the warrior fighting with righteous indignation the battle against the forces of evil and wickedness.[22]

The *Gita*'s active ideal, its calls to fight, and the interpretation of the battle as the struggle of reason against "the lower passions and temptations" and the battlefield, Kurukshetra, as the battlefield of life, provide scriptural support for Radhakrishnan's apologetic concern.

In response to the charge that the doctrine of karma results in fatalism, Radhakrishnan acknowledged the fatalistic attitude of Indians about him, criticized that attitude in terms of Vedanta, and argued that fatalism is far from its teaching. "But the cautious reader of the Bhagavadgita will find that the real meaning of karma does not exclude free will. In a verse of that famous book we find it said: 'Every sense has its affections and aversions to its objects fixed; one should not become subject to them, for they are one's opponents.' "[23] Though scholars debate whether or not the *Gita* is ultimately fatalistic, Radhakrishnan emphasizes those passages which call Arjuna to fight, to act, and to control his desires. He believes karma does condition one's current tendencies which are termed "affections" and "aversions," but one is able to play the hand that karma deals in this life; he will argue throughout his life that human beings are conditioned but not determined. Whereas, he argued in 1911, Kant provides only "the semblance of freedom" since necessity rules the phenomenal realm, in the Vedanta freedom is real, "even in the phenomenal realm, where we are powerful enough to check our impulses, to resist our passions, and lead a life of satisfied selfhood in which the lower passions are regulated by reason."[24]

The place of moral activity must be this phenomenal world and therefore, Radhakrishnan argued, the world is significant, not illusory. As he would assert throughout his life, the world has a reality, but it is not an independent one. The *Gita* provided support for his response. "The theory does not deny the reality of the world or the individual souls in it. The plurality of individual souls and the material universe are not 'real' in the absolute sense of the word, for they are subject to change. They are only relatively real."[25]

As it did for other modern Indian thinkers, for Radhakrishnan the *Gita* provided the concept of non-attachment, which defined the manner in which ethically appropriate action was to be performed. Just as the *Gita* had interpreted renunciation so that it was no longer renunciation of actions but renunciation of their results, Radhakrishnan rejected methods that renounced activity in the world. He promoted instead the active life, in which one does what one ought without attachment to the outcome. However, for Radhakrishnan this was not non-attachment to all results of actions but the doing of actions without any personal or selfish results in mind.

> The Bhagavadgita says: "Then treating alike pleasure and pain, gain and loss, success or defeat, prepare for the battle and thus wilt thou not incur sin" (II,38). This ideal of disinterested action is misconceived when it is confused with motiveless action. A rational being cannot act without motives, but can and ought to act disinterestedly. The Vedanta says, let not your selfish satisfaction be your motive. Anything you do, do because it is a necessary means of promoting the general welfare.[26]

Answering the charge that this promotes "reckless action," Radhakrishnan adds that careful consideration is called for before one acts. The Vedantic standard is here, as before, pictured in terms of philosophical reflection, the reliance upon one's conscience and reason. "If our conscience tells us that something is right, we must follow it, thoroughly prepared to meet fortune in all its moods."[27] Obedience is to be "thinking obedience," for rules are not universally valid, but guidelines for the active life. He rejects authoritarian morality with the exception of one "absolute moral rule." "It is obedience to reason and its ideal of service and sacrifice that is the one supreme law, and all others are subordinate to it."[28] This early apologetic argument for the rationality of Vedanta would not dominate his later use of the *Gita* as it does in these articles, his thesis, and his other work in this early period.

"The Theism of the Bhagavadgita"

Behind these apologetics was a metaphysical stance which Radhakrishnan called "Vedanta," "Hinduism" and later "religion of the spirit." Though designations for this position changed, the essential position remained the same throughout his life. Most influential in defining his position was the mature position of Swami Vivekananda (1863–1902), whose writings, Radhakrishnan remembered, had a great impact upon him as early as his college years, and who, Radhakrishnan believed, recovered the essence of 'Hinduism.' This suited well Radhakrishnan's values, as absorbed through his education, and his apologetic stance. "Vivekananda showed that the Hindu religion was both scientific and democratic, not the religion as we practise it, which is full of blemishes, but the religion which our great exponents intended it to be."[23] Radhakrishnan's metaphysical work, then, can be understood as a philosophical presentation of Vivekananda's position.

The earliest full presentation of that metaphysical position as it is attributed to the *Gita* is in the first volume of Radhakrishnan's *Indian Philosophy,* written by 1921 and published in 1923. This major work, to which Radhakrishnan would add a second volume in 1927, was not intended as a dispassionate presentation of the varieties of Indian thought. Its intent was to be critical and apologetic, to present an ideal scheme for understanding Indian thought. As an apologetic work it was meant to refute the idea that Indian thought contains "two or three 'silly' notions,"[30] particularly the charges that it is pessimistic, dogmatic, unprofitable, unprogressive, and non-ethical.[31] But it was also a critique of scholaticism in Indian thought, particularly in its present form. Concluding the second volume, Radhakrishnan lamented that: "India is no longer playing her historic role as the vanguard of higher knowledge in Asia."[32] This second concern was to move Indians themselves to the essence of their tradition as Radhakrishnan defined it and, thereby, to revive Indian philosophy, lifting it to an exalted place in the modern world. "The problem facing Indian Philosophy to-day is whether it is to be reduced to a cult, restricted in scope and with no application to the present facts, or whether it is to be made alive and real, so as to become what it should be, one of the great formative elements in human progress, by relating the immensely increased knowledge of modern science to the ancient ideals of India's philosophers."[33] Radhakrishnan's writings would regularly refer to the *Gita* to promote this revival.

Radhakrishnan entitled the sixty pages devoted to the *Gita* in *Indian Philosophy,* "The Theism of the Bhagavadgita." Dating the *Gita* in the fifth century B.C., his approach is to understand it as a popular religious text which adapted "the idealism of the Upaniṣads to a theistically minded people. . . ."[34] To say that it is "religious" is to underline its emphasis upon devotion, ethics, and a personal divine being. Yet, as a text of "Vedanta" its metaphysics ultimately were to be understood as Advaita, "non-dualism," in which the

Highest Reality, designated *brahman,* is a state of pure consciousness characterized by *saccidānanda,* pure existence, pure consciousness, and unlimited bliss. Though the *Gita,* therefore, is a "religious" text, in the metaphysical realm its "theism" must be understood in terms of this advaitin position, not an absolute theism but a relative one.[35] Thus, the hermeneutical principle involved in its understanding is that of the eighth century thinker Shankara.

This did not mean that he followed Shankara on all points. Radhakrishnan's interest in the importance of societal ethics and his emphasis upon this world, disagreed with Shankara's devaluation of the world in ultimate terms. For example, Radhakrishnan says: "Śaṁkara is not faithful to the intention of the author of the Gita when he says that 'aṁsá' [from 15.7], or part [in reference to the individual soul], indicates an imaginary or apparent part only. It is a real form of the Puruṣottama."[36] Radhakrishnan thereby preserves a more important status for the individual soul in the world and is faithful to the *Gita*'s affirmation of the reality of the individual soul. But he follows with a relativization of this verse by means of the *nirguṇa/saguṇa* distinction.

Shankara also believed that the liberated individual no longer performs actions. Since this is not what the *Gita* teaches, Shankara had to interpret passages that call for continual action as speaking on a lower level to the unenlightened. Radhakrishnan, however, does not wish to subordinate action to quietism as a path to liberation, due to his affirmation of ethics. "But karma performed as a sacrifice to God, and in a spirit of disinterestedness and impersonality, is quite as efficacious as any other method, and there is no need to subordinate it to the method of wisdom as Śaṁkara does, or that of devotion as Rāmānuja believes."[37]

Yet, an advaitin metaphysical position and its hermeneutical principle of higher and lower levels of understanding is Radhakrishnan's interpretative stance toward the *Gita*'s metaphysics. Though he notes that the *Gita*'s account of the nature of the Supreme Self is "rather puzzling,"[38] he concludes that: "In the spirit of the Upanisads the Gita identifies the two principles of the Atman and the Brahman."[39] The *Gita,* then, is an advaitin text at heart—"Vedanta" as Radhakrishnan defines it—and, thus, like the *Upanishads* as Radhakrishnan interprets them. "The Gita asserts the truth of an advaita or non-dualism in philosophy."[40] The key verse on which the *Gita*'s metaphysic is based, he says, is 2.16: "Of the unreal there is no being, and of the real there is no non-being."[41] Thus the ultimate is unchanging being, not that which is becoming, and it is best described without description, as *nirguṇa,* as the Absolute.

The *Gita,* however, speaks most often in terms of a lower level of understanding, a level on which the *Gita* renders the Absolute in terms of the limitations of the human condition. "The metaphysical idealism of the Upanisads is transformed in the Gita into a theistic religion, providing room for love, faith, prayer and devotion. So long as we do not have the vision of the absolute, but are working from the side of the empirical world, we can account for it only on the theory of the supreme godhead of Puruṣottama."[42] The term *puruṣottama,* used of Krishna in *Gita* 10.15; 11.3; 15.18, 19, means literally the "highest person," *uttama puruṣa,* in the important metaphysical passage 15.16–18. Yet, interpreted in terms of the Absolute, Brahman, the supreme reality, the Purushottama is merely the impersonal absolute "envisaged as Puruṣottama for the purposes of religion."[43] Metaphysically, Radhakrishnan says, the personal god is problematic and its relationship to the impersonal Absolute is unexplained since it is "intellectually insoluble."[44] Yet: "On ultimate analysis the assumption of the form of Puruṣottama by the absolute becomes less than real. It is therefore wrong to argue that according to the Gita the impersonal self is lower in reality than the personal Isvara, though it is true that the Gita considers the conception of a personal God to be more useful for religious purposes."[45] Consistent with the position Radhakrishnan will take throughout his life, the conception of the highest reality as personal is relativized and the "theism of the Bhagavadgita" is not absolute but subordinate to his metaphysical monism.[46]

Who then is Krishna, who the *Gita* declares to be the Lord and who stands before Arjuna, leading the dialogue with him on the field of battle? For Radhakrishnan the battlefield of Kurukshetra symbolizes the "life of the soul" whose enemies attempt to impede its progress toward perfection. Arjuna is "the representative man" who experiences the "dark night of the soul". Yet, contrary to earlier interpretation, the problem now is not reason versus the senses, but a confrontation with the intuititive: "Arjuna typifies the struggling individual who feels the burden and the mystery of the world. He has not yet built within himself a strong centre of spirit from which he can know not only the unreality of his own desires and passions, but also the true status of the world opposing him."[47]

Krishna is the divine within, "God in man," and in Radhakrishnan's understanding of the opinion of the *Gita* is identical with the Purushottama, the Lord, the Ultimate relativized.[48] In the fourth chapter of the *Gita,* however, Krishna refers to the concept of *avatāra,* "descent," in which he, though the unborn Lord of all, descends into the guise of a creature to protect the *dharma,* the right, whenever it languishes. Though Radhakrishnan recognizes the traditional theory of an avatar as a special event in history, he quickly moves to another interpretation. "An avatar is a descent of God into man, and not an ascent of man into God. Though every conscious being is such a descent, it is only a veiled manifestation." As Radhakrishnan understands it, there is a difference between Krishna and Arjuna: an avatar is "the self-conscious being of the divine," and the normal individual is "the same shrouded in ignorance." By this interpretation, the *avatāra* concept has been subordinated to the affirmation that Atman is Brahman, and ultimately becomes unnecessary for Radhakrishnan, except as a part of a text he wishes to affirm for other reasons. He concludes that: "It becomes indifferent, then, whether we say God limits Himself in the form of man or man rises to God working through his nature."[49] In fact, the latter is held to be more valuable.[50]

The world and the Absolute are related somehow, but we cannot ascertain the nature of this relationship. Radhakrishnan usually designates this relationship *māyā,* and admits that the *Gita* does not use the term *māyā* in this manner. Yet he affirms that the *Gita* implies this interpretation in any case.[51] Thus, the *Gita*'s affirmation of a non-illusory world whose change is based upon the ever-changing character of Nature, *prakṛti,* is enthusiastically affirmed by Radhakrishnan, who argued that that is what "Vedanta" taught. However, he believed the *Gita* does teach that the world is "only an effect of God, who is the cause," and, thus, it is less real than God.[52] In doing so, Radhakrishnan arrives at his previous understanding that the world is not false, but that it is not independently real either.

In "The Theism of the Bhagavadgita," Radhakrishnan's ethical interest continues. The *Gita*'s "central purpose is to solve the problem of life and stimulate right conduct. It is obviously an ethical treatise, a yoga sastra."[53] Taking, like Vivekananda, the three elements of the *Gita*'s path—non-attached action, realization of the self (*ātman*) as distinct from Nature (*prakṛti*), and sole devotion to Krishna as the Lord of the universe,—as three separate paths, he describes the *Gita*'s teaching as a "synthesis" of all paths. Each of the three ways, or *margas,* is suited to the temperament of a different type of individual, emphasizing either reason, will, or emotion.[54] All three reach the same goal, he taught and, thus, the *Gita* is understood as "tolerant" of other ways even though its "tone" is dogmatic.[55]

The path of knowledge, *jñāna,* is suitable for the person with a logical mind.[56] The logical investigations of the scientist are continued, but supplemented by intuitive knowledge, spiritual insight, and direct experience of the Truth. Theirs is, Radhakrishnan believes, not an uncritical conviction but one "supported by scientific judgment."[57] From this standpoint, then, he understands the climactic vision of Krishna's "lordly yoga," in *Gita* chapter eleven, as essentially an intuitive experience of Reality in which one realizes that Unity, not difference, is ultimate. The vision of the "universal-form" which graphically portrays the active Lord in relationship to the battle is interpreted in advaitin terms. "The viśvarūpa is a poetic exaggeration of the intuitional experience where the individual possessed by God sees all things in Him."[58] Likewise, the *Gita*'s discussion of meditative discipline and its delineation of the elements of Nature in the fashion of the traditional Yoga system of Patanjali, is interpreted by Radhakrishnan only ". . . as a means of mental training."[59]

The path of devotion, *bhakti,* is for the emotional being, but instead of the flights of emotion of some extreme theists, the *Gita* exalts a *bhakti* which is combined with wisdom as the highest form of life.[60] Instead of those who believe in the vicarious payment for one's sins, it never supercedes the law of karma, which requires just recompense for one's deeds ". . . since the law requires that even devotion should have its reward."[61] Though it ranks other objects of worship as lower than the Purushottama, Radhakrishnan believes it still "tolerates" them when understood as forms of the one or "out of a feeling of pity" for those who worship on a lower level.[62] But finally, and most importantly, Radhakrishnan subsumes the *Gita's bhakti* under the impersonal understanding of the Absolute as the highest object of devotion.

> The Gita, however, recognises nirguna bhakti, or devotion to the qualityless, as superior to all else. Then the absolute becomes the most ultimate category. When devotion is perfected, then the individual and his God become suffused into one spiritual ecstasy, and reveal themselves as aspects of one life. Absolute monism is therefore the completion of the dualism with which the devotional consciousness starts.[63]

As impersonal monism is the ultimate category in the paths of *jñāna* and *bhakti,* it is also in the path of karma. "Right conduct is whatever expresses our real unity with God, man, and nature; wrong conduct is whatever does not bring out this essential structure of reality."[64] As before, this meant the performance of action for the "service of humanity" without concern for personal results. Scriptural authority is the source of such action as the *Gita* says in 16.23–24, but the highest action is subjection to an "inner determination of the soul's freedom."[65] The *Gita* lays down some general schemes for such conduct such as caste (*varṇa*) division, and Radhakrishnan adds that the *Gita* also follows "the theory of the stages of life," the four *aśrama* found in the classical law books of India.[66] He cites no verses to support this latter claim, and *varṇa* is to be understood as not necessarily tied to birth, according to Radhakrishnan's interpretation, though birth is "the only available test." Radhakrishnan will continue to accept the four-fold division discussed in the *Gita* as an appropriate means for organizing society, and as dependent upon heredity, but, unlike the *Gita* itself, he will attempt to separate caste from birth in any limiting sense.[67]

Radhakrishnan's most difficult problem is interpretation of the *Gita*'s concept of liberation, *mokṣa,* using his advaitin hermeneutic. *Mokṣa* is "unity with the supreme self," yet, his interpretive problem is reflected in the statement: "[T]he Gita is not clear on the point whether there is any basis of individuality in the ultimate state."[68] Verses exist, he points out, on both sides of the issue, and, thus: "There are then two conflicting views in the Gita about the ultimate state. . . ." He, therefore, applies his hermeneutical principle of higher and lower understandings to the issue of liberation. "Adopting the same standpoint, we may say that the two views of the ultimate state of freedom are the intuitional and the intellectual ways of representing the one condition."[69] Since the *Gita* is a "religious work," emphasizing the relative, religious understanding of the Highest Reality, there is a confusion on this matter of liberation and the personal and impersonal are made out to be one. In this, then, and on other issues, Radhakrishnan's advaitin hermeneutic, based upon his belief that the *Gita* is a book of Vedanta and that Vedanta is advaitin, understands the "Theism of the Bhagavadgita" as a theism relative to the Upanisadic formula, *tat tvam asi,* "you are That," Atman is Brahman.

A COMMENTARY ON THE BHAGAVADGITA

From the time of Radhakrishnan's *Indian Philosophy* until the publication of his commentary on the *Bhagavadgita,* Radhakrishnan's speeches and writings, though not about the *Gita,* continue to use the *Gita* to support themes expounded in *Indian Philosophy* and fully developed in his commentary. His twofold purpose continues while his major works take a standard form in which "Vedanta, Hinduism" or "the religion of the spirit" is no longer merely defended but presented as the solution to the world's predicament.[70]

He continues to exhort Indians to approximate this ideal "Vedanta, Hinduism" and "religion of the spirit" because, he believes, it is the essence of their own religion and, now, the essence of others' as well (though "Hinduism" more fully manifests this essence). Thus, India is to wake up, turn from her ascetic, lazy ways and from attitudes of casteism, religious sectarianism, scholasticism, and fatalism, and recognize the greatness of her own tradition. The *Gita* contains texts to support this revival, he believed; to a Calcutta University audience he said:

> For the old maxims of flight from action, or wisdom or asceticism, the *Gita* substitutes "work free from attachment." Spiritual life is not a retreat from men and things, but is a consuming fire that burns away egoism, destroys bondage and penetrates everywhere. It is not the ascetic but the transfigured life radiant with power and energy that is exalted.[71]

In these speeches and writings the *Gita* is cited to support the universalism of religion, rebirth, the purposive nature of history, the reality of human freedom as opposed to determinism, the impersonal nature of the Absolute, the compatibility and desirability of the combination of work and wisdom, the ineffability of religious experience, and the efficacy of discipline, but not asceticism, on the path to liberation. The *Gita*'s message is, therefore, universal, not bound to the story of the text itself. To a Chinese audience he compared its teachings to Mahayana Buddhism: "Mahayana thought resembles that of the *Bhagavadgita* in the combination of metaphysical idealism and devotional faith."[72] In a sermon at Manchester College Chapel, he could move back and forth between the *Gita* and the New Testament: "God is the loving friend of all—*suhridam sarva-bhutanam,* [5.29], as the Bhagavadgita has it. If Jesus won for spirit the victory, it was not by force and greed, but by patient life and suffering."[73] The *Gita* was a text to which Radhakrishnan turned for scriptural support.

In 1947 Radhakrishnan's publisher in the West, George Allen & Unwin, Ltd., published his commentary on the *Gita*. This commentary was the first that Radhakrishnan wrote on what he later called India's four classics.[74] In 1950, his commentary on the Theravada Buddhist text *Dhammapada* appeared; in 1953, his commentary on eighteen *Upanishads;* and in 1960, his commentary on the *Brahma Sutra* attributed to Badarayana.[75] In the tradition of previous Vedantins before him, Radhakrishnan thereby commented upon the *prasthāna-traya,* "the triple foundation" of Vedanta thought[76] plus the *Dhammapada.*

By calling this tradition an "obligation," Radhakrishnan may be hinting at his own intentions: "The teachers of the Vedanta are obliged to justify their special doctrines by an appeal to these three authorities and so wrote commentaries on them expounding how the texts teach their special points of view."[77] Though Radhakrishnan would not call his teachings his own "special" point of view, that he followed in this "obligation" is significant as well as the fact that he believed that these texts taught, when understood correctly, his own position. In each of these three cases the commentary is preceded by an introduction which relates the text at hand to the tradition, but which, more importantly, expounds Radhakrishnan's position through the text.[78]

Radhakrishnan explained the purpose of his translation as: "It must be readable without being shallow, modern without being unsympathetic."[79] The manuscript was read by Professor M. Hiriyanna and Professor Franklin Edgerton, then Salisbury Professor of Sanskrit and Comparative Philosophy at Yale University whose own translation and study of the *Gita* had appeared in 1946. Edgerton's influence is particularly detectable in the translation, though the comments and introduction are clearly Radhakrishnan's own.

In December, 1947, Radhakrishnan went to Birla House in Delhi to seek Gandhi's permission to dedicate future editions to Gandhi. He had met Gandhi several times previously and had written about him, believing Gandhi affirmed Radhakrishnan's definition of "Hinduism, religion of the spirit." One report of Gandhi's words during the meeting is: "I know you will not write anything unworthy, but before that I want to ask you something. I am your Arjuna, you are my Krishna. I am like Arjuna—confused."[80] Radhakrishnan explained his understanding of the *Gita* and Gandhi agreed to the dedication, which reads simply, "To Mahatma Gandhi." Radhakrishnan also quotes words which express the solace Gandhi found in reading "a verse here and a verse there" of the *Gita,* but the only other reference is to Gandhi as a modern commentator; it merely says: "Gandhi has his own views."[81]

The purpose of the commentary, he says, is to emphasize the spiritual and ethical roots of "religion" in an age when science dominates human thinking. With the end of the second World War, Radhakrishnan saw a world which evidenced both hope and doom. Evolution had reached a stage when great possibilities were at hand. Yet, the world was also threatened as never before with annihilation by atomic weapons. His writings and speeches until his retirement reflect these two concerns, as well as the belief that his "religion of the spirit" could solve the problems of the human predicament by reconciling the diversities of humankind. Thus, his translation of the *Gita* accompanied by a truly contemporary commentary would make available "this great book which sets forth in precise and penetrating words the essential principles of a spiritual religion which are not contingent on ill-founded facts, unscientific dogmas or arbitrary fancies."[82]

The commentary had to be "contemporary" because, Radhakrishnan believed, scriptures consist of two elements: "one temporary and perishable, belonging to the ideas of the people of the period and the country in which it is produced, and the other eternal and imperishable, and applicable to all ages and countries."[83] The classical commentators spoke well to their contemporaries, but speak only faintly today, except where they touch on these eternal truths. Radhakrishnan's commentary, then, would not deal with the *Gita* as an historical document which is a product of its time, but as "a restatement of the truths of eternity in the accents of our time. . . ."[84] His hermeneutic, therefore, is less historical or even literal in thrust, but involves the discovery of what Radhakrishnan believes are these "eternal truths" in a text which he believes has them. Just as commentators in the past "speak to us from experience and express in a new form, a form relevant to their age and responsive to their needs, the ancient wisdom of scripture," so Radhakrishnan's hermeneutic is his own experience, and his form of expression is a modern one. Not surprisingly, much of his understanding of the eternal truths found in the *Gita* can be traced to Vivekananda.

His commentary is hortatory, "intended for the general reader who wishes to enlarge his spiritual environment rather than for the specialist."[85] Yet, Radhakrishnan believed that what he expounded in these pages was not private religion but the essence of all religions. This is reflected in his citation of a wide variety of foreign and Indian sources.[86] In other writings his arguments for the fact that his position was the essence of all religions vascilate between argument from an ineffable intuitive experience to argument from the conclusions of the comparative study of religion through which Radhakrishnan found his position in much the same manner as he found it in the *Gita*, by separating the eternal truths from the temporary and relative ones.[87]

The commentary and "Introductory Essay" elaborate upon but present little that is new in Radhakrishnan's understanding of the *Gita*. The purpose of the *Gita* is determined, he says, by noting the question with which the *Gita* opens, *upakrama,* and its conclusion, *upasaṃhāra:* "It raises the question whether action or renunciation of action is better and concludes that action is better."[88] He understands the *Gita* as first and foremost an ethical treatise affirming the ethical stance he previously enunciated.

As before, Radhakrishnan understands the *Gita* as a "religious classic," "a popular poem," and not a philosophical treatise. This is clearly the case, and for Radhakrishnan this understanding continues to function not merely to explain the structure of the text but to interpret its metaphysics. The *Gita,* thus, does not argue in support of its metaphysical position because "Only spiritual experience can provide us with proofs of the existence of Spirit."[91] At the heart of the *Gita,* as at the heart of Radhakrishnan's "religion of the spirit" is a religious experience which Radhakrishnan believes is an ineffable experience of Brahman, the impersonal absolute.

In interpreting metaphysical questions, the hermeneutical principle of higher and lower understandings is again used to maintain a consistent stance toward the text and to affirm an advaitin position. Radhakrishnan's language does not always evidence this principle and, thus, confusion over a number of issues and his use of terms is possible. Krishna is understood as the Divine within, "not a bygone personality but the indwelling spirit, an object for our spiritual consciousness."[90] In 9.34, as Radhakrishnan translates it, Krishna tells Arjuna: "On Me fix thy mind; to Me be devoted; worship Me; revere Me; thus having disciplined thyself, with Me as thy goal, to Me shalt thou come." But Radhakrishnan does not take this as an exhortation to recognize and experience Krishna as the Highest Lord, as God. His interpretative principle calls for another understanding and, therefore, he comments on the verse: "It is not the personal Krsna to whom we have to give ourselves up utterly but the Unborn, Beginningless, Eternal who speaks through Kṛṣṇa."[91] Likewise in the important phrase in *Gita* 14.27 where Krishna declares: "For I am the foundation of Brahman, the immortal, imperishable," Radhakrishnan translates "foundation," *pratiṣṭha* as "abode". He begins his comment on the verse: "Here the personal Lord is said to be the foundation of the Absolute Brahman." But he concludes with "Kṛṣṇa identifies Himself with the absolute, unconditioned Brahman."[92] Thus, he lets stand the view of ultimate reality of Madhusudana Saraswati, which suits Radhakrishnan's position well.

Again, his apparent confusion over the use of the terms "soul, self, *jīva*," as Stevenson points out, is explained in the comment at 13.1: "When we try to know the nature of the human soul, we may get to know it from above or below, from the divine principle or the elemental nature."[93] But the *Gita* emphasizes "the Supreme as the personal God,"[94] and particularly as the Indian god Vishnu, not because it is a sectarian document, Radhakrishnan says, but because: "The *Gita* is interested in the process of redeeming the world." The *trimūrti* concept is here the interpretative principle. Thus, of Brahman ("the Creator"), Vishnu ("the Preserver"), and Shiva ("the Destroyer"), since Vishnu is the form which "pours out His love and works with a patience matched only by His love," the *Gita,* which is a universalistic, non-sectarian treatise in Radhakrishnan's understanding, merely calls the Supreme Vishnu.[95]

In his commentary, more strongly than before, Radhakrishnan emphasizes that the *Gita,* is a universalistic, inclusive document. Thereby he affirms that it is suited for the needs of this age as well as the "religion of the spirit": "it attempts to reconcile varied and apparently antithetical forms of the religious consciousness and emphasizes the root conceptions of religion. . . ."[96] It teaches, as does "the Hindu tradition," that all paths are "mutually complementary and not contradictory."[97] The verse in the *Gita* used most often in later works to support this claim is 4.11, which Radhakrishnan translates: "As men approach me so do I accept them: men on all sides follow my path, O Partha (Arjuna)."[98] An extended comment includes his usual exposition of universalism: "The same God is worshipped by all. The differences of conception and approach are determined by local colouring and social adaptations."[99] The facts of religious experience are believed to be universal though they are conceptualized through different historical and racial temperaments.

Another emphasis is the commentary's argument against the ultimate authority of texts and teachers, and its advocacy of religious experience and rational reflection as the basis for knowledge of truth. Concerning religious teachers he laments:

> Today there are several teachers who require of their followers unthinking obedience to their dictates. They seem to believe that the death of intellect is the condition of the life of the spirit. Many credulous and simple-minded people are drawn to them not so much by their spiritual powers as by the publicity of their agents and the human weakness for novelty, curiosity and excitement. This is against the Hindu tradition which insists on jijñāsā of inquiry, manana or reflection or paripraśna in the words of the *Gita.*[100]

Scriptures are more helpful for the seeker, but only until one is awakened and "spontaneity becomes so great and absolute as to require no indirect help."[101]

Radhakrishnan continues to argue that the *Gita* affirms free will over against those critics that argue all is fatalistic. Thus, in chapter sixteen of the Gita, where two classes of persons are discussed by Krishna, those born to a demonic destiny and those to a divine destiny, though the text speaks of these as different people, Radhakrishnan understands them to be two natures found in all people. "In each man are these two kingdoms of light and darkness."[102] Even when the *Gita* declares that some will eventually go to the "lowest goal" after many rebirths and never attain Krishna, Radhakrishnan's comment is more positive, affirming free will and rejecting any final loss: "We are advised to shake off this demoniac nature. This does not mean predestination, for it is said that it is always open to us to turn godward and achieve perfection. It is not impossible at any stage."[103] Radhakrishnan elsewhere argues for this enduring chance for all, particularly against teachings of eternal loss, such as a Christian hell.

For Radhakrishnan, the commentary provides a place to argue that class and caste are not based ideally on birth but on one's propensities, talents, and personal characteristics. Central to this interpretation, here and in his later speeches and writings, is *Gita* 4.13, which he translates: "The fourfold order [*cāturvarṇyaṃ*] was created by Me according to the divisions of quality [*guṇa*] and work [*karman*]." His comment translates *guṇa* ("strand") as "aptitude" and *karman* as "function." More strongly than in his earlier discussions, he distinguishes caste or class (*varṇa*) from birth: "The varna or the order to which we belong is independent of sex, birth or breeding. A class determined by temperament and vocation is not a caste determined by birth and heredity."[104] Thus, unlike the *Gita* which believes that characteristics (*guṇa*) and karma are inseparable from birth, which calls caste characteristics in 18.42–43 one's inborn nature (*svabhāvaja,* "own-being born"), and which argues that Arjuna's duties are determined by the caste in which he was born; Radhakrishnan separates class or caste, its characteristics and required deeds, from birth.[105] He takes the *Gita* as egalitarian and the four castes as functional units within society, best conceived as an inter-related organism with membership in each unit determined by characteristics and talents but with those characteristics and talents not determined by the class in which one is born. "The present morbid condition of India broken into castes and subcastes is opposed to the unity taught by the *Gita,* which stands for an organic as against an atomistic conception of society."[106]

Overall, Radhakrishnan continues to argue that central to the *Gita* are issues of action and ethics, for the aim of the *Gita* is not to teach metaphysics, but "to enforce practice, dharma."[107] As before, right action is that performed without concern for personal, egoistic results, but "from a sense of duty."[108] Ultimately non-attachment should end any consciousness of toil and suffering, or the feeling that one's deed is an act of greatness. To act out of duty is to act out of love, which Radhakrishnan understands as promoting the good of all, that all may find their true nature, the image of the Divine.

Like the *Gita* itself, Radhakrishnan enumerates two goals of the religious life: the ultimate goal of personal liberation, and the promotion of society as it should be. For the *Gita* the first is foremost, and means individual liberation from karma and rebirth. Though the one liberated in this life will continue to work in society, his goal in that society will be to maintain it by maintaining the contemporary class order so there will be no confusion of classes. However, for Radhakrishnan, the social goal is not mere maintenance of the class order but active work in the world to bring all beings to perfection: "The two sides of religion, the personal and the social, are emphasized by the *Gita*. Personally, we should discover the Divine in us and let it penetrate the human; socially, society must be subdued to the image of the Divine."[109]

Radhakrishnan bases this understanding of the societal goal on two concepts he finds in the *Gita*. The first is Krishna's call to the yogin to "delight in the welfare of all beings," in passages such as *Gita* 5.25; 12.4. In the *Gita* this apparently has more the sense of not disturbing the social order, and thus Shankara understands it negatively as "injuring none," *ahiṃsaka ityathaḥ*. But Radhakrishnan takes this as a positive, loving interest in the promotion of the welfare and liberation of others, recognizing the dignity of each individual.[110] The second concept is based upon the term *lokasaṃgraha* (literally "the holding together of the world") in *Gita* 3.20, 25. In the *Gita* both Arjuna and Krishna are concerned with the maintenance of the social order of classes (both *varṇa* and *jāti* are used by the *Gita*). Their disagreement is over how Arjuna can best accomplish this, through fighting or not. But for Radhakrishnan *lokasaṃgraha,* which he translates as "the unity of the world, the interconnectedness of society, the welfare of the world," is the establishment of world brotherhood. Particularly this means ridding the world of war, but behind that goal is the attitude which sees all human beings as one family, and promotes spiritual solidarity among all nations. Describing the liberated one, he says: "All his activities are for the holding together of the world, *cikīrṣur lokasaṃgraham*. The liberated souls take upon themselves the burden of the redemption of the whole world."[111] Thus, as Radhakrishnan interprets non-attached action, it is attached to the welfare of the world, raising the world to that perfection which is the ultimate goal of the Divine in its evolution.

Radhakrishnan's comments on the eleventh chapter of the *Gita* are fewer than those on chapters which emphasize intuitive knowledge, meditation and action. Chapter eleven provides the great vision of Krishna's universal form, but Radhakrishnan says the vision is not the final goal of the *Gita,* for the book would have ended with chapter eleven if that were the case. A vision is never the end: "the knowledge acquired by the vision requires to be completed by the other elements of life."[112] Yet, this is not meant to lessen the importance of religious experience, for, as Radhakrishnan understands it, the vision is actually the essential religious experience behind all religion, the direct experience of "the One in the many and the many in the One."[113] He compares it to the transfiguration of Jesus, the vision of Saul on the road to Damascus, Constantine's vision of the cross, and Joan of Arc's visions.[114] It is described through poetic device and even exaggeration,[115] but the vision essentially reveals the potential Divinity of all Reality.[116]

Yet, the vision itself is less important to Radhakrishnan because the ethical life is his major concern. The commentary again and again returns to issues of ethics and, thus, the vision is preliminary to changing one's whole nature so as to serve the world.

> The *Gita* does not end after the tremendous experience of the celestial vision. The great secret of the Transcendental Atman, the source of all that is and yet itself unmoved for ever is seen. . . . Arjuna has seen this truth but he has to live in it by transmuting his whole nature into the willing acceptance of the Divine. A fleeting vision, however vivid and permanent its effects may be, is not complete attainment. The search for abiding reality, the quest of final truth cannot end, in emotional satisfaction or fitful experience.[117]

As *yoga śāstra,* then, the *Gita* provides Radhakrishnan with support for his religion of the spirit as an active ethical stance against criticisms of "Hindu" ethics. As such a support, a "living scripture" which shows its vitality in its ability to be used to support the religion of the spirit, he believes, it fulfills the requirements for such a religion. It must be scientific (not dogmatic but experiential), ethically active, and universal.[118]

THE GITA AND THE POLITICS OF INDEPENDENT INDIA

The publication of the Commentary on the *Gita* in 1948 occurred at the beginning of Radhakrishnan's direct activity in Indian politics. From 1946–1950 he was leader of the Indian delegation to UNESCO, but after the independence of India in 1947 his involvement in its government was direct and constant. Among other positions, he was a representative from the United Provinces to the Constituent Assembly until his resignation in August 1949 to become India's Ambassador to the U.S.S.R. He served until April 1952 when he became Vice President of the Indian Republic until 1962 when he was elected President. His retirement in 1967 from the presidentship ended his active public and literary life.

During this period he continued speaking in India and around the world as well as writing, and the *Gita* often supplied verses of support for his work. He recognized that the *Gita* was being used in the modern period to "regenerate" Indian civilization.[119] and that this regeneration, though spiritual, would have political consequences for India as a secular state. For him the *Gita* represented one of the proud jewels in the crown of India's past. Since India was essentially spiritual, in his mind, and the *Gita* represented that religion of the spirit, the *Gita* was a symbol of India's essential greatness. Thus, he proudly referred to the comments of the first Governor-General of British India, Warren Hastings, in Hasting's introduction to Charles Wilkins' translation of the *Gita:* "Though he started with a political motive he soon acquired admiration for the classics of India like the *Bhagavadgita,* which, he declared, would live 'when the British dominion in India has long ceased to exist and when the sources which it once yielded of wealth and power are lost to remembrance.' "[120] Similarly he referred to Oppenheimer's comment upon viewing the first atomic blast which quoted *Gita* 11.12, 32 as: "If the radiance of a thousand suns were to burst at once into the sky, that would be like the splendour of the Mighty One . . . I am become death, the shatterer of the worlds."[121]

While he was a representative of the Indian republic, his use of the *Gita,* which Radhakrishnan called a "religious" text and which he continued to say emphasized "the theistic side of religion,"[122] did not conflict with his work on behalf of a "secular" state. Radhakrishnan defined the Indian secular state not as areligious but as one which is not sectarian in its religion. He often attempted to clarify this understanding of India: "Secularism here does not mean irreligion or atheism or even stress on material comforts. It proclaims that it lays stress on the universality of spiritual values which may be attained by a variety of ways."[123] Since the *Gita* was non-sectarian but promoted the universal "religion of the spirit" which he believed was the essence of all religions, its use in political and educational as well as religious contexts was viewed as quite appropriate.

First and foremost, the *Gita* is referred to in many contexts to support non-sectarianism in religion and the belief that all religions are paths to the same end. Therefore, none must be despised. To make this point, President Radhakrishnan, in a speech delivered when laying the foundation-stone of Sri Sarada College, even adds the following sentence to *Gita* 4.11 when he quotes it: "The names may be different but the one goal they have is Me." He then comments: "That is what the *Gita* teaches us, catholicism, that you should not quarrel about dogmas, about ways of approach, . . . These differences are irrelevant. All men must be regarded as completely equal to one another."[124]

The *Gita* is also at hand to support a non-attached steadiness in all adversities, personal and national, a steadiness which holds onto brotherhood and love as its attitude. Such an attitude promotes mental health, he told the first convocation of the All India Institute of

Medical Sciences, quoting *Gita* 2.66 in Sanskrit: "For him that has no peace how can there be bliss?"[125] To Kerala University he quoted *Gita* 2.48 to support the contention that, "Any individual, if he wishes to regard himself as a truly educated one, must think freely, feel nobly, act rightly, be unattached."[126] "It is the *Gita,*" he tells them, "which tells us that love alone redeems our lives."[127]

To educators and university audiences he pointed out that the *Gita* teaches that practical knowledge and science are not enough. One must have right goals, ethics, and spiritual insight. Quoting the Sanskrit of *Gita* 2.28 to the national Council of Education, he added, "The ultimate questions are too deep or mysterious for science. We should recognize that we understand only a tiny fraction of the universe."[128] To the Indian Institute of Technology he said, "As the *Bhagavadgita* has it, we should aim at wisdom as well as knowledge, *jñanam vijñāna sahitam.*"[129] Citing *Gita* 4.39, he told the Bishop Cotton Schools in Bangalore, "And those who teach in institutions like this will have to take into account that their duty is not merely to give pupils knowledge or information but to train them in character, enable them to discipline themselves."[130]

To a variety of audiences the *Gita* was quoted to support the active life of humanitiarianism. "Wisdom" is to be combined with active service, and he saw this synthesis represented by Krishna and Arjuna in the *Gita.* He regularly referred to *Gita* 18.78 as support: "Where is Krsna the Lord of Yoga, and where is the Bowman, Son of Prtha, there fortune, victory, prosperity, and statecraft are firmly fixed, I ween."[131] This active life on the world scene must be based upon the goal of world solidarity. Thus, the *Gita* term *lokasaṃgraha* is included in speeches to UNESCO and other audiences. For example, to the Indian Branch of the Union for the Study of the Great Religions he advised: "World solidarity, *lokasaṃgraha,* is no more a pious dream. It is an urgent practical necessity."[132]

Other themes also continue. The *Gita* is quoted to support the use of personal judgment against the acceptance of external authorities. For example, even though the *Gita* disapproves of Arjuna's stand, Radhakrishnan supports Arjuna's stance as a refusal to merely accept outward demands. "When Arjuna in the opening chapter of the *Bhagavadgītā* declines to conform to the demands of society which impose on him as a ksatriya the obligation to fight, when Socrates says, 'Men of Athens, I will obey God rather than you,' they are taking their stand on inward integrity rather than on outward conformity."[133] In discussions of the class system in India, like his

"Inaugural Address" to the Seminar on Casteism and the Removal of Untouchability in 1955, *Gita* 4.13, with its reference to the fourfold class system "with distinction of strands (*guṇa*) and actions (*karma*)," provided the language supporting the recognition of persons by their abilities, not their birth.[134] "Our sacred literature repudiates discriminations based on birth or *jāti* and emphasizes *guṇa* and *karma*."[135]

However, a colophon later added to the *Gita* provided much support for Radhakrishnan, particularly the phrase *brahmavidaya yogaśāstra śrikṛṣṇārjunasaṃvāda* (the wisdom of brahman, the scripture of *yoga*, the dialogue of Sri Krishna and Arjuna), and the phrase *brahma saṃsparśa*, (touching Brahman). The colophon is referred to as support for the argument that the ideal life involves three elements: rational understanding, ethical discipline and direct experience,[136] and also to show that personal encounter with the Highest is essential to religion. Especially did the phrase *śrikṛṣṇārjunasaṃvāda*, "the dialogue of Krishna and Arjuna," refer to this according to Radhakrishnan, for though the term *saṃvāda* means "dialogue" (from *sam* + *vad*, "speak together"), Radhakrishnan offered another meaning: "It is not a question of dialogue; it is the communion of the individual soul with the soul of the Supreme Reality. It is something which cannot be given expression to."[137]

Another phrase which for Radhakrishnan emphasizes the centrality of religious experience is *brahma saṃsparśa*, "touching brahman," from *Gita* 6.28. Radhakrishnan used it as a key verse, as a *mahāvakya* not of the *Gita* but for understanding all religion: "The fulfilment of man consists in what the *Gītā* calls *brahma saṃsparśa*, touching God. It is an extensive feeling, it is a perpetual experience, it is intuitive communion with the Supreme."[138] This phrase encapsulated that essence of religion which he felt would provide the basis for world unity. He turned often then to it and to the colophon to support his argument for the experiential essence of religion.

For Radhakrishnan from the earliest reference to the *Bhagavadgita* until this political period, the *Gita* functioned as a text providing material for his homiletic interests. Particularly did it function to support his apologetic purposes, and especially to confirm that, as he defined "Hinduism," it was a religion interested in a positive, active ethical stance. Likewise, it supported his construction of "Hinduism, Vedanta, religion of the spirit," and was useful as reference for his neo-advaitin metaphysical position and the experiential and universalistic emphases he believed religion needed in the modern world. He felt his religion of the spirit would solve the problems of the modern world and the *Gita,* he believed, should inspire all humanity to that 'religion.'

CHAPTER NINE

Swami Sivananda and the Bhagavadgita

DAVID M. MILLER

In the yogic circles of the West, Swami Sivananda Sarasvati's name and reputation are well-known. Two of his most famous disciples, Swami Vishnudevananda (Canada) and Swami Satchidananda (U.S.A.) have had thousands of disciples in the more than thirty years that they have lived and worked in North America. Yet, among academics, Swami Sivananda receives scant reference. G. S. Ghurye in his classic work, *Indian Sadhus,* notes that: "among the living Paramahansas may be mentioned Swami Sivananda of Hrishikesh [sic]", and he lists Sivananda with such others as Shankara and Ramakrishna.[1] Agehananda Bharati holds Sivananda to be a key personality in the Hindu Renaissance and one of Vivekananda's "latter day imitators" who had a larger mass appeal in India than either Ramana Maharishi or Sri Aurobindo.[2] More recently Joel D. Mlecko cites Sivananda as "another important contemporary guru," after a discussion of Ramakrishna and Vivekananda.[3] Outside of articles that I have written earlier, these are, to my knowledge, the only references to Swami Sivananda in academic literature; yet each of the scholars who has made mention of Sivananda has placed him in excellent company, comparing Sivananda to such well-known gurus as Shankara, Ramakrishna, Vivekananda, Ramana Maharishi and Aurobindo. I must, therefore, begin with a brief introduction to the life and writings of Swami Sivananda.[4]

Swami Sivananda was born on September 8, 1887, in the village of Pattamadai, Tamil Nadu, as the third son of an upper-caste brahmin family. His father, P. S. Vengu Iyer, was a Tahsildar for the Raja of Ettiapuram, whose estate was located near Kanyakumari, the southern-most tip of India. In his *Autobiography,* published in 1958, Sivananda describes his father as "a virtuous pure soul, a Siva-Bhakta and a Jnani" who was descended from Appaya Dikshitar, a sixteenth-century pandit, "a giant among geniuses."[5]

Born into an orthodox family of high status, the son of devout and learned parents, and with an ancestry descended from a renowned pundit and Sanskritist,—a curious, if not contradictory detail is that Sivananda was given a modern, secular, education. In 1905 he graduated from a Jesuit College at Trichinopoly and entered Tanjore Medical Institute, in opposition to his orthodox family. Sivananda notes that: "At home my mother and brothers would persuade me to take up some work in some other line, but I was adamant in my resolve to stick to the medical line."[6] For some reason, which is left unexplained by Sivananda and by his biographers, he did not graduate from medical school, but he moved to Madras, where he was employed in a pharmacy and where he began an English medical journal, *Ambrosia,* that "was based on the teachings of the sages of yore."[7]

Throughout his early education and young adulthood, Sivananda makes no mention that he had training in Sanskrit; not does he record that he read traditional Hindu literature in English translation, although the format of his journal indicates that he was knowledgeable in Ayurvedic medicine. Rather, again and again, he stresses that he was educated in English, that he read English sources, and that he wrote in English. Furthermore, he and his biographers make it clear that to enter upon a career in "Western" medicine was not only a departure from the traditional orientation of his orthodox family, but it led to complete rupture with his family. Like Vivekananda, Sivananda was given a secular, British education, but unlike Vivekananda, Sivananda did not allow family loyalties, in particular, ties to his mother, to restrict his self-determined goals. We must remember that Sivananda was the third of three sons and that renunciation of family ties, even for secular goals, would have been impossible had he been the eldest or the only son.

In 1913, at the age of twenty-six, Sivananda sailed to Malaya and was employed as a doctor in a hospital on a rubber plantation in Seremban. Here he wrote articles on public health for the *Malaya Tribune,* a newspaper based in Singapore. He also became a member of the Royal Institute of Public Health, the Royal Sanitary Institute and the Royal Asiatic Society. In 1920, Sivananda left Seremban for Johore Bahru, near Singapore, where he entered into private practice with two English doctors. His life was that of an English gentleman with all of the luxuries that status and wealth can bring. He maintained an upper-middle class home, owned his own motorcycle and drove an automobile. He interjects, however, that he retained his brahmin purity and that he performed traditional religious duties and practices, sang bhajans and kirtans, and read "scripture," although what scripture and in what language is not made clear.

In 1923 Sivananda underwent a dramatic change of attitude. He writes of this period:

> Is there not a higher mission in life than the daily round of official duties, eating and drinking? Is there not any higher form of eternal happiness than these transitory and illusory pleasures? How uncertain is life here. How insecure is existence on this earthplane with various kinds of diseases, anxieties, worries, fears and disappointments. The world of names and forms is constantly changing. Time is fleeting. All hopes of happiness in this world terminate in pain, despair and sorrow. For hearing the Srutis, one should take Sannyas. The words of scriptures have great value. I renounced the life of ease and money-making and took to the life of a mendicant, a truc seeker after Truth. I left my luggage in Malaya with a friend . . . From Singapore I reached Banaras and had Darshan of Lord Shiva.[8]

At the age of thirty-six Sivananda renounced the lifestyle and the values of an affluent, middle-class doctor, whose first language was English and became a wandering samnyasin, who sought insight and inspiration from traditional Hindu scriptures, and who, according to custom, begged for his food.

From Banares, Sivananda travelled on foot along the banks of the Ganges River to Rishikesh, where on June 1, 1924, he took initiation into the Dashanami (Shankara) sannyasin suborder Sarasvati under Paramahansa Visvananda Sarasvati, a learned ascetic from Banares about whom Sivananda and his biographers provide little detail.[9] We are told by Venkatesananda that Sivananda "had Swami Viswanandaji's company only for a couple of hours," and Ananthanarayanan adds further that "the next day Swami Viswananda left for his native Varanasi. From there he wrote to his new disciple, giving the briefest of instruction about Sannyasa Dharma."[10] Sivananda, therefore, could have learned little from his guru, who was more a symbolic link in a spiritual lineage going back to the *achārya,* Shankara, than he was a teacher whose commentaries on and interpretations of the principal Vedantic scriptures could have influenced and guided Sivananda. This is an important point, for whatever else might be said, Sivananda's commentaries upon Vedantic sources, and in particular upon the *Bhagavadgita,* are uniquely his own, although he shares much in common with other so-called 'modernist' or Neo-Vedantic thinkers.

After his initiation into sannyasa, Sivananda established himself at Rishikesh in a small room that was part of a larger building owned by Svargashrama. Although for the next nine years Sivananda went on numerous pilgrimages about India, he spent considerable time in this room performing his *sādhanā,* meditating, reading, and writing. In a more limited way, he continued his medical practice by treating the sick and the ailing pilgrims and the sadhus who passed through Rishikesh. Sivananda describes his early ascetic life:

> I had the goal of my life as Self-Realization and determined to spend every bit of my energy and time in study, service and Sadhana . . . I paid special attention to simple living, high thinking, light food, deep study, silent meditation and regular prayers. I loved seclusion and observed Mowna . . . From the Ram Ashram library in Muniki-Reti I used to get some books for my study and devoted some time to study every day . . . Mahatmas and the poor villagers who were sick did not have proper medical aid. Thousands of pilgrims to Badrinath, Kedarnath also needed medical help. Therefore I starded a small dispensary . . . During my travels, I carried a bundle containing my ink-pot, pens, pencils, study books like Vivekachudamai, the Upanishads, the Gita and the Brahmasutras.[11]

Sivananda was then thirty-seven years of age, and this is the first reference that he makes in his *Autobiography* to the *Bhagavadgita,* but, again, he does not state in what language he read the *Gita*. My guess is that he knew some Sanskrit, and like many other upper-status brahmins, he had read the *Gita* in several languages and was able to recite much of it, if not all of it, in Sanskrit. From an examination of his early publications, however, it is certain that Sivananda did not "know" Sanskrit in the sense that he had shastric training.

Sometime between 1924 and 1933, Sivananda must have attained the experience of Self-realization that had become his ultimate concern. Yet, he remains absolutely silent on this most important event. His biographers have written chapters that describe in minutest detail Sivananda's daily life during this period, but they have nothing to say about Sivananda's enlightenment experience, nor do they provide any description of what the experience of *mokṣa* meant to Ṣivananda in those early years or even later. Ananthanarayanan glosses over the problem by stating:

> The Sivananda who cast a spell on vast audiences . . . who sang and danced his way into the hearts of tens of thousands . . . and threw them into high ecstasy, left no one in doubt about his being a realized soul. When and where he attained the Illumination, no one knew. It was a secret known only to Swamji and God.[12]

We do know that by the late 1920s, Sivananda had become recognized as one of the enlightened gurus of Rishikesh and that he began to attract a core of staunch disciples about him. One of his first tasks was to publish materials that he had written during his years of intense Sadhana. In 1929 Sivananda published *The Practice of Yoga,* the first of 340 books and pamphlets that were to follow over the next thirty-four years. In 1933 Sivananda completed his period of intermittent travel, and between 1933 and 1939 he and his disciples energetically supervised the publication of twenty-three books. The titles of some of the more significant works are instructive in that they give us an insight into Sivananda's preoccupation with and mastery of yogic systems:

> *Yoga By Japa* (1933); *Practice of Vedanta* (1934); *The Practice of Brahmacharya* (1934); *Dhyana Yoga* (1934); *The Science of Pranayama* (1935); *Yoga Asanas* (1935); *Kundalini Yoga* (1935); *Bhakti Yoga* (1935); *How to Get Vairagya* (1938); *Hatha Yoga* (1939); *Moksha Gita* (1939).

With the addition of *Gyana Yoga* (1944), *Raja Yoga* (1961) to this list we have a select bibliography of the principal contributions Sivananda made to yogic theory and practice. From his early years in Rishikesh until his death, Sivananda, the ascetic and recluse, remained the spiritual practitioner who sought to aid and comfort other seekers who had begun to tread those difficult paths that he had traveled many times. This concern with practicality and with teaching others through his example and his writing dominates every aspect of his life and work.

In 1939, Sivananda published the first edition of his classic, eight-hundred page translation of and commentary upon the *Bhagavadgita.* By Sivananda's death in 1963, his *Gita* had gone through six printings with 12,000 copies in the final 1962 edition. In 1941 Sivananda produced an anthology of selections from the *Upanishads,* and in 1949 the Ashrama press published his lengthy and complex commentary on the *Brahma Sutras,* which, in 1977, was revised and reprinted by Motilal Banarsidass, Delhi, one of India's leading Indological book publishers and dealers. The last major study, for the purpose of this paper at least, was his collection of articles, papers and lectures, entitled *Ethics of the Gita* published in 1957, but dating back to 1942.

Sivananda, in his commentaries upon the *Upanishads, the Brahma Sutras* and the *Bhagavadgita,* saw his task as that of a philosophical interpreter of Vedantic thought, practice and social theory, in the spiritual lineage (*guruparamparā*) of his acharya, Shankara. And, like Vivekananda, who was also deeply influenced by the tradition of Shankara, Sivananda sought to reconcile the different, often contradictory, philosophical understandings held by the various schools of Vedanta. Commenting upon *Gita* 7.17, in which Krishna says: "I hold the wise as verily myself," Sivananda argues:

> Here He speaks of identity. The doctrine of non-dualism is quite correct. Non-dualism is the highest realisation. The Lord gives instructions according to the type of the adhikari (qualified aspirant). Advaita philosophy can be grasped only by the microscopic few. So, He speaks of other kinds of philosophical doctrines in other places, to suit different kinds of aspirants. There is neither Jiva nor Self-realisation from the Absolute viewpoint. Brahman alone exists in reality. Dvaita (dualism), Visistadvaita (qualified monism), Suddha Advaita (pure monism) are different rungs in the ladder of realisation. The truth is that the Jiva and Brahman are One in essence. The Dvaitin and the Visistadvaitin eventually reach the Advaitic goal or Vedantic realisation of Oneness.[13]

In following the teaching of Krishna, Sivananda, as the guru, sought to vary his interpretation of the *Gita* to meet the spiritual needs and aspirations of his disciples, who were slowly climbing "the ladder of realisation," some having reached greater heights than others. This is, perhaps, the most significant difference between the systematic philosopher, such as Radhakrishnan, and the guru, such as Sivananda: the guru is not, nor does he seek to be, systematic in his presentation of philosophical tradition; rather, he must, like Krishna, make his teaching "suit different kinds of aspirants." Thus, in holding the *Gita* to be one of the principal sources of Vedantic philosophy, Sivananda understands its message to be allegorical and universal, speaking to all types of individuals in all times and places.

> The whole world is a big battlefield. The real Kuru-kshetra is within you. The battle of Mahabharata is still raging within you. Ignorance (avidya) is Dhrtarastra. The individual soul is Arjuna. The Indweller Who dwells in your heart is Lord Krishna, the charioteer. The body is your chariot. The senses (indriyas) are the horses. The mind, egoism, senses, samskaras (mental impressions), vasanas (latent tendencies), cravings, raga-dvesa (likes and dislikes), lust, jealousy, greed, pride, and hypocrisy are your dire enemies.[14]

I turn now to an examination of Sivananda's philosophical position and the relationship of his philosophical inquiry to social theory and religious practice.

Swami Sivananda's Philosophy and the Bhagavadgita

As the studies in this volume clearly illustrate the *Bhagavadgita* often means quite different and contradictory things to different people. Yet, whatever the philosophical position or approach taken, the interpreter of the *Gita* must take into account the philosophical system that underlies much of it. Sivananda's approach to the *Gita* is often that of an Advaita Vedantin or, perhaps more descriptively, that of a neo-Advaitin in the spiritual lineage of Shankara, whose work has inspired, and continues to inspire, commentary and critique. In my reading of Shankara's commentary on the *Brahma Sutra,* one passage seems to best summarize his position. Commenting upon BS 2.1.27, Shankara writes:

> By that [appearance] of plurality which is the [product] of ignorance, which is characterized by name and form, which is evolved as well as non-evolved, which is not to be defined either as the existing or the non-existing, Brahman becomes the basis of this entire apparent world with its changes, and so on, while in its true and real nature it at the same time remains unchanged, lifted above the phenomenal universe.[15]

I understand this passage to mean that the plurality or the multiplicity of the phenomenal world is grounded in ignoramce (*avidyā*) and that, in TRUTH, in the mystical experience of *jñāna* or non-dual knowledge, Brahman is 'seen' as it always has been, that is, non-dual (*advaita*), beyond Being (*sat*) and non-being (*asat*), and therefore without qualities (*nirguṇa*). The world of multiplicity, of individuality, of I-other relationships, including such dualities as soul/body and God/world, is ultimately illusory, the product of ignorance (*avidyā*). The causal base of all multiplicity or duality is, therefore, ignorance or *avidyā.* the key problem in Shankara's system is what is the 'reality' or 'truth value' that is assigned to *avidyā,* which Shankara says ". . . is not to be defined either as the existing or the non-existing." This problem has been stated by Daniel H.H. Ingalls in his article on *avidyā:*

> It is by the concept of *avidyā* that these monistic philosophers explain the apparent diversity of the world. They claim that in truth there is one indivisible reality, that the experience we have of diversity is due simply to *avidyā.* Now, the use of this concept leads to a logical dilemma. If this *avidyā* is a real entity, then monism ends. On the other hand, to say that it is an imaginary entity is to destroy the very doctrine of *avidyā.* . . . There are two ways out of this dilemma. One of them has been taken by most of Sankara's followers. . . . In this system a new truth-value is set up, *anirvacanīyatva,* that which cannot be said to be either true or false . . . There is, however, another way out of this dilemma, that is, not by solving but by avoiding it. This was the way chosen by Samkaracarya himself.[16]

At several points in his commentary on the *Gita* (1939) Sivananda appears to hold a position similar to that put forth by Shankara. For example, Sivananda interprets *Gita* 13.31, (which, if taken literally and historically, is Sankhyan philosophically), in the language of an Advaita Vedantin:

> The Supreme Self is beyond nature. Therefore He is without qualities. He is nirguna . . . the Supreme Self is one without a second . . . This world is a mere appearance. It is a mere figment of our imagination. It is superimposed on the Absolute on account of ignorance. An imaginary object has no independent existence apart from its substratum, just as the snake in the rope has no independent existence apart from its substratum, the rope . . . Brahman or the Supreme Self is beginningless. He is without a cause. He is self-existent. He is without parts. Therefore Brahman is imperishable.[17]

If one were to compare these statements with the philosophical position that Sivananda takes, rather consistently, in his equally lengthy and complex commentary on the *Brahma Sutra* (1949), it might be argued that Sivananda is a 'pure' Advaita Vedantin, closer philosophically to Gaudapada and to Shankara than to his contemporaries, such as Vivekananda. However, as is characteristic of other neo-Vedantic writers, in his commentary upon *Gita* 13.32–34 Sivananda slips quickly and quietly into a Vishishtadvaita ("qualified non-dualism") Vedanta interpretation as he states:

> The Supreme Self is one. He illumines the whole matter from the Unmanifested down to the blade of grass or a lump of clay, from the 'great elements' down to 'firmness' or 'fortitude'. (Cf. verses 5 and 6) . . . When ignorance is annihilated through the knowledge of the Self . . . then She (Nature) gives up Her play or dance in front of the Spirit. She has discharged all Her duties well for the sake of the enjoyment and the release (bhoga and apavarga) of the Purusa (spirit).[18]

The question might be asked: how can Sivananda move so easily and effortlessly from an Advaita Vedanta interpretation into a Vishishtadvaita Vedanta interpretation? In his defense Sivananda provides the classic epistemological answer of two levels of knowledge, *para-vidyā* (highest truth) and *apara-vidyā* (lower truth); see commentary on *Gita* 13.13–14 for example. *Para-vidyā* is *jñāna,* knowledge of Absolute Truth or of Brahman itself, whereas *apara-vidyā* is *avidyā* or ignorance of the highest truth (see commentary on *Gita* 13.31). If, however, from the standpoint of lower knowledge (*apara-vidyā*) the soul (*jīva*) and God (*Īśvara*) are said to exist over against matter (*prakṛti*), then to argue that these distinctions, in fact these separate entities, do not exist on the higher level of truth (*para-vidyā*) is simply to sidestep the basic problem. The final question for Sivananda and other neo-Vedantins remains unanswered: what is the reality or truth-value of *avidyā* or, indeed, what is the substratum that is the basis or cause of *avidyā*? Whatever else might be said, Ramanuja is quite emphatic in his rejection of Advaita Vedanta on this point:

> This entire theory rests on a fictitious foundation of altogether hollow and vicious arguments, incapable of being stated in definite logical alternatives. . . . The theory therefore must needs be rejected by all those who, through texts, perception and the other means of knowledge—assisted by sound reasoning—have an insight into the true nature of things.
>
> To enter into details.—Those who maintain the doctrine of a substance devoid of all difference have no right to assert

> that this or that is a proof of such a substance, for all means of right knowlege have for their object things affected with difference.[19]

The reason that Sivananda and other neo-vedantic writers slip back and forth between Advaita Vedanta and Vishishtadvaita Vedanta is they they do not deny the existence of the material or phenomenal world of multiplicity to which they attribute a far greater reality than their predecessors, whom Ingalls argues began the process of compromise in the first place. *Advaita,* for Sivananda, always means Oneness and not non-duality to the exclusion of all dualities. The world of multiplicity is, therefore 'real' for Sivananda, although that which is ultimately real is the Absolute Brahman.

What remains quite consistent, however, whether Sivananda interprets the *Bhagavadgita* from an Advaita or Vishishtadvaita position or perhaps from a synthesis of both, is that he reinterprets Sankhyan philosophy and categories in Vedantic terms and meanings. The best statement of his philosophical position is in his commentary upon *Gita* 13.19–20. I shall quote it at length:

> Till now the Lord expounded the knowledge of the field and the Self in accordance with the philosophy of the Upanisads. Now He explains the same knowledge in accordance with the Sankhya philosophy, but without accepting its dual nature in the form of discrimination between the Spirit and Nature . . . According to the Sankhya philosophy, Prakrti or Maya originates from Brahman and is, therefore, neither self-created nor independent. Isvara has maya under His perfect control. maya is His causal body. Maya is His illusory power. Matter and Spirit are the Natures of Isvara. Know that these two are beginningless. That which has no beginning is *anadi.* As Isvara is eternal . . . He causes the creation, preservation and destruction of the universe. Therefore He has the Lordship and rules over the universe.
>
> Purusa here means 'jiva' (the individual soul). . . . We can clearly infer the existence of the individual soul in the previous birth and that the individual soul is beginningless . . . Purusa, jiva, kshetrajna and bhokta are all synonymous terms. Purusa here referred to is not the Supreme Self. He is the conditioned soul, the soul subject to transmigration who experiences pleasure and pain. The Self or the Absolute is ever free from samsara and is unchanging. Prakrti and Purusa are the cause of samsara. Nature generates the body, life-force,

> mind, intellect and the senses. The soul experiences pleasure and pain. The soul is the samsarin.[20]

In these passages Sivananda used Vishishtadvaita Vedanta categories to re-interpret Sankhyan thought, and thus he avoids the difficulty of the Sankhyan contradiction that the *puruṣa (individual soul)* is, in ignorance, bound to matter when in Truth the *puruṣa* is, and always has been, eternally free from bondage to matter and hence not subject to rebirth. For Sivananda, rebirth, bondage, and release from rebirth and bondage are the three cardinal problems that form the core of the *Gita*. Beginning with *Gita* 13.21 he presents a langthy commentary developing a theory of rebirth and bondage (*saṃsāra*) that incorporates the Sankhyan theory of matter, made up of the three strands or qualities (*guṇas*): *sattva, rajas* and *tamas,* with the Vedantic understanding of karma (action) as the cause of rebirth. Sivananda uses what I shall call the *guṇa-karma* theory of rebirth to explain not only the hierarchy of the Indian social structure, but the whole of creation from the "highest" (most sattvic) evolved form of matter, which he identifies as the "Indian Yogi", down to "the whole mineral kingdom", in which *tamas guṇa* is predominate.[21]

The Guna-Karma Theory of Rebirth

The interrelatedness of the *guṇa* and the *karma* theories is central to Sivananda's commentary on the *Bhagavadgita,* and I am assuming that, on the basis of George Williams' work, Vivekananda held this concept of interrelatedness to be the core of his understanding of 'caste' (*varṇa*) as well.[22] But, what is striking is that western scholarship, for the most part, has missed this point, perhaps because the *guṇa-karma* theory of rebirth is only one theory of rebirth among many and perhaps also because the theory is, in its earliest form, part of Sankhya thought which has been of less interest to Westerners than the Vedantic schools.

In *Karma and Rebirth in Classical Indian Traditions* the only scholar who treats the *guṇa-karma* theory of rebirth is Ludo Rocher in his insightful article on "Karma and Rebirth in the *Dharmaśāstras*".[23] Rocher describes the *guṇa-karma* theory as "the second system" of five theories of rebirth that he locates in the *Dharmasastras*:

> Manu 12.24 introduces the three *guṇas* or inherent qualities of all matter: *sattva, rajas,* and *tamas* (goodness, passion, and darkness). After several stanzas dealing with aspects of the

> three *guṇas* which are less relevant for our purpose, stanza 12.39 introduces the transmigrations (*saṃsārāḥ*) resulting from them. Before doing so, the text (M. 12.41) further subdivides each of the three *guṇas* into three levels, which have been used on numerous occasions in the Dharmáśāstras: "low, middling, and high". The following nine stanzas (M. 12.42–50) list, within each of the nine subtypes, a number of possible forms of rebirth, starting from the low subtype of *tamas* up to the high subtype of *sattva* . . . each of the principal categories leads to a specific type of rebirth.[24]

In the table that follows his discussion, Rocher establishes a hierarchy of "living beings" with ascetics (*tāpasāḥ*), mendicants (*yatayaḥ*) and priests (*viprāḥ*) at the top and lower animals, murderous demons (*rākṣāṃsi*), and flesh-eating demons (*piśācāḥ*) at the bottom. In the middle category of this elaborate scheme he places kings (*rājānaḥ*), nobles (*kṣatriyāḥ*) and others within whom rajas (*activity*) is the predominant *guṇa.*[25] What is implied in Rocher's interpretation of *Manu* is that the hierarchy of living beings presupposes a dichotomy between the sattivic realm, which includes those with divine attributes, from the tamasic realm, which includes those with demonic or beastly attributes. The rajasic realm is, indeed, "the middle" in that it is a mixture made up of types, such as kings who are more sattivic than tamasic and goblins who are more tamasic than sattivic, yet all in this category are clearly distinguished by the dominant *guṇa, rajas.* Thus, Rocher's discussion of *Manu* 12. 24–50 gives us a detailed picture of the hierarchical ordering of the social structure that was existent at the time of *Manu* (ca. 200 B.C.) or, at least, that ideally existed in the minds of the brahmin authors of the *Dharmasaṣtras.* The fundamental principal upon which the brahmin authors based this complex ordering of society was the radical distinction between those in whom *sattva guṇa* was dominant and those in whom *tamas guṇa* was dominant.

Although Dumont in his study of the Indian social structure makes no reference to the *guṇa-karma* theory, he argues that the fundamental principle upon which the caste (*jāti*) system is based is:

> The opposition of the pure and impure. This opposition underlies hierarchy, which is the superiority of the pure to the impure, underlies separation because the pure and the impure must be kept separate, and underlies the division of labour because pure and impure occupations must likewise be kept separate. The whole is founded on the necessary and hierar-

> chical coexistence of the two opposites . . . This fact is of extreme importance, since it transports us at once into a purely structural universe: it is the whole which governs the parts, and this whole is very rigorously conceived as based on an opposition.[26]

If I were to translate "pure" by its Sanskrit equivalent "*sattva*" and "impure" by its Sanskrit equivalent "*tamas*", then what Dumont says of the caste or *jāti* system had its beginnings about the time in which the *Dharmasastras* and the *Bhagavadgita* were composed, a point which Dumont, in fact, acknowledges.[27] Although it is not my purpose here to extend this argument, the attitudes, the ways of thinking and acting, indeed, the food one eats, as described in *Manu* and in the *Gita* match exactly the characteristics of pure and impure as detailed by Dumont in his analysis of *jāti* system.

In Rocher's interpretation of *Manu* 12.24–50, the brahmins were held to be superior to the kshatriyas as the realm of *sattva guṇa* is superior to the realm of *rajas guṇa*; and both the brahmins and the *kshatriyas* ranked far above the *shudras,* who were placed in the realm of *tamas guṇa*. The hierarchy of the social structure that Rocher has reconstructed was a linear order from the highest, the ascetics (*tāpasāḥ*) down to the lowest, the flesh-eating demons (*piśācāḥ*), who had in this scheme, their human counterparts in the Camars, later to be called 'untouchables,' responsible for removing dead cattle.[28]

Dumont does not accept this view of hierarchical ordering; he argues:

> In theory, power is ultimately subordinated to priesthood, whereas in fact priesthood submits to power. Status and power, and consequently spiritual authority and temporal authority, are absolutely distinguished. . . . Thus in the theory of the *varnas* one finds that status and power are differentiated, just as the general consideration of hierarchy seemed to require. This fact is older than the castes, and it is fundamental to them in the sense that it is only once this differentiation has been made that hierarchy can manifest itself in a pure form.[29]

Thus, if the classical theory of the *varṇas* is combined with the social reality of the later *jāti* system, the fundamental principle underlying the Hindu social structure is and has been the radical separation of those who are 'pure' from those who are 'impure,' compromised, however, by those who hold power. That is, the kshatriyas have been allowed to violate brahmin values and standards: they have been allowed to eat meat, maintain polygamy, and they are, in fact, enjoined by their *dharma* to kill in pursuit of righteousness.[30]

Sivananda's interpretation of the *guṇa-karma* theory provides an excellent illustration of Dumont's thesis of the hierarchy of Indian social structure. This is a point that is not immediately obvious from the first reading of his commentary on the *Gita*. Sivananda is not systematic in his exposition of the *guṇa-karma* theory, but neither is the *Gita* a systematic text. The first oblique references that Sivananda makes to the *guṇa-karma* theory of rebirth occur in his commentary upon 3.27 and 3.34. In regard to the latter verse he writes:

> Nature which contains the sum-total of one's Samskaras or the latent self-productive impressions of the past actions of merit and demerit draws a man to its course through the two currents, attachment and aversion.[31]

In his commentary upon 18.14 Sivananda expands upon this earlier reference:

> Karma is action arising from and fashioned by past thoughts and desires. The gunas cannot manifest themselves without a cause. Nature is the tendency, Samskara or Vasana in living beings. This is acquired by them in the past births. This manifests in the present birth and produces its effects. This nature is the source of the gunas. Every man or woman is born with his or her own svabhava (nature). The gunas operate according to the respective natural tendencies of man which impel him to perform his own duties as their natural effects. The duties are allotted to the four classes or castes in accordance with the gunas of persons (cf. IV. 13).[32]

As pointed out above, the *jīva* or the *puruṣa* as the individual soul is subject to transmigration and experiences pleasure and pain. Thus, for Sivananda the *jīva* or soul is the bearer of "the sum-total of one's *saṃskāras* or latent self-productive impressions of the past action of merit or demerit." The *saṃskāras,* in turn, cause the *jīva* to be reborn and determine the exact type of rebirth, depending upon whether one's actions in the previous life were meritorious (dharmic) or non-meritorious (adharmic).

In his commentary upon 13.21 Sivananda adds:

> The soul's attachment to the qualities of pleasure, pain and delusion is the chief cause of this birth. If you add the word samsara to the second half of the verse, it will mean: "Attachment to the qualities is the cause of his samsara through births in good and evil wombs." Good wombs (sat yoni) are those of the gods and the like; evil wombs (asat yoni) are those of lower animals. The human womb is partly good and partly evil on account of mixed karmas.[33]

The interrelatedness of the karma and the *guṇa* theories is thus that the *saṃskāras,* which are the residues of past actions (karma), cause the *jīva* to be reborn, and the *saṃskāras* determine the type of womb into which the *jīva* will be reborn. "Good wombs," here, mean those whose karma has been good (dharmic) and in whom *sattva* is predominate; "evil wombs" are those whose karma has been evil (adharmic) and in whom *tamas* predominates. Throughout the *guṇa-karma* theory, therefore, a series of dichotomies are operative: meritorious action (*dharma*) and non-meritorious action (*adharma*); good wombs (*sat yoni*) and evil wombs (*asat yoni*); and finally *sattva guṇa* and *tamas guṇa.* No mention is made of *rajas guṇa.*

Although Dumont does not use Sanskrit terminology, this dichothomous structure is the core principle that, he argues, underlies both the *varṇa* and *jāti* systems. Dumont holds that the principle upon which the caste or *jāti* system is based is the dichotomy of pure (which I have translated as *sattva*) and impure (which I have translated as *tamas*). In regard to the hierarchical ordering of the class or *varṇa* system, Dumont argues:

> Thanks to Hocard and, more precisely, to Dumezil, the hierarchy of the Varnas can be seen not as a linear order, but as a series of successive dichotomies or inclusions. The set of the four Varnas divides into two: the last category, that of the Shudras, is opposed to the block of the first three, whose members are 'twice-born' in the sense that they participate in initiation, second birth, and in religious life in general. These twice-born in turn divide into two: the Vaishyas are opposed to the block formed by the Kshatriyas and the Brahmans, which in turn divides into two . . . Let us simply say that the lot of the Shudras is to serve and that the Vaishyas are the grazers of cattle and the farmers, the 'purveyors' of sacrifice, as Hocart says, who have been given dominion over the animals, whereas the Brahmans-Kshatriyas have been given dominion over 'all creatures'. We shall return to the solidarity

between the two highest classes and the distinction between them: the Kshatriya can order a sacrifice as can the Vaishya, but only the Brahman may perform it. The king is thus deprived of any sacerdotal function. It can be seen that the series of dichotomies on which this hierarchy rests is formally somewhat similar to caste hierarchy, and it also is essentially religious; but it is less systematic and its principles are different.[34]

In his commentary on *Gita* 4.13 Sivananda notes briefly that: "the four castes (Brahmana, Kshatriya, Vaisya and Sudra) are classified according to the differentiation of *guṇa* and *karma*." Toward the end of the *Gita,* at 18.41, Sivananda provides a more detailed commentary that supports Dumont's argument of "a series of dichotomies on which this hierarchy rests." Sivananda, however, extends his theory of social order to include all of humankind:

> Brahmanas, Kshatriyas and Vaisyas are qualified to practise the Vedic rites. The members of the fourth class, O Arjuna, have no claim to these rites, for their profession is to serve the members of the first three. They are not allowed to study the Vedas or perform yajnas. There is organization of mankind into the four castes and each man's life is divided into four stages, according to the nature of the gunas and the degree of the growth or evolution. I will now explain the specific duties of these castes according to the qualities by means of which, freeing themselves from the grip of birth and death, they can attain Self-realization or knowledge of the Self . . . the one human race has been divided into four castes based upon the three qualities. The duties are allotted to each according to the qualities born of Nature . . . Nature (svabhava) is Isvara's Prakrti (Maya) constituted of the three qualities—Sattva, Rajas and Tamas. The Brahmana's nature is Sattva. So he is serene. The nature of the Kshatriya is Rajas and Sattva. Sattva is subordinate to Rajas. Rajas predominates. Therefore he possesses lordliness. The nature of the Vaisya is Rajas and Tamas. Tamas is subordinate to Rajas. so he does various sorts of activities or business to earn money. The nature of the Sudra is Tamas, with subordinate Rajas. He is dull.[35]

In *Practice of Karma Yoga* (1961), which is supported by seventy references to the *Gita,* Sivananda illustrates the range of the human hierarchy:

> The conscience of a savage speaks of a language entirely different from that of a civilised European. The conscience of an African Negro speaks a language entirely different from that of an ethically developed Yogi of India.[36]

Later, in the same work, Sivananda becomes more specific and identifies "an African Negro" with "the cannibals" of Central Africa.[37] One might assume that Sivananda has in mind "a linear order" similiar to that which Rocher found in *Manu* 12. 24–50. Sivananda's "yogis" are Rocher's "ascetics" (*tāpasāḥ*) and "mendicants" (*yatayaḥ*) and his "African cannibals" could be identified with "flesh eating demons" (*piśācāḥ*), meateaters of the lowest type. But if one were to look deeper, it is clear that Sivananda's theory of social order presupposes a principle of hierarchy similar to Dumont's, based on the dichotomy of pure and impure, but compromised by power. One of the characteristics of the individual in whom *sattva* predominates is that he lives by the value of *ahiṃsā* or noninjury to all living creatures. A kshatriya, such as Arjuna, in order to fulfill his *dharma,* must kill in battle; this, of course, is one of the basic problems in the *Gita.* Much has been written on this problem, despite the fact that it disappears when seen in the context of the *guṇakarma* theory of rebirth and when related to *dharma.* Sivananda is emphatic on this point in his commentary upon the famous passage of *Gita* 3.35:

> It is indeed better for man to die discharging his own duty though destitute of merit than for him to live doing the duty of another though performed in a perfect manner. For the duty of another has its pitfalls. The duty of a Kshatriya is to fight in a righteous battle. Arjuna must fight. This is his duty. Even if he dies in the discharge of his own duty, it is better for him. He will go to heaven. He should not do the duty of another man. This will bring him peril. He should not stop from fighting and enter the path of renunciation. (cf. 18.43).[38]

Sivananda's reference to chapter eighteen brings us back to our previous discussion of the Hindu social hierarchy. Although many of the characteristics and virtues of a kshatriya, described by Sivananda in his commentary on *Gita* 18.43 are in opposition to brahmin values, nevertheless he lauds the righteous (dharmic) kshatriya for doing his duty.

> it is the first duty of a Kshatriya (man of the warrior class or of royal blood) to be brave and chivalrous. Bravery is that sublime virtue through which one is naturally strong, vigorous

> and courageous. In the face of the most terrible calamity the mind will not be in the least perturbed. He is firm under any unfavourable or trying conditions or circumstances . . . He will ever avoid turning his back to them on the field of battle. He is absolutely fearless. Just as a tree gives away its flower and fruits freely to whoever desires them, as the jasmine sends out its sweet fragrance in every direction, so will a Kshatriya generously give to another whatever may be asked of him. His charity is boundless . . . A Kshatriya king enjoys sovereignty over his subjects owing to the sure protection he grants them, exercises ruling power over his subjects who are to be ruled, and raises the rod of chastisement to punish the unrightous or the wicked.[39]

In the *Ethics of the Bhagavadgita* (1957) Sivananda reinforces this last point as he relates political-military theory to the problem that confronts Arjuna in the *Gita*.

> He must have a sharp, subtle intellect, that would grasp matters at once; and he must have well developed discrimination that would promptly arrive at a decision and at the right way of executing it. All these would become easy only if the ruler is guided by the *Eternal Dharma,* and by the advice of saints and sages, his own Guru. For the sake of the preservation of Dharma, the Kshatriya is allowed to wage war. But, in this connection, it is good to bear in mind the Lord's own example: a study of the Mahabharata would reveal that the Lord, though He was omniscient and knew that war was inevitable, did endeavour to avoid the war and come to a peaceful settlement with the enemy, and that he advised war only when this was inevitable . . . (The Kasatriya) is the Lord of the people placed by God under his care. He protects them. He is really an Amsa of God as he performs here the divine duty which the Lord has imposed upon Himself, viz, protection of the righteous, subdual of the wicked, and the preservation of Dharma. This is the Kshatriya's foremost duty.[40]

The brahmins and kshatriyas, whose respective *dharmas* differ radically and whose values often stand at opposite poles, nevertheless together form a group from all other groups: God has given the brahmins and kshatriyas "dominion over all creatures." Sivananda goes into lengthy descriptions of the duties of the other *varṇas.* As noted above, he affirms the injunction stated in *Gita* 3.35 and repeated in *Gita* 18.47: "Better is one's own duty, though devoid of merit than the duty of another well discharged."

To sum up, one's previous karma and its residues, the *saṃskāras,* determine the rebirth and the *guṇa* makeup of the body into which the *jīva* is born. And the family, caste, and class into which the individual is born determine his *dharma,* which he must fulfill in spite of, or perhaps, in conflict with other value orientations and considerations. The karma theory, therefore, explains the inequalities of birth; the *guṇa* theory accounts for differences in personality and character structure among individuals; and the *dharma* theory dictates the duties that one must perform in life. This seemingly fatalistic and deterministic picture of the human social order is complicated by one last factor: *prārabdha karma* or action to be worked out in this present life. Sivananda writes:

> The karmas (prarabdha) which have already started their operation by producing this present birth do not perish, notwithstanding the dawn of the knowledge of the Self. When an arrow is once sent out from a bow at a mark, it . . . continues to act till it falls to the ground when the full force with which it was discharged is exhausted. Even so the prarabdha karma which has given rise to the body continues to act till the inherent force is fully exhausted, although the sage has attained Self realisation.[41]

With the words "Self realisation" Sivananda paints in a ray of light, of hope, that brightens this otherwise dark and gloomy canvas depicting the human social order and the human situation. He says this most forcefully in *Practice of Karma Yoga:*

> The doctrine of Karma is diametrically opposed to the doctrine of fatalism. Fatalism causes inertia, lethargy, weakness of will and bondage. Fatalism annihilates faith. It induces terrible fear in the people. It destroys ethics. It checks growth and evolution, whereas the doctrine of Karma is an incentive to action to better one's condition. It is a source of solace. It gives man an assurance of a broader and happier life. It presupposes freedom of the will. Freedom is the essence of Karma. It gives opportunities for growth and evolution. The doctrine of Karma affords a most rational and scientific explanation of what is called fate . . . Determinism is the doctrine that all things, including the will, are determined (limited) by causes. This is the converse of free will . . . man has power to choose between the alternatives which fate brings before him. In choosing between these he may either follow his

> tendencies produced by his past actions or struggle against them. The will of a man is always free.[42]

Therefore, to attain "Self-realization" one must act according to one's free will and according to theories of action that Sivananda establishes in his commentary on chapters three and eighteen. The individual who attains "Self-realization" gains release (*mokṣa*) from the wheel of birth and rebirth (*saṃsāra*) and hence from the bonds of karma and the controlling activities of the *guṇas.* All human beings, as individuals, from the yogi on down to the cannibal possess radical free will and the ability to change or at least better their situations, without, however, altering their *dharma.*

MOKṢA AND YOGIC THEORY

The very words "Self realization" reflect an advaitin interpretation of *mokṣa* (release), despite the fact that Sivananda uses Vishishtadvaita Vedanta categories to reinterpret Sankhya philosophy. Sivananda takes *mokṣa* to mean realization (*jñāna*) of the Absolute Oneness of the Self (Atman/Brahman) and not union of the individual soul (*jīva*) with God (*Īśvara*). In his commentary on *Gita* 13.26 he says:

> On account of lack of discrimination of their real nature, the attributes of the Self are transferred to the body and vice versa. The insentient body is mistaken for the sentient Self. The activities of the body or Nature are transferred to the silent, actionless Self. This sort of illusion or superimposition will disappear when one attains knowledge of the Self, when he knows the distinction between the field and its knower, when he is able to separate the field from the knower like the reed from the munja grass, when he realises that Brahman which is free from all limiting adjuncts is his own immortal Self, and that the field is a mere appearance like the snake in the rope, silver in the mother-of-pearl, an imaginary city in the sky . . . the sage who has the knowledge of the Self is not born again.[43]

Yet, Sivananda does not accept the more radical position of the Advaitin tradition that denies all duality and hence the reality of the phenomenal world of multiplicity. A few lines later Sivananda states:

> But the sage has knowledge of the Self or true knowledge and so he beholds the one Self in all beings . . . Knowledge

> of the Self leads to liberation or salvation. Knowledge of the Absolute annihilates the ignorance in toto. If the ignorance is destroyed and false knowledge is also destroyed, all evils are simultaneously destroyed. Those who have realised that unity of the Self in all these diverse forms are never caught in the meshes of birth and death. They attain the state of Turiya (the fourth state beyond waking, dreaming, and deep sleep) where form and sound do not exist.[44]

It is clear from these passages that knowledge (*jñāna*) of the Self (Atman) or of the Absolute Oneness of all that exists brings about release (*mokṣa*), but we are again left with the question noted earlier that was posed by Ingalls: what is the reality or truth-value of *avidyā*? And, again, what happens to the *jīva* in release? And what is the purpose of detailing the *guṇa-karma* theory of rebirth if "the field is mere appearance like the snake in the rope . . ."? These questions, problems, and indeed, contradictions are of no importance to the sage, the *jīvanmukta,* the one-liberated-in-life. The *jīvanmukta* transcends the limitations and the bondage of the *guṇa-karma* theory; the *jīvanmukta* is free from rebirth and is identical with the Absolute, the Self. The *jīvanmukta,* is "the Ultimate Paradox"; he transcends the phenomenal world of multiplicity and yet lives and works within it. Sivananda writes of the *jīvanmukta* in his commentary upon *Gita* 13.2:

> But the sage who knows that the kshetrajna or the knower of the field or the Self is distinct from the body is not swayed by likes and dislikes. He identifies himself with the pure, eternal Absolute or the Supreme Self and is always happy and 'actionless' though he performs actions for the welfare of humanity.[45]

Or again at *Gita* 13.11:

> The liberated sage has constant awareness of the Self. He knows that knowledge of the Self alone is permanent and all other learning relating to this world is ignorance. He knows that the knowledge which leads to the realisation of the Self is the only truth. The fruit of this knowledge of the Self is deliverance from the round of births and deaths.[46]

And finally at *Gita* 13.25:

> He keeps a balanced mind in honour and dishonour. He is the same to friend and foe. He is not affected by the dual

> throng. He has risen above the gunas. He rests in his own essential nature as Existence-knowledge-bliss Absolute. He abides in his own Self. He is a gunatita (one who has transcended the qualities of Nature) who is not affected by the play of the qualities.[47]

The *jivanmukta* somehow lives at the level of *paravidyā,* but continues to act at the level of *aparavidyā* and, like his Buddhist counterpart, the Bodhisattva, compassionately helps others to attain *jñāna.* Sivananda's interest in philosophy, therefore, is similar to that of Shankara, about whom Ingalls writes:

> Samkara's approach to truth is psychological and religious. His interest in metaphysics and logic is always subordinated to the center of his attention.[48]

Sivananda is the skilled surgeon who treats each individual according to the severity of his/her ailment—or to put it in philosophical terminology—according to the darkness (*tamas*) of the individual's ignorance (*avidyā*). He therefore focuses on one philosophical position and then on another without attempting to solve the intellectual problems involved in such radical shifts. As Ingalls notes in regard to Shankara, such shifts of focus are "not philosophically exact, but pedagogically impressive."[49] The frustration caused by these radical shifts in philosophical position is a problem for the interpreter of Sivananda's thought, just as the problem of the reality or the truth-value of *avidyā* is a problem for the one who asks the question. Sivananda himself, as the *jīvanmukta,* has no patience with such problems and questions.

One last consideration remains: What are the theories of action by which the individual attains Self-realization? Volumes have been written about yogic theory and practice, and it is impossible to do justice to Sivananda's interpretation of the various yogas in a few pages. Therefore, I shall limit discussion to a few points in which Sivananda differs from many other interpreters of the *Bhagavadgita.* Since *jñāna* or knowledge of the Oneness of the Self brings about *mokṣa,* Sivananda holds *jñāna-yoga* to be the highest or the best yogic discipline. *Raja-yoga* (the discipline of meditation) and *karma-yoga* (the discipline of unattached action) are placed at lower levels. Thus, in his commentary upon *Gita* 13.24 Sivananda states:

> Sankhya yoga is jnana yoga. The aspirant does vicara (analysis, reflection) and separates himself from the three qualities

> of nature . . . Those who practise Sankhya Yoga are the highest class of spiritual aspirants. Those who practise the Yoga of meditation are aspirants of the middling class. Those who practise Karma alone are the lowest class of spiritual aspirants. The aspirants of the middling and lowest class soon become aspirants of the highest class through rigorous sadhana or spiritual practices.[50]

However, earlier in his commentary on *Gita* 3.3 Sivananda had argued that *karma-yoga* was "a means to an end"; that is, by following *karma-yoga* the individual, in time, realizes *jñāna,* the Oneness of all that exists. If this be the case, then *jñāna-yoga, raja-yoga* and *karma-yoga* are not ranked in a linear order, but rather *raja-yoga* and *karma-yoga* are parallel disciplines that lead to the realization of *jñāna.* Furthermore, Sivananda holds that *karma-yoga,* as expounded in the *Gita,* is the only teaching that fits the situation in which Arjuna found himself.

Sivananda sermonizes in one of his lectures entitled "Lessons from the Gita:"

> May it be that there was some meaning in His choosing the battle-field for the Gita-teachings? (Krishna) wanted to point out to us that wisdom should not recline on the armchair. If his wisdom did not accompany a man to the field of battle, it was no wisdom at all! Any man could talk philosophy after dinner; any man could discourse upon the most intricate points in the Yoga Sutras sitting comfortably near the fireplace. But that is no wisdom at all: it is lip-service to the Supreme Science of Knowledge of the Self. It is hypocrisy. These people generally fail when they face a trial, when their wisdom is put to the acid test of practical demonstration, when they find themselves in a crisis. Krishna's Panchajanya roars a big NO! No, No. That is not wisdom: real wisdom will serve you right in the battle-field, right in a crisis, and will enable you to surmount the obstacle, resist the temptation, arise victoriously from the trial. You will convert the trial into a great opportunity for revealing your genius. For, genius is often made by crisis.[51]

Karma-yoga is, therefore, the discipline to be followed by the man of action in whom *rajas guṇa* is dominant; *rāja yoga* is the discipline to be followed by the individual who has renounced all action, the Sannyasin, in whom *sattva guṇa* is dominate. (See his commentary on *Gita* 13.10).

Sivananda places *bhakti-yoga* below *rāja-yoga* and *karma-yoga* as a preparatory stage for higher stages of religious development. Although he is hardly consistent on this point, Sivananda concludes that *bhakti-yoga* does not lead directly to *jñāna*. This, of course, supports his ultimate orientation as an Advaita Vedantin, but what is equally interesting is that in his earlier work entitled *Bhakti Yoga* (1935) he cites only four references to the *Gita*. In chapter three of his commentary on the *Gita*, Sivananda expresses his attitude toward *bhakti-yoga:*

> An ignorant man says to himself, "I shall do this action and thereby enjoy its fruit." A wise man should not unsettle his belief. On the contrary he himself should set an example by performing his duties diligently but without attachment. The wise man should also persuade the ignorant never to neglect their duties. If need be, he should place before them in vivid colour the happiness they would enjoy here and hereafter by discharging such duties. When their hearts get purified in the course of time, the wise man could sow the seeds of Karma Yoga (selfless service without desire) in them.[52]

Sivananda's emphasis upon the free will of the individual to change his situation by self-effort is so strong that he places in a subordinate position any system, such as *bhakti-yoga,* which requires the aid of a higher power in attaining *mokṣa*. Indeed, from the standpoint of *paravidyā* or *jñāna,* God (*Īśvara*) is seen to be as much a fiction or an illusion as 'the snake in the rope.' The grace (*prasāda*) of God as a necessary prerequisite for *mokṣa* is, from this standpoint an equally illusory category; however, Sivananda adds: "a wise man should not unsettle . . . the ignorant." Sivananda, again, as the skilled surgeon, and like the *jīvanmukta* and the Bodhisattva, encourages devotional practices, worship of God, and, of course, performance of one's *dharma,* until such time as the individual gains the spiritual strength required to enter upon either the path of *rāja-yoga* or the path of *karma-yoga*. The *Bhagavadgita* is, for Sivananda, a manual for the *karma-yogi* who finds himself in a situation in which he must act; he must act, as Krishna argues throughout the *Gita,* without attachment to the results of his actions and without concern for the "pairs of opposites."

Karma-yoga, as the discipline of unattached action, has been a subject of commentary for almost every interpreter of the *Gita*. Sivananda, like Vivekananda and many other Neo-Vedantins, however, provides a more positive dynamic in his interpretation of *karma-yoga,* which becomes for him the discipline of selfless service; that is, all ego-attachment to the result of one's action is renounced or denied, exactly like the older or more traditional interpretation of *karma-yoga.* But once this is accomplished, service is to be rendered to all of humankind, because all humanity, and indeed, all creation is one. Arjuna, by engaging in a righteous (dharmic) war is selflessly fulfilling his *dharma* as a kshatriya on behalf of those whom he is enjoined to protect. Furthermore, for the neo-Vedantins the theory of *karma-yoga,* if taken away from the battlefield and applied to every aspect of daily life, becomes a way of life to be followed by all, regardless of one's *dharma.* Thus, Sivananda writes in *Practice of Karma Yoga:*

> Ignorant people say that one cannot work without any motive. It is a great pity that they have not understood the essence and truth of Karma Yoga . . . When the thought of doing good becomes part and parcel of a man's very being, he will not entertain any motive at all. He takes immense delight in serving others, in doing good to others . . . The Karma Yogi gets inner spiritual strength and power by performing motiveless and selfless actions . . . Look at the stupendous and magnanimous work turned out by Lord Buddha, Sri Sankara and other Karma Yogis of yore . . . they lived for doing service to others. They were examples of absolute self-abnegation.[53]

The old conception of *karma-yoga* is the discipline of unattached action related only to the individual who was engaged in performing action. The new concept of *karma-yoga* as the discipline of selfless-service directs the energies of the actor toward the good of all humanity and toward the welfare of others. This re-interpretation of *karma-yoga* is the core of neo-Vedantic ethics and is the theoretical basis for such welfare institutions as the Ramakrishna Mission and the Divine Life Society.[54] The neo-Vedantic re-interpretation of *karma-yoga* provides Sivananda and others with a way of translating neo-Vedantic thought into the practicality of the work-a-day world. And this is the importance of the living guru within Hindu society: he remains the exemplary model whose thought and action continue to guide and to affect the lives of millions within Indian society, just as "other Karma Yogis of yore."

Although Bharati says that "the sadhu, as itinerant or *āśram*-bound full-time religious specialist . . . is indeed at the helm of things" in the Hindu Renaissance,[55] he argues that the Indian interest in the *Bhagavadgita* is an excellent example of what he entitles "the pizza-effect"; like the pizza in Italy, the *Bhagavadgita* only became popular in India *after* it had received wide acclaim in the West. He states in defense of this position that:

> But the informed Hindu must contest the *Bhagavadgītā's* Renaissance status: it is not canonical like the Vedas or the Upanisads; it is *smṛti,* belonging to a category of texts the acceptance of which is not incumbent on the Hindu. The leaders of the Renaissance have blurred this distinction. Most modern Hindus, unless they happen to be Sanskritists, assume that the *Gītā* is a canonical text. Historically seen, the suzerain status ascribed to it is another paradigm of the pizza-effect.[56]

Bharati places too much emphasis upon the distinction between *śrūti* and *smṛti,* which are categories that Western interpreters of Hindu tradition hold to be exclusive of each other, but which Hindus have never held to be exclusive, at least as far as the *Gita* is concerned. Bharati also forgets to add that the *Bhagavadgita* has been, at least since the time of Shankara, one of the three principal sources for Vedantic philosophy—the other two sources being certain *Upanishads* and the *Brahma Sutras.* The *Gita,* was therefore central to Indian philosophical thought and debate centuries *before* the Hindu Renaissance. Gurus like Swami Sivananda, who trace their spiritual lineage back to Shankara are therefore characteristic of a tradition that began with the founder of their school. This is what makes the study of the life and writings of Swami Sivananda important; perhaps better known than many other gurus, he does not rank, in terms of originality of thought and in terms of the creation of a 'new' philosophical position with such intellectual giants as Swami Vivekananda and Sri Aurobindo. But, Sivananda is typical of thousands of other gurus whose writings and commentaries upon Vedantic texts have influenced the values and actions of millions of Hindus. Indeed, as Kushwant Singh has stated:

> The number of saintly men and women in India are beyond enumeration. Every district has its quota of living saints to whom people turn for advice on spiritual and worldly matters . . . And everyone will come for their darsan. Of the living saints the most famous is Anandamayee Ma. Prime Minister Indira Gandhi has visited her on many occasions.[57]

If we take this statement by India's leading journalist seriously, we must place, as does Bharati, the contemporary Guru at "the helm of things," as one of the most important agents of change in the process of modernization that is taking place in India. And, we must further acknowledge that one of the principal sources of the philosophical base of modern India is and will continue to be the *Bhagavadgita* as it is interpreted and re-interpreted by the contemporary guru.

CHAPTER TEN

Swami Bhaktivedanta and the Bhagavadgita *"As it Is"*

ROBERT D. BAIRD

The encounter between the scholar and the believer is always an interesting one. Frequently in historical studies, however, the believers whom one studies are gone and therefore unable to respond to scholarly analyses of their work and thought. Sometimes the tradition itself is dead and there are not even any followers with whom one must reckon. This is not true for the subject at hand, for the movement founded by Swami Bhaktivedanta is a thriving and self-conscious movement today. It will become clear that Swami Bhaktivedanta has some exceedingly uncomplimentary things to say about the world of scholarship and the academic interest in the *Bhagavadgita* in particular. The gulf between Swami Bhaktivedanta's presentation and that of the scholarly exegete is unbridgable, for their purposes operate on different levels.

One way to deal with the gulf is to seek to circumvent it by crossing at another point, as does Edward Dimock in his "Foreword" to Bhaktivedanta's commentary. Dimock sees Bhaktivedanta's interpretation as an authentic interpretation within the Gaudiya Vaishnava tradition. My task, however, in this context, is not merely to see Swami Bhaktivedanta as an authentic proponent of Vaishnavism, but to inquire how he interprets the *Gita.* And it must be assumed that this examination is to be done within the context of academic scholarship and not as part of a devotional commitment. This also assumes that there are two objects to be considered. The first is the *Gita* itself, and the second is Swami Bhaktivedanta's interpretation of it. While the devotee may be expected to merge the two, particularly when it is believed that the interpreter is in disciplic succession *(paramparā),* such an assumption is not permitted for the historian of religions. Hence, although from the standpoint of the devotee, the scholar's approach may lack integrity, the academic is bound by a scholarly integrity of his own.

The historian is interested in learning precisely what the text has to say. He wants to understand everything that might be implied in the words of the text without importing anything that is not actually there. Furthermore, he is interested in understanding the *ślokas* in their historical setting. Exoteric meaning is his only realm, for the esoteric tradition is closed to him. With this in mind we will turn to an examination of several passages and Swami Bhaktivedanta's interpretation of them. The passages are chosen to illustrate points or trends that are common in Swami Bhaktivedanta's handling of the *Gita*. Since Swami Bhaktivedanta's purports go well beyond the exoteric meaning of the texts to which they are attached, they indicate some of the themes that are emphasized in his thought.

Treatment of the Text

Promulgation of Krishna Consciousness.

Many scholars see some degree of progression within the *Bhagavadgita*. It is recognized that chapters one through six deal with unattached action and place little emphasis on the place of Krishna as supreme Lord of the universe. Chapters seven through twelve expound the supreme nature of Krishna, while chapters thirteen through eighteen return again to an emphasis on unattached action. While these are not mutually exclusive, they are clear emphases. Whether this difference in tone is to be explained as progressive teaching on the part of the author or as the result of the use of different source materials is a matter for discussion.[1] However, one of the striking features of Swami Bhaktivedanta's approach to the *Gita* is that he reads the complete teaching of the book, indeed of vedic literature generally, into any passage. There is no recognition given to the possibility of progressive teaching in the text. This is particularly striking in some of the early passages of the book.

In chapter two the *Gita* seems to be teaching that Arjuna will finally be unable to avoid action. Since action is inevitable, the key to liberation is action without attachment to the fruits. In 2.48 this is how yoga is defined. It is actions performed without attachment, indifferent to success or failure *(samatvaṃ yoga ucyate)*. Yoga, then, is defined as indifference or evenness of mind. This would seem to be confirmed in 3.3 where *jñānayoga* is identified with *saṅkhya* (not necessarily the classical system by that name—*jñāna yogena sāṅkhyānāṃ),* while the term yoga is identified with *karmayoga (karma yogena yoginām).* Already, Swami Bhaktivedanta takes *karmayoga* not merely as unattached action, but in the light of later passages in the *Gita,* as "devotional work."

This whole chapter which emphasizes unattached work as the means to liberation is infused with Krishna consciousness. The reference to Krishna as the object of meditation is taken as a reference to Krishna consciousness. R.C. Zaehner points out that in 2.61 we have the first instance in the *Gita* in which Krishna mentions himself. And, he points out that it is in connection with exercises that are essentially "Buddhistic and Sāṁkhya-Yoga" in nature. He continues:

> He is not at all offering Himself as an object of living devotion and veneration, but merely as a definite object on which to direct what is elsewhere called 'one-pointed' (*ekāgra,* cf. *Yoga-sutras* 3.11,12) concentration.[2]

Zaehner goes so far as to say that "Hence, at the end of this chapter which from now on describes the ascent of the self to full liberation, there is no further mention of Krishna as God: the goal is not God, but Nirvāna, the Buddha's goal."[3] Whether one wants to follow Zaehner in saying that the goal specified is the Buddha's goal, it certainly does not articulate a liberation in terms of Krishna consciousness. Yet in 2.61 where Krishna is the object of meditation, Swami Bhaktivedanta comments: "that the highest conception of *yoga* perfection is Kṛṣṇa consciousness is *clearly* [emphasis mine] explained in this verse."[4]

In 2.67 where the text merely states that the senses are roving and are capable of carrying away a person's mentality, Swami Bhaktivedanta comments that to avoid this, all the senses are to be "engaged in the service of the Lord" and that "all the senses must be engaged in Kṛṣṇa consciousness, for that is the correct technique for controlling the mind."[5] In 2.68 which says only that withdrawing the senses from the objects of sense stabilizes the mentality *(prajñā),* Swami Bhaktivedanta introduces not only Krishna consciousness, but also the need for a bona fide spiritual master. ". . . Only by Kṛṣṇa consciousness is one really established in intelligence and . . . one should practice this art under the guidance of a bona fide spiritual master. . . ."[6] In 2.70 the text (even by Swami Bhaktivedanta's translation) likens the person who is able to achieve peace to the ocean which has rivers emptying into it while remaining still. Swami Bhaktivedanta comments that this is true of the person

> . . . fixed in Kṛṣṇa consciousness. As long as one has the material body, the demands of the body for sense gratification will continue. The devotee, however, is not disturbed by such desires because of his fullness. A Kṛṣṇa conscious man is not in need of anything because the Lord fulfills all his material necessities.[7]

When 2.71 says that the man goes to peace who is free from self interest and egoism *(nirmamo nirahaṅkāraḥ sa śāntim adhigacchati),* Swami Bhaktivedanta comments: "To become desireless means not to desire anything for sense gratification. In other words, desire for becoming Kṛṣṇa conscious is actually desirelessness."[8] He then goes on to describe the Krishna conscious person as the eternal servitor of Krishna. There is certainly no explicit reference to Krishna in verses 62 through 71. Yet, when liberation is described as *brahma nirvāṇam* it is understood by Swami Bhaktivedanta as equivalent to Krishna consciousness and being elevated to the spiritual plane in devotional service to the Lord.[9]

It would appear, then, that Swami Bhaktivedanta reads the notion of Krishna consciousness into the second chapter where the text itself says much less. This tendency is found repeatedly in his interpretation of the *Gita.* It suggests that he considers it legitimate to interpret any verse in the light of the whole system found in the *Gita* whether it is explicitly mentioned in that verse of the *Gita* or not.

Inculcation of a Vaishnava Life Style.

Not only does Swami Bhaktivedanta seem to disavow any principle of progression in the *Gita,* but he also goes beyond specific texts and the *Gita* itself when he makes it the occasion for the inculcation of a Vaishnava life style. In several places Swami Bhaktivedanta credits Caitanya (1486–1534) with instituting the chanting of the *mahāmantra.* Yet in numerous places in his purports on specific verses, which never mention this practice of chanting, Swami Bhaktivedanta recommends it as the best way of achieving the goal of the text in the present age, *kali yuga.* In 4.39 the text says that one who has knowledge and has controlled the senses soon goes to the highest peace. Swami Bhaktivedanta says that such knowledge can be achieved by one who believes firmly in Krishna and that this faith is achieved by acting in Krishna consciousness and by chanting the *mahāmantra*.[10]

In 6.34 Arjuna calls attention to the fickle nature of the mind which is as difficult to restrain as the wind. In his purport, Swami Bhaktivedanta recommends chanting as the best method for restraining the mind. "The easiest way to control the mind, as suggested by Lord Caitanya, is chanting 'Hare Kṛṣṇa,' the great *mantra* for deliverance, in all humanity.'[11] In 6.35 it is admitted by Krishna that it is very difficult to control the mind, but it is said that it is possible through practice *(abhyāsena)* and detachment *(vairāgyeṇa)*. The text does not specify precisely what practice is, but Swami Bhaktivedanta does in some detail. It is the practice of Krishna consciousness and engaging in "nine types of devotional service to the Lord. The first and foremost of such devotional engagements is hearing about Kṛṣṇa."[12] This can purge the mind of all misgivings.

In 8.5 the text indicates that liberation to Krishna's estate is guaranteed for one who remembers Krishna alone at the time of death. However, Swami Bhaktivedanta reminds his readers that this is not possible for the "impure person" who has not practiced Krishna consciousness and devotional service. The way to be certain is to chant the *mahāmantra*.

> To remember Kṛṣṇa one should chant the *mahāmantra,* Hare Kṛṣṇa, Hare Kṛṣṇa, Kṛṣṇa Kṛṣṇa, Hare Hare/ Hare Rama, Hare Rama, Rama Rama, Hare Hare, incessantly, following in the footsteps of Lord Caitanya, being more tolerant than the tree, humbler than the grass and offering all respect to others without requiring respect in return. In such a way one will be able to depart from the body successfully remembering Kṛṣṇa and so attain the supreme goal.[13]

This same advice about the *mahāmantra* is repeated in the purports for verses 7 and 8 as a means of remembering Krishna even though the text itself says nothing about chanting. In 12.6–7, the text also indicates that one should work with the mind fixed on Krishna, the means to which Bhaktivedanta again sees as chanting the *mahāmantra*. He recommends that one engage in one's vocation and at the same time chant the *mahāmantra*.

In 16.1–3 he indicates, as does the text, that sacrifice is useful. He says that one should perform vedic sacrifices, but because of the tremendous expense it is not really possible. The best sacrifice that one can offer in this age is the *mahāmantra*. Nowhere is this stated or implied in the text. A similar imposition is clear in 6.11–12 since the text recommends one thing and Swami Bhaktivedanta cancels that and offers the *mahāmantra.* This text tells how one should select the best place for meditation and go to a sacred place. Swami Bhaktivedanta indicates that this is fine in India, but that in Western societies it is not possible. Therefore, the *Brihan-Naradiya Purana* says that in the *kali yuga* when people in general are short-lived, slow in spiritual realization and always disturbed by anxieties, the best means of spiritual realization is chanting the name of the Lord. "In this age of quarrel and hypocrisy the only means of deliverance is chanting the holy name of the Lord. There is no other way. There is no other way. There is no other way."[14] So, although nowhere in the text of the *Bhagavadgita* is there any explicit mention of chanting the *mahāmantra,* it is recommended repeatedly as the best method in this age, and indeed as the *only* means of adequately concentrating the mind on the Lord.

Swami Bhaktivedanta also takes a number of occasions to proclaim the teachings of ISKCON (International Society for Krishna Consciousness) of vegetarianism, of offering all food to Krishna, and of eating *prasādam.* In 6.16 the text warns of eating too much or too little or sleeping too much. It is a good text to show how Swami Bhaktivedanta is more interested in expounding the principles of Krishna consciousness than in merely explicating the text at hand. For, although the text also warns against those who do not eat at all, Bhaktivedanta does not comment on that. He does, however, expound on the Krishna consciousness principles of not eating too much and eating only foods offered to Krishna (not mentioned at all in the text), and not sleeping over six hours. He even indicates that eating animals is unnecessary and the result of one's being in the mode of ignorance. He uses 9.26 to enumerate some of the foods that are acceptable and unacceptable to Krishna. Since ISKCON members eat only food offered to Krishna *(prasādam)* it is also a list of acceptable food for them as well. Actually, 9.26 lists some of the physical things that are commonly offered to the image in *bhakti* worship. Swami Bhaktivedanta's translation is: "If one offers Me with love and devotion a leaf, a flower, fruit or water, I will accept it." The Krishna conscious person will avoid anything that the Lord does not ask for and will limit his offering to the things specified. Thus, Swami Bhaktivedanta concludes that "meat, fish and eggs should not be offered to Kṛṣṇa. If He desired such things as offerings, He would have said so."[15] He continues: "Vegetables, grains, fruits, milk and water are the proper foods for human beings and are prescribed by Lord Kṛṣṇa Himself. Whatever else we eat cannot be offered to Him, since He will not accept it."[16] It is clear, however, that the text mentions flowers which are generally not eaten and makes no mention of vegetables, grains or milk. Nevertheless, Swami Bhaktivedanta uses the text to teach the dietary principles of ISKCON. Leaves, flowers, fruit and water hardly exhaust even the ISKCON diet.

In 17.8–10 various foods are classified according to the three *guṇas*. The text speaks of sattvic foods as being fattening. Swami Bhaktivedanta takes this to mean not animal fat, and goes to great length to indicate that one can get all the animal fat that one needs through milk, which rules out the need for killing innocent animals. None of this is mentioned in the text. Moreover, the text indicates that food that is cooked more than three hours before it is eaten is tamasic food. Although this is all that the text says, Swami Bhaktivedanta notes parenthetically "except *prasādam,* food offered to the Lord."[17] He also notes that remnants of food can be eaten only if they were first offered to the Lord or eaten first by saintly persons. Food that is offered to the Lord is transcendental and therefore not obliged to be eaten within three hours. This is all in keeping with the principles of ISKCON, but is not part of the text. In the purport to 18.3 which reports a difference of opinion about the usefulness of sacrifices, Swami Bhaktivedanta concedes that animal sacrifice is recommended in the vedic literature, but that the animal is not actually killed! "The sacrifice is to give a new life to the animal. Sometimes the animal is given a new animal life after being killed in the sacrifice, and sometimes the animal is promoted immediately to the human form of life."[18]

Another important principle for ISKCON is the strict regulation of sexuality. Since 4.26 talks about offering up the senses in the fire of restraint, Swami Bhaktivedanta takes the opportunity to talk about how the *brahmacārī* does this through Krishna consciousness, and how the householder does this through regulation of the senses dealing with intoxication, meat eating, and sexuality according to Krishna consciousness principles. In the midst of a long list in which Krishna is seen as the best of all categories, he is in 7.11 the might of the mighty (free from desire and passion), and he is also desire in creatures (so far as it is not inconsistent with right). Swami Bhaktivedanta's purport on this verse is short, but it is the occasion for teaching the regulation of sex. "Similarly, sex life, according to religious principles *(dharma)*, should be for the propogation of children, not otherwise. The responsibility of parents is then to make their offspring Kṛṣṇa consciousness."[19] Since both *kāma* and *dharma* are in the text, he fills them with his content.

Articulation of a Theology of Krishna.

Swami Bhaktivedanta does not develop his theological themes in a systematic manner, but one can see in his purports the use of the text to present aspects of his theology of Krishna. An interesting passage is 4.6–8, since it shows how Swami Bhaktivedanta's theology is brought to bear on a text on which scholars have generally agreed. Here in verse 6 the text is translated by Edgerton, Deutsch, and Zaehner to indicate that though Krishna's *ātman* is eternal and unborn, by his own mysterious power *(māyā)*, he does take on *prakṛti*.[20] The next verse indicates that this happens when *dharma* languishes and *adharma* thrives. Swami Bhaktivedanta takes this to mean that although unborn, Krishna's transcendental body never deteriorates. *Prakṛti* is taken as transcendental form. This means that although Krishna appears he does not assume a new body as living entities do. When the Lord appears, he does so in the same original body, by his internal potency *(ātma-māyayā)*.

> In other words, Kṛṣṇa appears in this material world in His original external form, with two hands, holding a flute. He appears exactly in His eternal body, uncontaminated by this material world. Although He appears in the same transcendental body and is Lord of the universe, it still appears that He takes His birth like an ordinary living entity.[21]

However, Swami Bhaktivedanta comments, although the Lord grows from childhood to boyhood, he never goes beyond youth.

> At the time of the Battle of Kurukṣetra, He had many grandchildren at home; or, in other words, He had sufficiently aged by material calculations. Still He looked just like a young man twenty or twenty-five years old. We never see a picture of Kṛṣṇa in old age because He never grows old like us, although He is the oldest person in the whole creation—past, present, and future.[22]

In 4.7 it is stated that Krishna incarnates when *dharma* declines and *adharma* ascends. According to Bhaktivedanta, the principles of religion are laid down in the *Vedas* and any discrepancy in executing the rules of the *Vedas* makes one irreligious, i.e. adharmic. These principles are clearly indicated throughout the *Gita* and the highest principle at the end of the *Gita* is to surrender to Krishna only, nothing more. Swami Bhaktivedanta relies on the *Bhagavatam* and holds that Buddha was an incarnation oif Krishna. In Buddha's time, materialists were claiming the authority of the *Vedas* while participating in animal sacrifices contrary to vedic principles. So Buddha appeared to establish the vedic principle of nonviolence. Each *avatāra* has its own purpose, but no *avatāra* should be accepted as such unless it is specifically referred to in scriptures.

In 3.11 it would seem that the text is sketching the vedic view of sacrifice. The sacrifices are offered to the *devas*. For Swami Bhaktivedanta the *devas* are the demigods who are the administrators of material affairs under the supreme Lordship of Krishna. He goes into some detail to indicate how the demigods each have their realm of responsibility, but that they serve under Krishna and that even though some *yajñas* are for their benefit, it is ultimately Lord Krishna who is the beneficiary of the *yajñas*. Now the text explicitly says none of this. "Some of the *yajñas* are meant to satisfy particular demigods; but even in so doing, Lord Viṣṇu is worshipped in all *yajñas* as the chief beneficiary."[23]

Krishna Consciousness as the Fulfillment of Religion.

In addition to using texts of the *Gita* to teach Vaishnava life style and thought, Bhaktivedanta often seeks to show the superiority of the Vaishnava position and the error of other positions. Sometimes, he asserts, the positions are wrong, occasionally he holds those who hold them are ignorant or lacking intelligence, and if they do not recognize the ultimate reality of Krishna as the personal god, they are preliminary positions that are fulfilled in Krishna consciousness. The position that is attacked with the most regularity and vigor is that of Advaita Vedanta. Its advocates are called mayavadins, impersonalists, or monists.

In the path to spiritual realization there are three stages which are outlined. The first is an experience of the impersonal Brahman, the second is the experience of God as localized Supersoul, while the third is the experience of the Supreme Personality of Godhead. Apparently, the text does not need to refer to impersonalism for Swami Bhaktivedanta to clarify the error of impersonalism or the preliminary nature of its experience. In 7.19 the text indicates that after many rebirths the man of knowledge finally comes to Krishna. Swami Bhaktivedanta takes the occasion to point out that early in one's attempt to give up attachment to materialism there is an experience of impersonalism, but as one becomes more advanced spiritually he surrenders to Krishna.[24] In 18.53–54 one is described as *brahma-bhūtaḥ,* which Edgerton translates as "becoming Brahman." Swami Bhaktivedanta takes this as an impersonal experience that is merely the first stage.

> To the impersonalist, achieving the *brahma-bhūta* stage, becoming one with the Absolute, is the last word. But for the personalist, or pure devotee, one has to go still further to become engaged in pure devotional service. This means that one who is engaged in pure devotional service to the Supreme Lord is already in a state of liberation, called *brahma-bhūta,* oneness with the Absolute.[25]

There are passages which seem to support Swami Bhaktivedanta's interpretation but which make no mention of other views as being inferior. One of them would seem to be 13.23. Here Swami Bhaktivedanta takes the occasion to show that this text supports his view more than that of the monists, who take the knower of the body to be one and hence fail to distinguish between the individual soul and the Supersoul.

> The individual soul enjoys the activities of a particular field, but the Supersoul is present not as finite enjoyer nor as one taking part in bodily activities, but as the witness, overseer, permitter and supreme enjoyer. His name is *Paramātmā,* not *ātmā;* and He is transcendental. It is distinctly clear that the *ātmā* and *Paramātmā* are different.[26]

In the purport to 7.24, Swami Bhaktivedanta makes it clear that the impersonalists who think that they have experienced the final truth do not yet know the ultimate feature of the Absolute (which is personal). He is even harder on modern impersonalists who, unlike Shankara, do not recognize Krishna as the Supreme Personality of Godhead.

> Persons who are under the impression that the Absolute Truth is impersonal are described as *asuras,* which means one who does not know the ultimate feature of the Absolute Truth. In the *Śrīmad-Bhāgavatam* it is stated that supreme realization begins from the impersonal Brahman and then rises

> to the localized Supersoul—but the ultimate word in the Absolute Truth is the Personality of Godhead. Modern impersonalists are still less intelligent, for they do not even follow their great predecessor, Śaṅkarācārya, who has specifically stated that Kṛṣṇa is the Supreme Personality of Godhead.[27]

Swami Bhaktivedanta goes on to indicate that the truth cannot be realized through mental speculation, but that one can only come to know Krishna through devotion and that one should begin to practice it by chanting the *mahāmantra.* He continues; "Nondevotee impersonalists think that Kṛṣṇa has a body made of this material nature and that all His activities, His form and everything, are *māyā.* These impersonalists are known as Māyāvādī. They do know the ultimate truth."[28] Devotional service is not a temporary activity that is only preliminary to liberation. Actual devotional service continues after liberation, indeed, one can even say that in the best sense it does not begin until liberation.[29]

That it is difficult to achieve liberation through renunciation without yoga is indicated in 5.6. Swami Bhaktivedanta takes this occasion to show the inferiority of the mayavadin view. Studying *sāṅkhya* and *vedānta* and engaging in speculation, they do not place much stock in devotional service. But since their speculation becomes tedius, they sometimes revert to the *Bhagavatam,* although they do not properly understand it. They also have the tendency to fall from the path of realization and enter materialistic activities of a philanthropic and altruistic nature which are merely material entanglements.[30] "Therefore, the conclusion is that those who are engaged in Kṛṣṇa consciousness are better situated than the *sannyāsīs* engaged in simple Brahman speculation, although they too come to Kṛṣṇa consciousness, after many births."[31]

Swami Bhaktivedanta, then, does not deny that the mayavadins have a valid experience. The impersonal Brahman is real, but it is merely the "personal effulgence of Kṛṣṇa."[32] It is the personal god who is the cause of everything. All the incarnations are only expansions of the Lord as are the living entities which are part and parcel of the Supreme Lord. The mayavadins do not properly understand this truth. "The Māyāvādī philosophers wrongly think that Kṛṣṇa loses His own separate existence in His many expansions. This thought is material in nature."[33] *Māyā* does not teach that the distinctions that are made are unreal, but that living entities think that they are separate from Krishna.

> For want of sufficient knowledge in the absolute science, we are now covered with illusion, and therefore we think that we are separate from Kṛṣṇa. Although we are separated parts of Kṛṣṇa, we are nevertheless not different from Him. . . . The whole teaching of the *Gītā* is targeted toward this end: that a living being, as His eternal servitor, cannot be separated from Kṛṣṇa, and his sense of being an identity apart from Kṛṣṇa is called *māyā.*[34]

Since the liberation of the impersonalists is only partial, they stand the risk of returning again to this material world.[35] A text such as 4.11 does not have to mention the impersonalists to providẹ Swami Bhaktivedanta with an opportunity to criticize them. Krishna helps even them by absorbing them into his effulgence, but they "return to this material field to exhibit their dormant desires for activities."[36]

Not only is Advaita only fulfilled in the personal god, but in 6.46–47 Swami Bhaktivedanta sees *bhakti-yoga* as the fulfillment of all other yogas. Although the text indicates that of all yogis, the ones who revere Krishna with faith are the best, Bhaktivedanta makes use of this to teach that *bhakti-yoga* is best. "The culmination of all kinds of *yoga* practices lies in *bhakti-yoga.* All other *yogas* are but means to come to the point of *bhakti* in *bhakti-yoga. Yoga* actually means *bhakti-yoga;* all other *yogas* are progressions toward the destination of *bhakti-yoga.*"[37]

In 4.29 Swami Bhaktivedanta explains the purposes of *prānṇāyāma,* of inhalation and exhalation, and how its practice can prolong life by many years. However, the person who is Krishna conscious is seen as accomplishing all that this is intended to accomplish and more. Even the practice of reducing the intake of food is done automatically when the devotee limits his intake of food to *prasādam.* In the purport to 6.3, Swami points out that the practice of the eight-fold yoga is particularly difficult in the *kali yuga.* Also, early attempts at such practice are only fruitive activities and only near the end of such practice do disturbing mental activities cease. A Krishna conscious person is superior since from the very beginning he thinks only of Krishna. The purpose of yoga, then, is fulfilled in Krishna consciousness.

> Kṛṣṇa is realized in different degrees as Brahman, Paramātmā and the Supreme Personality of Godhead. Kṛṣṇa consciousness means, concisely, to be always engaged in the transcendental loving service of the Lord. But those who are attached to the impersonal Brahman or the localized Supersoul are also par-

> tially Kṛṣṇa conscious, because impersonal Brahman is the spiritual ray of Kṛṣṇa and Supersoul is the all-pervading partial expansion of Kṛṣṇa. Thus the impersonalist and the meditator are also indirectly Kṛṣṇa conscious. A directly Kṛṣṇa conscious person is the topmost transcendentalist because such a devotee knows what is meant by Brahman or Paramātmā. His knowledge of the Absolute Truth is perfect, whereas the impersonalist and the meditative *yogī* are imperfectly Kṛṣṇa conscious.[38]

THEORETICAL BACKGROUND FOR SWAMI BHAKTIVEDANTA'S APPROACH

If Swami Bhaktivedanta does not interpret the text of the *Gita* in the manner of modern scholars, and if we find in his purports discussions that go beyond the context of the text itself, we must ask if there are any principles at work which will explain why he takes this approach without any evidence of discomfort. There are a number of such principles which provide such an explanation, and to those we now turn.

The Nature and Extent of Vedic Literature.

The *Vedas* are eternal, are given by Krishna, and have the knowledge of Krishna as their end.[39] However, when Swami Bhaktivedanta speaks of the *Vedas* he means more than the four *Vedas;* vedic literature extends to include all of what is commonly taken as *śruti* as well as much of *smṛti.* For example, the vedic literature is seen as including the four *Vedas, Vedanta-sutras,* the *Upanishads* and *Puranas.* "In all Vedic literature, beginning from the four *Vedas, Vedānta-sūtra* and the *Upaniṣads* and *Purāṇas,* the glories of the Supreme Lord are celebrated."[40] "*Veda* refers to all kinds of Vedic literature, namely the four *Vedas (Ṛk, Yajus, Sāma* and *Atharva)* and the eighteen *Purāṇas* and Upaniṣads, and *Vedānta-sūtra.*"[41] Also included in vedic literature are the *Mahabharata* and certain other authorized texts in the Vaishnava tradition (e.g. *Caitanya-Caritamrita*). Krishna is the source of the whole corpus of vedic literature and is the final author of it all. Swami Bhaktivedanta indicates the relative purposes of the texts as follows:

> First, He divided the *Vedas* into four, then He explained them in the *Purāṇas,* and for less capable people He wrote the *Ma-*

hābhārata. In the *Mahābhārata* there is given the *Bhagavad-gītā.* Then all Vedic literature is summarized in the *Vedānta-sūtra,* and for future guidance He gave a natural commentation on the *Vedānta-sūtra,* called *Śrīmad-Bhāgavatam.*[42]

Of all the revealed scriptures, however, the *Bhagavadgita* is best.[43] The reason for this is that "it is the essence of all Vedic literature and . . . is spoken by the Supreme Personality of Godhead."[44] Furthermore, the only aim of the *Vedas* is to enable devotees to gain Krishna consciousness, to realize that they are part and parcel of the Lord, to go back to Godhead. That is not only true of the *Bhagavadgita* and *Bhagavata Purana* which are explicit in this regard. It is also true of the four *Vedas,* the *Upanishads,* and the *Vedanta-sutras.* "All the *Vedas,* therefore, aim only toward Kṛṣṇa. Whatever we want to know through the *Vedas* is but a progressive step to understand Kṛṣṇa."[45] Since the Lord in his incarnation as Vyasadeva is the author of the texts, it stands to reason that even the earliest ones will have the same message as the later ones. "The *Vedas* offer knowledge of the Supreme Personality of Godhead, Kṛṣṇa, and Kṛṣṇa in His incarnation as Vyāsadeva is the compiler of the *Vedānta-sūtra.* The commentation on the *Vedānta-sūtra* by Vyāsadeva in the *Śrīmad-Bhāgavatam* gives the real understanding of *Vedānta-sūtra.*"[46] Not only is the *Gita* the best for the reasons indicated above, but one can come to the goal of vedic literature by reading it alone. Furthermore, if one comes to Krishna consciousness and acts in Krishna consciousness, one also automatically fulfills all other vedic injunctions and sacrifices.

Use of Other Texts to Explain the Gita.

If the extent of vedic literature is as we have indicated, and if the end of it all is Krishna, then it could be expected that Swami Bhaktivedanta would quote from these other texts to indicate what the intention of the *Gita* is. This is in fact the case and some of the texts that Swami Bhaktivedanta quotes come before and some after the composition of the *Gita.* But these texts are used in such a way that they are not referred to merely to illuminate the text, but are quoted as though they have the same authority as the *Gita* itself. They are used in much the same way that later passages of the *Gita* are used to explain the meaning of earlier passages. The time line is erased in their use.

In 3.9 the Sanskrit is as follows:

yajñārthāt karmaṇo'nyatra
loko-'yaṁ karma-bandhanaḥ

This is rendered by Edgerton as: "Except action for the purpose of worship, this world is bound by actions." The point seems to be that karma or work is binding except when it is done as a sacrifice. Swami Bhaktivedanta, however, sees *yajña* as referring to Vishnu, and interprets the passage as follows: "*Yajña* means Lord Viṣṇu, or sacrificial performances. All sacrificial performances also are meant for the satisfaction of Lord Viṣṇu. The *Vedas* enjoin: *yajño vai viṣṇuḥ*. In other words, the same purpose is served whether one performs prescribed *yajñas* or directly serves Lord Viṣṇu."[47] Swami Bhaktivedanta then continues by saying that the *varnāśrama* institution was created for the purpose of serving Lord Vishnu. This is supported by a text in the *Vishnu Purana* (3.8.8). The conclusion is that "one has to work in Kṛṣṇa consciousness to satisfy Kṛṣṇa (or Viṣṇu); and while performing such activities one is in a liberaged stage."[48]

In the following verse (3.10), *Prajāpati*, the Lord of creatures, is taken as an equivalent of Vishnu by Swami Bhaktivedanta. The *yajñas* which he created are seen as sacrifices to Vishnu. The principle of the vedic hymns is to understand Krishna, and when it is found in *Bhagavatam* 2.4.20 that Lord Vishnu is described as *pati* in many ways, it becomes clear that *Prajāpati* is Vishnu. There are many yajñas which are prescribed for worship of Krishna in the vedic literature, but perhaps the best for the *kali yuga* is the *saṅkīrtana-yajña*. This is mentioned in the *Bhagavatam* and was introduced by Caitanya who was an incarnation of Lord Krishna.

> In this age of Kali, the *saṅkīrtana-yajña (the chanting of the names of God) is recommended by the Vedic scriptures, and this transcendental system was introduced by Lord Caitanya for the deliverance of all men in this age. Saṇkīrtana-yajña* and Kṛṣṇa consciousness go well together. Lord Kṛṣṇa in his devotional form (as Lord Caitanya) is mentioned in the *Śrī-mad-Bhāgavatam*. . . .[49]

In 3.22, Krishna tells Arjuna that although he is not bound to do anything in the three worlds, he acts anyway. Swami Bhaktivedanta quotes a lengthy passage from the *Shvetashvatara Upanishad* (6.7–8) to illuminate the nature of the one who so acts.

> The Supreme Lord is the controller of all other controllers, and He is the greatest of all the diverse planetary leaders. Everyone is under His control. All entities are delegated with

particular power only by the Supreme Lord; they are not supreme themselves. He is also worshipable by all demigods and is the supreme director of all directors. Therefore, He is transcendental to all kinds of material leaders and controllers and is worshipable by all. There is no one greater than Him, and He is the supreme cause of all causes.

He does not possess bodily form like that of an ordinary living entity. There is no difference between His body and His soul. He is absolute. All His senses are transcendental. Any one of His senses can perform the action of any other sense. Therefore, no one is greater than Him or equal to Him. His potencies are multifarious, and thus His deeds are automatically performed as a natural sequence.

In 4.8 the text indicates that Krishna incarnates himself to annihilate the evil doers and to protect the good *(sādhūnām)*. According to Swami Bhaktivedanta a *sādhu* or holy man is a man in Krishna consciousness. An evil doer *(duṣkṛtam)* refers to one who does not care for Krishna consciousness. He then quotes from the *Caitanya-Caritamrita* of Krishnadasa Kaviraja for amplification. He delineates the various kinds of *avatāras* according to Vaishnava theology, while emphasizing that Lord Krishna is the fountainhead of all *avatāras.* He then appeals to the *Srimad-Bhagavatam* for support for the view that the incarnation of the Lord in the *kali yuga* is Lord Caitanya. That Caitanya is an incarnation of Krishna is in earlier vedic texts even though it is not stated openly, but secretly.

> Lord Caitanya as the incarnation of Kṛṣṇa, the Personality of Godhead, is described secretly but not directly in the confidential parts of the revealed scriptures, such as the *Upaniṣads, Mahābhārata, Bhāgavatam,* etc. The devotees of Lord Kṛṣṇa are much attracted by the *saṅkīrtana* movement of Lord Caitanya. This *avatāra* of the Lord does not kill the miscreants but delivers them by the causeless mercy of the Lord.[50]

Sometimes the puranic stories are used to illustrate the point of the text as in 6.43. But for Swami Bhaktivedanta this is not mythology at all but literal history.

In 2.17 the text states that the soul is indestructable, and that it pervades the body. Swami Bhaktivedanta uses both the *Shvetashvatara Upanishad* (5.9) and the *Bhagavatam* (no reference given) to confirm that the soul is the size of one ten thousandth of the upper portion of the hair point. This is further confirmed by a quotation from the *Mundaka Upanishad* (3.1.9). The *Katha Upanishad* (1.2.20) is quoted to support the distinction between the soul and the Supersoul. The *Vedanta-sutras* are also referred to without any specific reference given. In all, a wide range of texts are used to serve as authorities for understanding the *Gita*. Swami Bhaktivedanta not only treats specific texts in a way that would be unusual among Western scholars, but he sees specific texts in the light of the *Vedas* in general.

The History of the Gita.

That Krishna first instructed Vivasvan who instructed Manu who in turn taught this teaching to Ikshvaku is found in 4.1. Swami Bhaktivedanta expands on this and thereby indicates his understanding of the history of the *Gita* itself. In this millenium the sun god is known as Vivasvan who is the origin of the planets within the solar system. The *Gita,* therefore, is not a speculative treatise but knowledge direct from the Supreme Personality of Godhead from remote time. How remote is indicated in Swami's interpretation of the following passage from the *Mahabharata* (*Santiparva* 348.51–52):

> In the beginning of the Tretā-yuga [millenium] this science of the relationship with the Supreme was delivered by Vivasvān to Manu. Manu, being the father of mankind, gave it to his son Mahārāja Ikṣvāku, the King of this earth planet and forefather of the Raghu dynasty in which Lord Rāmacandra appeared. Therefore, *Bhagavad-gītā* existed in the human society from the time of Mahārāja Ikṣvāku.[51]

Swami Bhaktivedanta comments:

> At the present moment we have just passed through five thousand years of the Kali-yuga, which lasts 432,000 years. Before this there was Dvāpara-yuga (800,000 years), and before that there was Tretā-yuga (1,200,000 years). Thus, some 2,005,000 years ago, Manu spoke the *Bhagavad-gītā* to his disciple and son Mahārāja Iksvāku, the King of this planet earth. The age of the current Manu is calculated to last some 305,300,000 years, of which 120,400,000 have passed. Accepting that before the birth of Manu, the *Gītā* was spoken by the Lord to His disciple, the sun-god Vivasvān, a rough estimate is that the *Gītā* was spoken at least 120,400,000 years ago; and in human society it has been extant for two million years.[52]

Five thousand years ago it was observed by Krishna that the disciplic succession was broken and that the purpose of the *Gita* was lost. So, he spoke it again to Arjuna to reestablish the disciplic succession. It is the *Gita* as understood in this disciplic succession that accounts for the title of Swami Bhaktivedanta's commentary. It is the *Gita* as it is from the hands of disciplic succession *(paramparā)* and not as the result of mental speculation or unaided academic interpretation.[53]

It should be noted that Arjuna is a devotee of the Lord, one of those devotees who is a constant companion of the Lord and was therefore incarnated whenever the Lord incarnated. This means that he was present when Krishna spoke the message of the *Gita* to the sun god Vivasvan. When Arjuna questions Krishna, then, it is not so much for himself as for those who do not believe in the Supreme Personality of Godhead.

> Arjuna is an accepted devotee of the Lord, so how could he not believe in Kṛṣṇa's words? The fact is that Arjuna is not inquiring for himself but for those who do not believe in the Supreme Personality of Godhead or for the demons who do not like the idea that Kṛṣṇa should be accepted as the Supreme Personality of Godhead; for them only Arjuna inquires on this point, as if he were himself not aware of the Personality of Godhead, or Kṛṣṇa.[54]

The Structure of the Gita.

It should not come as a surprise to learn that Swami Bhaktivedanta does not seem to be interested in giving a great deal of attention to the establishment of the overall structure of the text. It is true that often either at the beginning or end of a chapter he indicates what he considers the essential purport of the chapter, and sometimes refers to previous chapters as a point of reference. Nevertheless, at no point in the commentary, not even in the introduction, does he offer an outline of the book. This is understandable if one recognizes that for Swami Bhaktivedanta, "In every chapter of *Bhagavad-gītā,* Lord Kṛṣṇa stresses that devotional service unto the Supreme Personality of Godhead is the ultimate goal of life."[55] Structure shows a sense of progression, and while there is some development as Swami Bhaktivedanta sees it, the purpose of *Gītā* study is not to offer textual analysis but spiritual development.

Swami Bhaktivedanta, however, does see the *Gita* as broadly falling into three sections of six chapters each. But, while some commentators see devotion to Krishna as not prevalent in the first six chapters,

Swami Bhaktivedanta sees it everywhere. He characterizes the first six chapters of the *Gita,* then, as dealing with "the knower of the body, the living entity, *and* [emphasis mine] the position by which he can understand the Supreme Lord . . ."[56] In the middle six chapters (which Bhaktivedanta considers of prime importance), "the Supreme Personality of Godhead and the relationship between the individual soul and the Supersoul in regard to devotional service are described."[57] In the final six chapters, "how the living entity comes into contact with material nature, how he is delivered by the Supreme Lord through the different methods of fruitive activities, cultivation of knowledge, and the discharge of devotional service are explained."[58] It is clear from this that there are different emphases in the content of the *Gita* in each of the units, but that each unit in one way or another aims at Krishna consciousness.

There are places where Swami Bhaktivedanta singles out a certain section or a certain chapter as a high point. But given the frequency with which several texts are seen as the "essence" of the *Gita,* we quickly realize that it is not structure that is the object of concern. In the purport to 4.35, he comments: "The whole teaching of the *Gītā* is targeted toward this end: that a living being, as His eternal servitor, cannot be separated from Kṛṣṇa, and his sense of being an identity apart from Kṛṣṇa is called *māyā.*"[59]

Swami Bhaktivedanta starts his purport on 7.1 by saying that "In this Seventh Chapter of *Bhagavad-gītā,* the nature of Kṛṣṇa consciousness is fully described."[60] And, at the end of chapter eight he indicates that the middle chapters of the *Gita* are "the essence of the *Gītā.*"[61] But chapter nine begins with the comment that "This chapter of *Bhagavad-gītā* is called the king of education because it is the essence of all doctrines and philosophies explained before."[62] Yet in his purport to 14.1, Swami Bhaktivedanta sees Krishna further enlightening Arjuna, and says, "The knowledge explained in this chapter is proclaimed by the Supreme Lord to be superior to the knowledge given so far in other chapters."[63] And further, "Thus it is expected that one who understands this Fourteenth Chapter will attain perfection."[64]

Chapter 11, which contains the 'vision' of Krishna in his universal form, is sometimes seen as the high point of the *Gita.* But it is not so singled out by Swami Bhaktivedanta. Indeed, there is a sense in which it is less significant than many other chapters. The text indicates that Arjuna has heard of the nature of Krishna, but that now he desires "to see thy form as god" (Edgerton). Arjuna's request comes through even in Swami Bhaktivedanta's rendering: " I yet wish to see how you have entered into this cosmic manifestation."[65] Swami Bhaktivedanta, however, explains in his purport that Arjuna is not asking for himself, but to convince others in the future who might have some doubt.[66] Of course, Krishna knows this too. The explanation is as follows:

> Arjuna's asking the Lord's permission is also significant. since the Lord is the Supreme Personality of Godhead, He is present within Arjuna himself; therefore He knows the desire of Arjuna, and He can understand that Arjuna has no special desire to see Him in His universal form, for he is completely satisfied to see Him in His personal form of Kṛṣṇa. But He can understand also that Arjuna wants to see the universal form to convince others.[67]

Since this is the beginning of a new *paramparā* it is particularly important that this confirmation be made so that it will be less easy for imposters to pose as incarnations of the Lord. Furthermore, the true devotee is not concerned to see this universal form.[68] The purports on this chapter are frequently short, something that comes as an initial surprise until one understands the relative unimportance of the chapter. The form that is revealed in chapter eleven is on the material level; hence it is only temporary and not the highest knowledge. "This universal form is material and temporary, as the material world is temporary. But in the Vaikuṇṭha planets He has His transcendental form with four hands as Narāyana."[69] This also explains why the universal form "is not attractive for pure devotees, who are in love with the Lord in different transcendental relationships."[70] Actually those who think this form is wonderful are those who are "involved in elevating themselves by fruitive activities."[71]

It comes as a bit of a surprise, then, to find that 11.55 is "the essence of *Bhagavad-gītā*."[72] Again, this is not a comment on the structure of the *Gita*. Rather, it is its essence, just as are chapters six through eleven, and several other passages, indeed, wherever Krishna consciousness is clearly taught. Here at the end of chapter eleven, since the text teaches that if one is engaged in devotional service to Krishna and without attachment and "mental speculation," one will come to Krishna, it teaches the essence of the *Gita*.

Qualifications for Understanding the Gita.

As we have seen, for Bhaktivedanta the ultimate goal of vedic literature and of the *Gita* which is its essence, is to bring people back to the Supreme Personality of Godhead, to get them to surrender to the Lord, and thereby live in Krishna consciousness as part and parcel of the Lord. However, not everyone is equally qualified to interpret, to understand, or to teach the *Bhagavadgita.* Scholars in particular come under Swami Bhaktivedanta's condemnation because they are merely "mental speculators." They are also called "mundane wranglers" (4.1), "insignificant" (4.1), "demonic persons" (4.2), "foolish and ignorant" (9.11), and persons who are engaged in "foolish speculation" (10.2), and "speculative reasoning" (13.26). Since these scholars are not surrendered to Krishna, they are not Krishna conscious; they are merely offering their own ideas rather than the truth within the *paramparā* system.

> The next class of *duṣkṛtina* is called *māyayapāhṛta-jñāna,* or those persons whose erudite knowledge has been nullified by the influence of material illusory energy. They are mostly very learned fellows—great philosophers, poets, literati, scientists, etc.—but the illusory energy misguides them, and therefore they disobey the Supreme Lord.
>
> There are a great number of *māyayapāhrta-jñāna* at the present moment, even amongst the scholars of the *Gītā.*[73]

There are numerous statements in the *Gita* which indicate that Krishna is the Supreme Personality of Godhead, but these scholars deride the Supreme Lord by considering him as simply another human being. The result is that their work on the *Gita* is not only not illuminating, but a distinct barrier in the path of spiritual understanding.

> All the unauthorized interpretations of the *Gītā* by the class of *māyayapāhṛta-jñāna,* outside the purview of the *paramparā* system, are so many stumbling blocks in the path of spiritual understanding. The deluded interpreters do not surrender unto the lotus feet of Śrī Kṛṣṇa, nor do they teach others to follow this principle.[74]

Ordinary knowledge like that offered in the university is on the level of matter and is not that to which the *Gita* aspires.[75] Hence it is unlikely that one will find a true understanding of the *Gita* there. Such are not simply passing remarks, but are repeated with such frequency that one must see them as a major concern on the part of Swami Bhaktivedanta. Even in texts where one would be hard pressed to draw the inference (6.8), the purport rails against "mundane scholarship" and "mere academic knowledge."[76] The Krishna conscious person is above all of this. "He is transcendental because he has nothing to do with mundane scholarship. For him mundane scholarship and mental speculation, which may be as good as gold to others, are of no greater value than pebbles or stones."[77]

There would seem to be two qualifications if one is to understand the *Bhagavadgita* "as it is." The first qualification resides with the teacher while the second resides with the disciple. First, then, is to be taught the meaning of the *Gita* by one who is in disciplic succession *(paramparā).* Any teaching other than this is mental speculation and not the *Bhagavadgita* "as it is." This is very important, for Krishna took the trouble to reestablish this succession some 5000 years ago when it was clear that it had been broken. "If we want to understand *Bhagavad-Gītā,* we should accept the statements in these two verses [10.12–13]. This is called the *paramparā* system, acceptance of the disciplic succession. Unless one is in the disciplic succession, he cannot understand *Bhagavad-gītā.*"[78] On the part of the disciple, the essential requirement is submission to a bona fide spiritual master. The *Gita*'s teachings should also be heard in the company of other devotees. A striking quality of Swami Bhaktivedanta's treatment of the *Gita* is now understandable. He points out the errors of other positions, and makes it clear that those who do not hold to his position are in error. But he seldom engages in the kind of argumentation that scholars are accustomed to when deciding between alternative interpretations. Most commonly he merely announces what is correct. For if he were using "mundane scholarship" he would have to present arguments, but a spiritual master within disciplic succession merely declares. If the hearer surrenders and accepts, he will ultimately achieve liberation. If he does not, he will sink lower and lower into material bondage and degradation. Not only, then, can one in disciplic succession properly interpret the *Gita,* but only a devotee can understand it.[79] Others are like bees licking on a bottle of honey!

Conclusion

ROBERT N. MINOR

Because the modern Indian thinkers studied in this volume believed that the message of the *Gita* transcended its historical circumstances, their approach to the text included methods which differ from those Orientalists who seek to place the text in its historical context. Each thinker sought the true meaning, not merely its meaning in the circumstances of its authorship as determined by scholarly study. Their personal twentieth century experiences of what they were convinced was true called for other methods. They did not believe, however, that they were relativists, that what they understood as the true meaning of the text was merely a twentieth century interpretation. They believed they had found meanings which also transcended their own circumstances, and that, since these were essential meanings of the *Gita*, that the *Gita* too transcended its circumstances.

The allegorical method which the Theosophists believed brought correct understanding of the *Gita*, as a battle between the higher and lower elements of a reality in spiritual evolution, of the human monad versus its lower passions, explained for them the inner meaning of the battle narrated in the text. Arjuna has dropped his bow, refusing to fight in a battle which threatens both branches of his family. Arrayed against him are relatives and gurus. In chapter two Krishna encourages him to fight, arguing that even if he destroys their bodies, he can never touch their immortal souls. Thus, without concern for the outcome, or for the killing itself, Arjuna is advised to perform his duty as a *kṣatriya* and fight in a battle that is pictured as a world war. Most of these interpreters use the allegorical method to interpret the battle, thereby preserving the *Gita* as a document that teaches *ahiṃsā*. For these thinkers *ahiṃsā* is a positive spirit of loving aid to all creatures, not merely "non-injury."

The allegorical method, however, is not used throughout the *Gita*. When in chapter two its discussion turns to matters of metaphysics or the mental attitude with which Arjuna is to fight, allegory is put aside without comment. Except for Theosophical understandings, the allegorical method is limited to interpretation of the battle.

Tilak's and Bhaktivedanta's works are exceptions to this allegorical interpretation of the battle. Besides being a religious text, for Bhaktivedanta the battle is an historical event. It is not mere mythology, for it took place in space and time, albeit 5,000 years ago. Tilak, Stevenson notes, took the battle literally and believed that the *Gita* raised the true karmayogin above the limitations of conventional morality and the law. Evil in the end may have to be repaid with evil, and killing can be without blame for the one who kills if it is accompanied by non-attachment to the results.

This attitude inspired a number of terrorists in the Nationalist cause. For example, another Chitpavan Brahmin named Damodar Hari Chapekar, who was touched by Tilak's appreciation of the Maratha Empire, took the *Gita* with him when he and his brother murdered a British official named Rand for insults they believed the British had heaped upon Poona during a plague. While awaiting trial in 1897, Chapekar dictated an autobiography in which he noted that "we had no ill-feeling against Mr. Rand." Instead, they clearly admired his character.[1] Another who took the *Gita*'s battle literally and used it so was V.D. Savarkar, a Mahrattha Brahmin and President of the Hindu Mahasabha from 1937–43. As a Hindu nationalist, he wrote to those who would fight for Mother India, that they should do so: ". . . with Shree Krishna for Thy redoubtable Charioteer, and Shree Ram to lead, and thirty crores of soldiers to fight under thy banner."[2] By the beginning of the twentieth century British authorities identified people in possession of more than one copy of the *Gita* as revolutionaries.

Although historians of religion like the authors of these essays are sympathetic with, though not advocates of, the methods of these interpreters, they approach the *Gita* on the basis of historical and public evidence and, therefore often interpret the actual text in a different manner. The difference, the modern interpreters often claim, is their own access to an esoteric interpretation historians do not consider relevant. These modern thinkers believe that in a variety of ways they are in touch with Truth or truths which provide an esoteric understanding of the text, an understanding which by definition is 'truer' than that discovered by the Orientalist historian. Neufeldt argues that Theosophy, with its occult ties from the time of H.P. Blavatsky, had a truth which functioned as a controlling orthodoxy in its interpretation of the *Gita*, at least implicitly. Though Tilak's interpretation, as Stevenson points out, is a combination of traditional interpretations and modern scholarship, Tilak entitled his result *Gita Rahasya*, "the Esoteric Import of the *Gita*." For Gandhi, as Jordens notes, the esoteric interpretation was based upon one's living the *Gita* in one's own life, so that the philosophy based upon his own experiences, which he confidently believed were "experiments with Truth," provided the correct interpretation. For Bhave, Wilson writes, the real meaning of the *Gita* is not always evident to the average reader. It may even involve the alteration of the text itself. Aurobindo brings his experiences of higher levels of consciousness to the *Gita* and, thus, claims experiences of Truth which ultimately leave the *Gita* behind, while Bhaktivedanta, as Baird points out, claims the insights of correct disciplic succession as opposed to "mundane scholarship." As a guru himself, Shivananda also claims an authentic line of succession, and his own self-realization within that spiritual inheritance, Miller suggests, is the apparent basis for his interpretations. Though Vivekananda and Radhakrishnan are less interested in esoteric interpretations, Radhakrishnan speaks of the "eternal truths" of the *Gita* which need recognition apart from its historical teachings, and these, he believes, are based upon an essential religious experience found in all traditions, but best expressed by *tat tvam asi*, "you are That," or Atman is Brahman. Only Bankim, whose goal was to be a model of Western argument and logic, did not seem to claim a special knowledge for interpreting the *Gita*. Limiting knowledge to such categories would in itself need justification in the midst of the claims of the other interpreters, unless one were not taking a normative stance toward the text.

In each case, whether the claim to esoteric knowledge is made directly or not, most of the interpreters do not limit the tools of their interpretations as historians do. There is an esoteric interpretation which comes closer to what each believes is true, and though it is potentially open to all, those who refuse to follow the recommended path miss what these interpreters believe are the keys to the *Gita*.

Many modern and contemporary Indian interpreters including those studied in this volume, with Bhaktivedanta, Aurobindo, and possibly Bankim as exceptions, take the text as in some essential manner a treatise close to Advaita Vedanta, or non-dualism, what Bhaktivedanta calls "impersonalism." It was Advaita Vedanta which had most impressed Western philosophers about Indian thought due to similarities they saw with Kantian philosophy. This provided a contrast to the usual Western criticism of India. The Kantian and neo-Hegelian milieu of these interpreters established the basis for a more positive acceptance of Indian versions of idealism and, of Advaita Vedanta. Neo-advaitin interpretations appear dominant and the apparent non-Advaitin elements in the *Gita* are in a few cases credited to the fact that the *Gita* is a "religious poem" (Gandhi) or "a popular religious text" (Radhakrishnan).

But what is essential to the text is often determined by the identification of what has traditionally been called the *mahāvākya* or "great utterance" of the text. This traditional principle of interpretation provides the "law" which for many is behind what has been called a "lawless individualism" in Indian textual interpretation. Thus, as Jordens notes, Gandhi finds the "great utterance" in the last twenty verses of chapter two, as does his disciple Bhave. Aurobindo uses 15.16–17 as his *mahāvākya*, and Radhakrishnan in *Indian Philosophy* emphasizes 2.16 as the basis for the *Gita*'s metaphysics. For Tilak, however, the key is a principle, *karmayoga,* not a verse, and Bhaktivedanta in a similar manner uses the principle of Krishna-consciousness to understand the *Gita*'s purport. Vivekananda emphasizes the reconciliation of all paths to the Divine and *karmayoga,* as French points out, using verses such as 4.11 and 6.5, but no one particular text. Had Bankim's commentary proceeded beyond *Gita* 4.19, he too might have preferred a *mahāvākya,* but his interest in Western and logical interpretations may have been best fulfilled by the early chapters, which enabled him to discuss ethics without delving too deeply into the more metaphysical passages. For him Krishna was "the ideal man," not the Lord of the Universe of which later chapters speak.

Strikingly absent from these interpretations with Bhaktivedanta again the exception, is the centrality of *bhakti* that moves the *Gita* from its discussions of non-attached action to Arjuna's experience of the universal Krishna in chapter eleven, which Zaehner calls "the climax of the Gita.[3] Even Bhaktivedanta, as Baird notes, shows little interest in chapter eleven. For the others, however, advaitin interpretations have taken priority, and, thus, devotion to a personal divine being is less valuable than action, intuitive knowledge of the Atman, and the experience of the Unity behind all duality. One expects less emphasis on devotion to Krishna among these thinkers, and interpretations of the idea of *avatāra* or "descent" of the god to restore *dharma* suit their advaitin understanding much better than they do those of theistic thinkers.

It should be kept in mind that of all the phenomena of Indian religions, the devotional elements often received the greatest condemnation from Western critics in India who confronted these thinkers in their formative years. Many of their criticisms of Indian religions were repeated by other Indian reform movements such as the Brahmo Samaj and the Aıya Samaj, and descriptions of polytheism, devotional excesses, animal sacrifices, and idolotry, whether used appropriately or not by the Western critics and the Indian reformers, resonated in the minds of most of these thinkers. They took them seriously as criticisms and defended 'Hinduism' against these charges as though they were charges of deficiency or ignobility. They usually did so by denying that these elements were essential to "Hinduism" as each defined it. With the *Gita* understood as essential to the tradition they affirmed, *bhakti* was interpreted as service of all humanity by those like Bhave, relegated to a path for those of a less intellectual temperament as Vivekananda and Radhakrishnan do, considered a preliminary to *karma-yoga* as Tilak does, reinterpreted by those like Bankim as worship merely of an ideal, or simply deemphasized or ignored in the manner of Gandhi. Except for Bhaktivedanta, then, no matter how crucial devotion might be to the *Gita* in the eyes of some interpreters and historians, for the majority of figures discussed in this volume, it ranges from less significant to unimportant.

The understandings represented in this volume at times vary widely from what the original author or authors of the *Gita* may have meant to say; indeed, this variance might not bother the thinkers studied here at all. More than likely, however, they would regard any perception of variance by the authors of these essays as evidence that they do not understand the *real Gita*. The authors of these essays are from departments of religious studies who are interested in studying religion *as* religion, as the study of the ultimate concerns of human beings. They are suspicious of any possibility of reductionism that may reduce the religious person's understanding to other categories. As the essays of historians of religions, not theologians, philosophers or religious thinkers, they, therefore, claim historical verifiability. On that basis, studies of the *Gita* in its own historical context produce claims that diverge from those of many of these modern thinkers. Still, one can hear almost all of the thinkers here studied say something like Swami Tapasyananda: "A researcher, because he has no sense of a purport, of an appreciation of a profound meaningfulness functioning through all the meandering movements of thought and obscurities of archaic symbolisms, creates only a learned confusion in regard to the totality of the teaching, while shedding much light on particular parts and ideas, as in the interpretation of the words of a sentence."[4]

In any case from an historical standpoint, the interpreters studied in this volume differ at times considerably from the author of the *Gita*, even to the extent of affirming another *Weltanschauung* altogether. And to these historians of religions, that difference is accounted for by a number of factors: political, societal and educational, as well as religious. Religious change, for whatever reasons, is to be observed in modern India, and that entails changes in the understanding of a sacred text. That inspite of these changes, or because of them, the text remains central to these interpreters, indicates their desire to remain within their scriptural traditions as each one sees them. But that may mean that the text must be stretched quite far in order for these interpreters to affirm the truth of worldviews which are at least chronologically a part of the changes and concerns of the modern period, and still affirm that those worldviews are somehow to be found in a two thousand year old religious classic like the *Bhagavadgita*.

Conclusion

[illegible] confusion in regard to the totality of the teaching, while shedding much light on particular parts and verses, as in the interpretation of the words of a sentence.

[illegible] historical standpoint, the interpreters studied in this volume differ at times considerably from the author of the [illegible] even to the extent of offering another [illegible] altogether. And to these historians of religions, this difference is [illegible] by a number of factors [illegible] social and [illegible] questions. [illegible] Kṛṣṇa's change, for whatever reasons, is to be [illegible] in modern India and that entails changes in the understanding of [illegible] of these changes [illegible] of them, the text remains central to these interpreters in all their desire to [illegible] their scriptural tradition [illegible] them. [illegible] that the text must be stretched quite far in order for these interpreters to [illegible] the [illegible] views which are at least [illegible] a part of the changes and concerns of the modern period, and still affirm that these worldviews are [illegible] to be found in [illegible] religious classic, the Bhagavadgītā.

Notes

Introduction

1. Norvin Hein, "Hindu Formulas for the Facilitation of Change" in *Traditions in Contact and Change: Selected Proceedings of the XIVth Congress of the International Association for the History of Religions,* ed. by Peter Slater and Donald Wiebe (Waterloo: Wilfred Laurier University Press, 1983), 39–52.

2. For discussions of matters of date and the relationship of the *Gita* to the *Mahabharata,* see J. A. B. van Buitenen, *The Bhagavadgītā in the Mahābhārata* (Chicago: University of Chicago Press, 1981), 1–6, and Robert N. Minor, *Bhagavad-gītā:An Exegetical Commentary* (Columbia, Mo: South Asia Books, 1982), xxi–1. For surveys of the commentarial traditions on the *Gita* see Surendranath Dasgupta, *A History of Indian Philosophy* (Cambridge: University Press, 1932), II, 430–43; or Minor, xv–xxi.

3. For one scholar who questions the idea that it was characteristic of Vedantins to feel obligated to comment on the *prasthāna-traya,* see Daya Krishna, "Vedanta—Does it Really Mean Anything?" *Conspectus* II, No. 2 (1966), 20–8.

4. Robert N. Minor, "The *Gītā*'s Way as the Only Way," *Philosophy East and West,* XXX, No. 3 (July, 1980), 339–54.

5. Ursula King, "The Iconography of the Bhagavad Gītā," *Journal of Dharma* VII, No. 2 (April-June, 1982), 150.

6. Rai Bahadur Lala Baijnath, *The Bhagavadgita in Modern Life* (Meerut: Vaishya Hitkari, 1908), 50.

7. Ralph L. Rusk, ed. *The Letters of Ralph Waldo Emerson* (New York: Columbia University Press, 1939), III, 290. On early Western interpretations of the *Gita* see Eric J. Sharpe, "Some Western Interpretations of the Bhagavad Gita, 1785–1885," *The Journal of Studies in the Bhagavadgita* I (1981), 1–28; and Eric J. Sharpe, *The Universal Gita: Western Images of the Bhagavad Gita, a Bicentennial Survey* (New York: Open Court, 1985). The *Gita* was also used to support nationalistic causes in the West. For an example of its use in 1934 to support German nationalism see Sharpe, *Universal Gita,* 129.

8. *An Autobiography: The Story of My Experiments With Truth* (Boston: Beacon Press, 1957), 33.

CHAPTER ONE

*I am indebted to Mr. Ted Davy, the Secretary of the Canadian Theosophical Society for his careful reading of the text, his criticisms, and his suggestions for revisions.

1. Eric J. Sharpe, "Early Theosophists and the Interpretation of the Bhagavad Gītā," *Theosophy in Australia,* September, 1979. See pp. 51–52 for a list of references.

2. *Ibid.,* 52.

3. William Q. Judge, *Bhagavad Gītā Recension Combined with Essays on the Gita* (Pasadena: Theosophical University Press, 1969), "Foreward" by James A. Long.

4. Sharpe, "Early Theosophists," 52.

5. Subba Row, *The Philosophy of the Bhagavad Gītā* (Madras; Theosophical Publishing House, 1921), 2, 41–42.

6. *Ibid.,* 3–4.

7. *Ibid.,* 126–27.

8. *Ibid.,* 5–7.

9. *Ibid.,* 8–17.

10. *Ibid.,* 18, 27.

11. *Ibid.,* 33–35.

12. *Ibid.,* 42–43.

13. *Ibid.,* 46, 60–61.

14. *Ibid.,* 99.

15. *Ibid.,* 69, 78.

16. *Ibid.,* 74–76.

17. *Ibid.,* 122–25.

18. Sharpe, "Early Theosophists," 54.

19. Mohini M. Chatterji, *The Bhagavad Gītā or The Lord's Lay* (New York: Julian Press Inc., 1960), 4–5.

20. *Ibid.,* 6.

21. *Ibid.,* 21–23.

22. *Ibid.,* 26.

23. *Ibid.,* 37.

24. *Ibid.,* 37–38.

25. *Ibid.,* 30.

26. *Ibid.,* 50.

27. *Ibid.,* 80–81.

28. *Ibid.,* 47.

29. *Ibid.,* 63–64.

30. *Ibid.,* 96.

31. A. Brahmin, F. T. S. *Thoughts on the Bhagavad Gītā. A Series of Twelve Lectures Read Before the Branch Theosophical Society Kumbhakonam* (Kumbhakonam: Kumbhakonam Branch Theosophical Society, 1893), I, 2–3.

32. *Ibid.,* 3.

33. *Ibid.,* 7–8.

34. *Ibid.,* 8–9.

35. *Ibid.,* 29–30.

36. *Ibid.,* 8.
37. *Ibid.,* 16.
38. *Ibid.,* 8.
39. *Ibid.,* 112.
40. *Ibid.,* 117.
41. *Ibid.*
42. *Ibid.,* 119.
43. *Ibid.,* 26.
44. *Ibid.,* 41, 91.
45. *Ibid.,* 59–62.
46. Traditionally The Dreamer was identified as Upendranath Basu. According to a note in *The Canadian Theosophist,* XL, No. 4 (Sept-Oct. 1959), p. 81, the traditional identification is wrong.
47. The Dreamer. *Studies in the Bhagavad Gītā. The Yoga of Discrimination.* (London: Theosophical Publishing Society, 1902), 6.
48. *Ibid.,* 7.
49. *Ibid.,* 15–16.
50. *Ibid.,* 12.
51. *Ibid.,* 18.
52. *Ibid.,* 25–27.
53. *Ibid.,* 29–30.
54. *Ibid.,* 54–57.
55. *Ibid.,* 111.
56. The Dreamer, *Studies in the Bhagavad Gītā. The Path of Initiation* (London: The Theosophical Publishing Society, 1904), 124.
57. *Ibid.,* 126.
58. Pandit Bhavani Shankar, *The Doctrine of the Bhagavad Gītā* (Bombay: Popular Prakashan, 1966), 4.
59. *Ibid.,* 14–25.
60. *Ibid.,* 64.
61. *Ibid.,* 28.
62. *Ibid.,* 53, 56.
63. William Q. Judge, *Bhagavad Gītā, Recension Combined with Essays on the Gita* (Pasadena: Theosophical University Press, 1969), 108.
64. *Ibid.,* 110–11.
65. *Ibid.,* 112–14. The most obvious words would be *dharma* and *kurukṣetra;* references would have to do with the "bright and dark sides of the moon" and the "eating of ambrosia."
66. *Ibid.,* v–vi, 115–17.
67. *Ibid.,* vi.
68. *Ibid.,* vii.
69. *Ibid.,* 118–19.
70. *Ibid.,* ix.
71. *Ibid.,* 124.
72. *Ibid.,* 133.
73. *Ibid.,* 146.
74. *Ibid.,* 152.
75. *Ibid.,* 157.

76. *Ibid.,* 175.
77. *Ibid.,* 191.
78. Annie Besant, *Hints on the Study of the Bhagavad Gītā* (London and Benares: Theosophical Publishing Society, 1908), 2.
79. *Ibid.,* 1.
80. *Ibid.,* 5.
81. *Ibid.,* 6–7.
82. *Ibid.,* 9–10.
83. *Ibid.,* 11.
84. *Ibid.,* 11–15.
85. *Ibid.,* 26–27.
86. *Ibid.,* 28–30.
87. *Ibid.,* 38–39, 42.
88. *Ibid.,* 44.
89. *Ibid.,* 48–49.
90. *Ibid.,* 51.
91. *Ibid.,* 53.
92. *Ibid.,* 82–83.
93. *Ibid.,* 128–29.
94. Charles Johnston, *Bhagavad Gītā, The Songs of the Master* (London: John M. Watkins, 1965), 7.
95. *Ibid.,* 9–10.
96. *Ibid.,* 12–15.
97. *Ibid.,* 10.
98. *Ibid.,* 20.
99. *Ibid.,* 21.
100. *Ibid.,* 22.
101. *Ibid.,* 29.
102. *Ibid.,* 16–17.
103. *Ibid.,* 75.
104. *Ibid.,* 86–87.
105. *Ibid.,* 124.
106. T. Subba Row, *Notes on the Bhagavad Gītā* (Point Loma, California: Theosophical University Press, 1934).
107. *Ibid.,* 4.

CHAPTER TWO

1. C.E. Buckland, *Bengal under the Lieutenant Governors* (Calcutta: K. Bose, 1902), II, 1078–9.
2. Nirad C. Chaudhuri, *The Autobiography of the Unknown Indian* (London: Macmillan, 1951), 188.
3. M. K. Halder, ed., *Renaissance and Reaction in Nineteenth Century Bengal: Bankim Chandra Chattopadhyay* (Calcutta: Minerva Associates, 1977), 90.
4. Tara Chand, *History of the Freedom Movement in India* (Delhi: Publications Division, Government of India, 1967), II, 410.
5. With Rev. Hestie, Principal of the General Assemblies Institution.

6. *The Statesman,* Calcutta, October 28, 1882.
7. *Ibid.*
8. Bankim Chandra Chatterji, "Devatattva o Hindudharma" in his *Bibidha* (Calcutta: Bangiya Sahitya Parishad, 1950), 208. All translations from the Bengali are the author's own except where indicated.
9. Chand, *Freedom Movement,* 410.
10. *The Statesman,* October 28, 1882.
11. *Ibid.*
12. Bankim Chandra Chatterji, "Letter to Kumar Binayakrishna Deb," in *Bibidha,* 383.
13. Chatterji, "Devatattva o Hindudharma," 187.
14. Chatterji, "Letter to Kumar Kinayakrishna Deb," 383.
15. Bankim Chandra Chatterji, *Krishnacaritra* (Calcutta: Bangiya Sahitya Parishad, 1961), 288.
16. Bankim Chandra Chatterji, *Dharmatattva* (Calcutta: Bangiya Sahitya Parishad, 1965), 22.
17. Bipin Chandra Pal, *Memories of My Life and Times* (Calcutta: Modern Book Agency, 1950), 26–28.
18. Bankim Chandra Chatterji, *Śrīmadbhagavadgītā* (Calcutta: Bangiya Sahitya Parishad, 1950), 26–28.
19. *Ibid.,* 29–48.
20. *Ibid.,* 49.
21 Chatterji, "Devatattva o Hindudharma," 246.
22. *Gita,* 12.5 (Tr. Radhakrishnan).
23. Halder, 114.
24. Chatterji, *Śrīmadbhagavadgītā,* 28.
25. Halder, 144.
26 Chatterji, *Krishnacaritra,* 287
27. *Ibid.,* 286.
28. Chatterji, *Dharmatattva,* 19.

Chapter Three

1. Bal Gangadhar Tilak, *Śrīmad Bhagavadgītā Rahasya,* or *Karma-Yoga-Śāstra,* trans. B. S. Sukthankar, 2 vols. (Poona: Tilak Bros., 1935), hereafter abbreviated T. GR. in notes.
2. Biographical material is drawn from: Ram Gopal, *Lokamanaya Tilak, a Biography* (Bombay: Asia Publishing House, 1956); Valentine Chirol, *Indian Unrest* (London: Macmillan and Co., Limited, 1910); Theodore L. Shay, *The Legacy of the Lokamanya: The Political Philosophy of Bal Gangadhar Tilak* (London: Oxford University Press, 1956); D. V. Tahmankar, *Lokamanya Tilak, Father of Indian Unrest and Maker of Modern India* (London: John Murray, 1956), (this is an "authorized biography" sponsored by the Kesari Mahratta Trust, Poona); Stanley A. Wolpert, *Tilak and Gokhale: Revolution and Reform in the Making of Modern India* (Berkeley: University of California Press, 1962).
3. Tilak wrote three books and they gained him much respect among Hindus. In addition to his work on the *Gita,* he wrote *The Orion, or*

Researches into the Antiquity of the Vedas (Bombay: Mrs. Radhabhai Atmaram Sagoon, 1893); and *The Arctic Home in the Vedas* (Poona: Messrs. Tilak Bros., 1956), first published in 1903. *The Orion* sought, through astronomical analysis, to establish the composition of the Vedas so early in human history as to link their authors with the origins of civilization. *The Arctic Home* used geological analysis to locate the original and civilized Aryans in the northern polar regions prior to 8,000 B.C. Reaction to Tilak's scholarship is mixed. It has been suggested that these works achieved the practical goal of providing Hindus with an ancestry that placed them second to no culture or civilization.

4. Aurobindo Ghose, "An Aappreciation by Babu Aurobindo Ghose," *Bal Gangadhar Tilak, His Writings and Speeches,* 3rd ed. (Madras: Gasesh & Co. 1922), 7.

5. *Bal Gangadhar Tilak,* 70.

6. *Ibid.,* 46.

7. *Ibid.,* 164.

8. *Keshari,* 1 January, 1907, p. 4, quoted in Wolpert, *Tilak and Gokhale,* 192.

9. *Mahratta,* 14 January, 1906, pp. 22–23, quoted in Wolpert, 179. Ram Gopal, 250, quotes some of the same material, including sections that make the point of Hindu unity based upon the *Vedas* even more strongly.

10. *Keshari,* 10 July, 1906, p. 4, quoted in Wolpert, 218.

11. These general characteristics of the Congress Moderates have been discussed by many authors. E.g., Charles Heimsath, *Indian Nationalism and Hindu Social Reform* (Princeton: Princeton University Press, 1964), 58, 190–91; Shay, 48; Wolpert, passim.

12. Chirol, 41.

13. Tahmankar, 320.

14. T. GR., I, xliii–xlv.

15. These unidentified commentaries must have included those by Shankara and Ramanuja, Jnaneshvar, Madhva and Shridhara, all of which are mentioned in T. GR., or in his letters from Mandalay prison. See M. D. Vidwans, ed., *Letters of Lokamanya Tilak* (Poona: Kesari Prakashan, 1966), passim.

16. He says that he "got out of the clutches of the commentators," in order to get at the *Gita*'s and only the *Gita*'s meaning. "If as a result of this straightforward translation [of the *Gita*] . . . my exposition assumes a doctrine-supporting character, then such character is of the *Gītā* and not mine."

17. *Ibid.,* I, xliv.

18. *Ibid.,* I, v.

19. *Ibid.,* I, and II, 1–714.

20. *Ibid.,* II, 851–1210.

21. *Ibid.,* II, 716–831.

22. J. A. B. van Buitenen, *Rāmānuja on the Bhagavadgītā,* 2nd ed. (Delhi: Motilal Banarsidass, 1968), 29 ff.; and S. K. Belvalkar, *Vedanta Philosophy,* Part 1 (Poona: Bilvakunja Publishing House, 1929), 12.

23. T. GR., I, xliv. Energism is synonymous with *pravṛtti* (*ibid.,* I, 17). Tilak claims also that his work may be called " . . . the first comparative exposition of the *Gītā* in support of Right Action," since the *karmayoga* interpretations criticized in chapter three of Shankara's *Gitabhashya* are no longer extant! (*ibid.,* I, lii)

24. *Ibid.,* I, 13.

25. *Ibid.,* I, xlvi.

26. *Ibid.,* I, 325.

27. A discussion of Shankara and Tilak on these points is contained in my doctoral dissertation for Harvard University: *Historical Change in Scriptural Interpretation: A Comparative Study of Classical and Contemporary Commentaries on the Bhagavadgita,* (1975), 84–93 and 132–44.

28. T. GR., I, 505.

29. *Ibid.,* I, 472–73.

30. Length of a chapter's commentary has been calculated by dividing the number of lines of commentary in the chapter by the number of verses. The result, a rough estimate of the average number of lines of commentary per verse in the chapter, is a useful indicator for purposes of comparison. Measurement of individual passages by number of pages (in the next para.) also provides a useful relative method of comparison.

31. T. GR., II 967.

32. *Ibid.,* II, 953–62.

33. *Ibid.,* II, 1001, re. *Gita.* 6.35–36.

34. *Ibid.,* II, 1007–8.

35. *Ibid.,* II, 975, re. *Gita.* 5.14–15; II, 872–73, re. *Gita.* 2.14–15; 907–8, re. *Gita.* 2.72.

36. *Ibid.,* I, 230; II, 1185–86, re. *Gita.* 18.20.

37. *Ibid.,* I, 72–75 and commentary at *Gita.* 5.8–9 and 3.5.

38. *Ibid.,* I, 76–83; II, 896–97, re. *Gita.* 2.50.

39. *Ibid.,* II, 910, re. *Gita.* 3.3.

40. It is possible to be a *jīvanmukta* says Tilak: T. GR. II, 977, re. *Gita.* 5.18–20 and I, 413–15.

41. *Ibid.,* I, 342–44.

42. *Ibid.,* 978–79, re. *Gita.* 5.24.

43. *Ibid.,* I, 366 and II, 911–13, re. *Gita.* 3.4–5; II, 973, re. *Gita.* 5.8–9.

44. *Ibid.,* I, 463–64; II, 697; II, 1159 ff., re. *Gita.* 17.2 ff; II, 1184 ff., re. *Gita.* 18–19 ff.

45. *Ibid.,* II, 911–12, re. *Gita.* 3.4–5.

46. *Ibid.,* II, 901–3, re. *Gita.* 2.55–62; II, 913, re. *Gita.* 3.4–5; II, 933–34, re. *Gita.* 3.33–34; II, 937, re. *Gita.* 3.42–43.

47. *Ibid.,* II, 899–900, re. *Gita.* 2.54 ff.; II, 904, re. *Gita.* 2.64–65.

48. *Ibid.,* II, 907–8, re. *Gita.* 2.72.

49. The flame of knowledge consumes uncommenced *karma. Ibid.,*II, 952, re. *Gita.* 4.19; II, 964, re. *Gita.* 4.37.

50. *Ibid.,* II, 913, re. *Gita.* 3.4–5.

51. *Ibid.,* II, 927, re. *Gita.* 3.20. For Shankara on the other hand, Janaka's activity is incidental to the main fact that he was a *jñānin.* Tilak describes the *Gita*'s ethical doctrine in *ibid.,* I, 534 ff.

52. *Ibid.*, II, 643. See also I, 492, item 2.

53. *Ibid.*, II, 929, re. *Gita*. 3.22–24.

54. *Ibid.*, II, 1197–99, re. *Gita*. 18.47–49.

55. *Ibid.*, II, 982–83, re. *Gita*. 6. Intro., and 1–2. The argument is further elaborated in Tilak's discussion of *saṃnyāsa* and *tyāga* at the beginning of *Gita*. 18.

56. *Ibid.*, I, 572.

57. *Ibid.*, II, 1097–98, re. *Gita*. 12.6, ". . . *sarvāṇi karmāṇi mayī saṃnyāsa* . . ."; and see also II, 1057–58, re. *Gita*. 9.27.

58. E.g., *Bhagavata Purana* 7.5.23: *śravanam kīrtanam viṣṇoḥ smaraṇam pādasevanam/arcanaṃ vandanaṃ dāsyaṃ sakhyaṃ ātmanivedanam.* Quoted in T. GR., I, 573.

59. T. GR., II, 1045, re. *Gita*. 9.1. Tilak often asserts the comparative easiness of *bhakti*, e.g., at *Gita*. 7.16.16–19, 12.2–6, etc.

60. *Ibid.*, II, 650.

61. *Ibid.*, I, 600 ff.

62. *Ibid.*, II, 1022, re. *Gita*. 7.20–23; see also *Gita*. 9.23.

63. *Ibid.*, II, 1095, re. *Gita*. 12. Intro.

64. *Ibid.*, I, 577.

65. *Ibid.*, II, 638–39.

66. R. W. Stevenson, *Historical Change* . . ., 257–73.

67. T. GR., II, 965, re. *Gita*. 4.36–40 vs. II, 901–2, re. *Gita*. 2.60–61.

68. *Ibid.*, II, 907–8, re. *Gita*. 2.72; II, 904, re. *Gita*. 2.64–65; II, 899–900, re. *Gita*. 2.54 ff.; see also I, 158.

69. *Ibid.*, I, 424; II, 972, re. *Gita*. 5.4–6.

70. *Ibid.*, II, 913, re. *Gita*. 3.4–5, II, 981, re. *Gita*. 6. Intro.

71. *Ibid.*, II, 1100, re. *Gita*. 12.9–12.

72. *Ibid.*, I, 596–97.

73. *Ibid.*, II, 996, re. *Gita*. 6.20–23 (see also 992–93, re. *Gita*. 6.15) and II, 1120, re. *Gita*. 13.24–25.

74. *Ibid.*, I, 34–37.

75. *Ibid.*, II, 871 ff.; re. *Gita*. 2.13 ff., II, 1086, re. *Gita*. 11.33–34.

76. *Ibid.*, I, 516–18, 519.

77. *Ibid.*, II, 1183, re. *Gita*. 8.17.

78. *Keshari,* 15 June, 1897, quoted more fully in Wolpert, *Tilak and Gokhale,* 86–87.

79. T.GR., I, 553–54.

80. It is intriguing to note that Tilak maintains the evil karma of a violent act falls not upon the *karmayogin* (whose actions can produce no karmic effects because they are desireless) but upon the head of the one who makes the act necessary. *Ibid.*, I, 554.

81. *Ibid.*, II, 881, re. *Gita*. 2.30; II, 934, re. *Gita*. 3.35.

82. *Ibid.*, II, 1198, re. *Gita*. 18:47–49.

83. *Ibid.*, II, 697 and 935, re. *Gita*. 3.35.

84. *Bal Gangadhar Tilak* . . ., 164–65. Shay has devoloped these points at some length, 1–25, 98–104.

CHAPTER FOUR

1. There are numerous introductions to Aurobindo's thought. For a listing, as well as a study of his thought in terms of the various periods of his life, see Robert N. Minor, *Sri Aurobindo: The Perfect and the Good* (Columbia: South Asia Books, 1979). An appreciative, yet the most complete, biography is K. R. Srinivasa Iyengar, *Sri Aurobindo: A Biography and a History,* 3rd ed. (Pondicherry: Sri Aurobindo International Center of Education, 1972).

2. *Sri Aurobindo Birth Centenary Library* (Pondicherry: Sri Aurobindo Ashram Trust, 1972), II, 401. Hereafter, this set of Aurobindo's complete works will be abbreviated *BCL.*

3. *BCL.* XXII, 70 and XXVI, 126. Cf. XXII, 69.

4. Studies of his *Essays* are: Thomas J. Hopkins, "The Vision of the Purushottama in *Essays on the Gita,* " in *Six Pillars: Introduction to the Major Works of Sri Aurobindo,* ed. by Robert A. McDermott (Chambersburg: Wilson Books, 1974), 61–96; J. Feys, *The Yogi and the Mystic: A Study in the Spirituality of Sri Aurobindo and Teilhard De Chardin* (Calcutta: Firma KLM Private Limited, 1977); K. C. Varadachari, "Aurobindo on the Bhagavadgita," in *Gītā Samīkṣā,* ed. by E. R. Sreekrishna Sarma (Tirupati: Sri Venkateswara University, 1971), 141–47.

5. *BCL.* XII, 1–60. For his thought in the Baroda period see Minor, *Sri Aurobindo,* pp. 20–38.

6. *BCL. III, 115.*

7. *Ibid.,* 116.

8. *BCL.* XII, 53. Cf. III, 116–17.

9. *BCL.* III, 118.

10. *Ibid.,* 169. Brackets mine.

11. *Ibid.,* 174.

12. *Ibid.,* 170.

13. See Robert N. Minor, *Bhagavad Gītā: An Exegetical Commentary* (Columbia: South Asia Books, 1982), 362–68.

14. *BCL.* III, 168.

15. *Ibid.,* 174.

16. See David L. Johnson, *The Religious Roots of Indian Nationalism: Aurobindo's Early Political Thought* (Calcutta: Firma KLM Mukhopadhyay, 1974); and Minor, *Sri Aurobindo,* 44–74.

17. *BCL.* I, 235.

18. *Ibid.,* 98. Cf. his later statement in *BCL.* XXVI, 22.

19. *BCL.* XXVI, 64.

20. *Ibid.,* 68. See Robert N. Minor, "Sri Aurobindo and Experience: Yogic and Otherwise," in *Religion in Modern India,* ed. by Robert D. Baird (New Delhi: Manohar, 1981), 277–304.

21. *BCL.* XXVI, 79.

22. *BCL.* I, 652.

23. *Ibid.,* 653.

24. *Ibid.,* 764.

25. *Ibid.,* 658.

26. Feys, 15–22. Cf. also Aurobindo's 1923 statement quoted in A.B. Purani, *The Life of Sri Aurobindo: A Source Book* (Pondicherry: Sri Aurobindo Ashram, 1964), 116.

27. *BCL.* XXVI, 83–84.

28. For example see *BCL.* I, 659, 665.

29. *BCL.* XXVI, 64.

30. *BCL.* II, 10. See Minor, *Sri Aurobindo,* 74–90.

31. *Ibid.,* 3.

32. *Ibid.,* 7.

33. *Ibid.,* 3.

34. *Ibid.,* 5.

35. *Ibid.,* 6.

36. *Ibid.,* 8–9.

37. *Ibid.,* 13–14.

38. The critics include Feys, 15–22 and June O'Conner, *The Quest for Political and Spiritual Liberation: A Study in the Thought of Sri Aurobindo Ghose* (Cranbury, N.J.: Farleigh Dickinson Press, 1976), 134–40. For a discussion of Sri Aurobindo's position, see Minor, *Sri Aurobindo,* 100–101, 161–62.

39. *BCL.* II, 401.

40. *BCL.* IV, 57.

41. *Ibid.,* 66–110.

42. *Ibid.,* IV, 125.

43. *BCL.* II, 19.

44. *BCL.* III, 343. Cf. *BCL.* IV, 60–62.

45. *Ibid.,* 344.

46. *BCL.* II, 36.

47. *Ibid.,* 105.

48. *BCL.* IV, 90–96.

49. *BCL.* III, 345. Cf. *BCL.* IV, 57.

50. Aurobindo's translation in *ibid.,* 353.

51. *Ibid.,* 355.

52. *Ibid.,* 356. Cf. *BCL.* IV, 69.

53. *Ibid.,* 364.

54. *Ibid.,* 354. Brackets mine.

55. *BCL.* II, 427.

56. *Ibid.,* 428. Cf. *BCL.* IV, 58.

57. *Ibid.,* 425.

58. *Ibid.,* 426.

59. As noted by Hopkins, 86–87.

60. *BCL.* III, 369. Aurobindo's own testimony is that this problem was the major one he needed to solve in his own *sādhana* to enable him to apply his yoga to transform the multiplicity into perfect multiplicity. See, for example, *BCL.* XXVI, 86.

61. *Ibid.,* 370.

62. *Ibid.* Brackets mine.

63. *Muṇḍaka Upanishad* 3.1.1–3; *Śvetāśvatara Upanishad* 4.6–7.

64. *BCL.* III, 370.

65. *BCL.* XIII, 72–3, 117; XVIII, 145–47; etc.
66. *BCL.* III, 371.
67. See Minor, *Sri Aurobindo,* 102, 109.
68. "Purna yoga" is also used of Aurobindo's yoga in an undated manuscript in *BCL.* XVII, 61–69, which may be from this early period at Pondicherry.
69. *BCL.* XVI, 413.
70. Feys, 38–49.
71. *BCL.* XVI, 416.
72. *BCL.* XXVI, 79.
73. *BCL.* XVI, 416. Brackets mine.
74. *BCL.* XXVI, 78; Feys, 47.
75. *Ibid.,* 64.
76. In an undated letter, which the editors of *BCL* date to 1913, Aurobindo speaks of a specific experience; (*BCL* XXVII, 433):

> 15th August is usually a turning point or a notable day for me personally either in Sadhana or life,—indirectly only for others. This time it has been very important for me. My subjective Sadhana may be said to have received its final seal and something like its consummation by a prolonged realisation and dwelling in Parabrahman for many hours. Since then, egoism is dead for all in me except the Annamaya Atma,—the physical self which awaits one farther realisation before it is entirely liberated from occasional visitings or external touches of the old separated existence.

Yet, this does not suit at all the description of the Purushottama or the third experience of the process of seeing God in all things in "The Yoga and Its Objects." It is still preliminary to Purushottama or, later, Supermind.
77. *BCL.* XVI, 416.
78. *BCL.* XXVI, 64.
79. *Ibid.,* 136.
80. *Ibid.,* 136–37.
81. The latest edition is *BCL.* XX, XXI.
82. For his own discussions of the addition of Overmind and later levels see *BCL.* XXVI, 369–70 and XXII, 261, 263.
83. *BCL.* XIII, 1.
84. *Ibid.,* 2–3.
85. See Minor, *Sri Aurobindo,* 113–15.
86. *BCL.* XIII, 3–4.
87. *Ibid.,* 62.
88. *Ibid.,* 27–35. It is unlikely that Aurobindo read Tilak's *Gītā-rahasya.* In a review of the *Gītā-rahasya* in the first issue of the *Ayra* (Vol. 1 [August 15, 1914] 59–61; reprinted in *BCL* XVII, 265–6), Aurobindo's belief that Tilak has missed the higher point is based only on an account of Tilak's work. Had he read the work, it is unlikely that his critique would have taken this turn.
89. Feys, 22.
90. *BCL.* XIII, 128.
91. *Ibid.,* 34.

92. *Ibid.,* 35.

93. Cf. *ibid.,* 72–73, 117–18, 127, 131–32, 133, 218–22, 228, 233, 236, 256–57, 265, 271, 275, 279–80, 342, 396–97, 419, 421–34, 440–41, 478, 502, 511–17, 530, 538.

94. *Ibid.,* 73.

95. *BCL.* XVIII, 322.

96. *BCL.* XIII, 73.

97. *Ibid.,* 84.

98. *Ibid.,* 85.

99. *Ibid.,* 275.

100. *Ibid.,* 523. Brackets mine.

101. Robert N. Minor, "The *Gītā*'s Way as the Only Way," *Philosophy East and West,* XXX, No. 3 (July, 1980), 345–46.

102. *BCL.* XIII, 228. Cf. 256.

103. *Ibid.,* 177.

104. See Minor, *Sri Aurobindo,* 108–12 and notes.

105. *BCL.* XIII, 553.

106. *Ibid.,* 18. Cf. 17–18, 165; XXII, 71–72.

107. *Ibid.,* 37.

108. *Ibid.,* 41–42.

109. For his attitude toward World War II, see Iyengar, *Sri Aurobindo,* 1267–74, and Aurobindo's own messages in *BCL.* XXVI, 393–399.

110. *BCL.* XIII, 48.

111. *BCL.* XXII, 69. Cf. 70; *BCL.* XXVI, 126–27.

112. *Ibid.*

113. Robert N. Minor, "In Defense of Karma and Rebirth: Evolutionary Karma," in *Karma and Rebirth: Post Classical Developments,* ed. by Ronald W. Neufeldt, (Albany: SUNY Press, 1986), 15–40.

CHAPTER FIVE

1. *The Collected Works of Mahatma Gandhi* (Ahmedabad: Navajivan), XXXII, 94. Henceforth, the Collected Works will be referred to as *CW,* the Roman figure indicating the volume, and the Arabic figure the page.

2. *CW* XLI, 90.

3. *CW* XLIX, 111.

4. M. K. Gandhi, *An Autobiography, or the Story of my Experiments with Truth,* tr. by Mahadev Desai (Ahmedabad: Navajivan, 1927), 48.

5. *Ibid.,* 194.

6. *CW* VII, 96 and 375.

7. *CW* XV, 288.

8. *Ibid.,* 313.

9. Cf. *CW* XIII, 131; XXV, 83–85.

10. This was published in 1936 by Navajivan Publishing House under the title *Gītāpadhārtakosh.*

11. *CW* XXVIII, 315–21.

12. *Autobiography,* 88ff, 97ff.

13. *Ibid.,* 99.

14. *Ibid.*
15. *CW* XXIX, 444.
16. *CW* XXXII, 329.
17. *CW* LII, 9.
18. *Ibid.*, 410.
19. *CW* LIII, 370.
20. *CW* LXIV, 75.
21. *CW* XXV, 86.
22. *CW* LII, 9.
23. *CW* LXIV, 397.
24. *CW* XXXI, 156.
25. *CW* XXXV, 98.
26. D. G. Tendulkar, *Mahatma, Life of Mohandas Karamchand Gandhi,* (Ahmedabad: Navajivan, 1952), IV, 75.
27. *CW* XXXII, 228.
28. Tendulkar, 75.
29. *CW* XLI, 98.
30. *CW* LII, 9.
31. *CW* LI, 384; see also *CW* XXXII, 329.
32. *CW* LII, 370.
33. *CW* LXIII, 286.
34. *CW* LVII, 7.
35. *CW* XV, 317.
36. *CW* XXXIII, 384.
37. *CW* LII, 9.
38. *CW* XXVIII, 316.
39. *CW* LI, 344.
40. *CW* LVI, 341.
41. *CW* LIII, 396.
42. *CW* LI, 344.
43. *CW* XXXIV, 395.
44. *CW* LXXI, 30.
45. *Ibid.*
46. *CW* LI, 344.
47. *CW* XXXIV, 395.
48. Tendulkar, VII, 77.
49. *CW* LXIV, 75.
50. *CW* LVI, 341.
51. *CW* XXVIII, 31.
52. *CW* XLI, 98.
53. *CW* LXXI, 29.
54. *CW* XXXII, 146.
55. *Ibid.*, 31.
56. *CW* XXVIII, 316.
57. *CW* XXVI, 289.
58. *CW* XXVIII, 318.
59. *CW* LVIII, 141.
60. *CW* XXXII, 100, 154.

61. *CW* LXIII, 399.
62. *CW* XXXII, 154.
63. *CW* XXXIV, 89.
64. *Ibid.*
65. *CW* XLIII, 85.
66. *CW* XV, 313.
67. *CW* XXVIII, 316–17.
68. *CW* XXXIV, 89.
69. *CW* XXVII, 316.
70. *CW* XLI, 92.
71. *CW* XLIII, 85.
72. *CW* XLI, 100.
73. *CW* XLV, 96.
74. *CW* LXXI, 304.
75. *CW* XXVI, 140.
76. *CW* XV, 288.
77. *CW* XVIII, 125.
78. *CW* XX, 129; cf. also XXI, 515.
79. *CW* XXV, 86.
80. *Ibid.*, 86–87.
81. *Ibid.*
82. *CW* XXVIII, 318.
83. *Gita*, 18.68.
84. *CW* XLI, 94.
85. *CW* XII, 126–27.
86. *Ibid.*, 126.
87. *CW* XXVI, 335. See also XXVII, 317; XLI, 339; LXIII, 45.
88. *CW* XII, 126.
89. *CW* LIV, 112.
90. *CW* XIV, 175.
91. *CW* XLI, 339.
92. *CW* XLI, 94.
93. *Ibid.*, 339.
94. *CW* LIV, 471.
95. *Gita*, 4.6.
96. *CW* XXXII, 189.
97. *CW* XLI, 95.
98. *Ibid.*
99. *Ibid.*; see also XXXII. 351.
100. Cf. Mulji, Karsondas (publ. anon), *History of the Sect of the Maharajas or Vallabhacharyas of Western India* (London, 1891); *Report of the Maharaj Libel Case and of the Bhattia Conspiracy Case Connection with it* (Bombay: Gazette Press, 1862).
101. *CW* XLI, 96.
102. *Ibid.*
103. *CW* XXXII, 305.
104. *CW* XII, 126.
105. *CW* XLIX, 327–28.

106. Quoted by S. N. Hay, 'Jain Influences on Gandhi's Early Thought,' in S. N. Ray, ed., *Gandhi, India and the World* (Bombay, 1970), 21.

107. Agehananda Bharati, 'Gandhi's Interpretation of the *Gita:* An Anthropological Analysis,' in S. N. Ray, 46.

108. Cf. Pyarelal, *The Early Phase,* I, 321–27.

109. Anna Kingsford and Edward Maitland, *The Perfect Way, or The Finding of Christ,* fourth ed., pref. S. H. Hart (London: John M. Watkins, 1909), 28.

110. *Ibid.,* 225.

111. *Ibid.,* 230.

112. *Ibid.,* 112.

113. *Ibid.,* 248.

114. *Autobiography,* 99.

115. *CW* XXXII, 593–603 contains both the questions of Gandhi, and a translation of Raychand's answers. S. N. Hay's chapter in S. N. Ray gives a close analysis of various aspects of the influence of Raychand on Gandhi.

116. *Ibid.,* 598.

117. *Ibid.,* 601.

118. *Ibid.*

119. *CW* XXXII, 2,6,7.

120. *CW* XLIX, 327.

121. For the reader's information, I refer to the one substantial work in English on the subject of this chapter, which I acquired after finalizing my own writing: Ramesh Betai, *Gita and Gandhiji, Gujarat Vidyapith,* (Ahmedabad, 1970) XII, 2931.

CHAPTER SIX

1. Gandhi shortened Bhave's name to Vinoba and it was this appellation he carried with him to his death.

2. *The Overseas Hindustan Times* (New Delhi), 23 December 1982, 8.

3. P. D. Tandon, ed., *Vinoba Bhave; The Man and His Mission* (Bombay: Vora, 1954), 22. Some think Vinoba gave the Satyagraha movement its philosophical underpinnings because of his thorough knowledge of Indian literature and philosophy.

4. Vasant Nargolkar, *The Cread of Saint Vinoba* (Bombay: Bharatiya Vidya Bhavan, 1963), 40–41. "The *Gita Talks,* however, is not a verse-by-verse commentary. The eighteen discourses together do contain the core of the teaching of the *Gita* as Vinobaji sees it. But each chapter of the original poem provides only a basis for the unhindered flight of Vinobaji's power of expansion." *Ibid.,* 42.

5. Vinoba Bhave, *The Dhammapada: Nava Samhita,* trans, Srikrishna Datta Bhatta, (Varanasi: Sarva Seva Sangh Prakahan, 1967), 7.

6. *The Overseas Hindustan Times* (New Delhi), 23 December 1982, 8.

7. Hallam Tennyson, *India's Walking Saint* (Garden City: Doubleday), 54f; cf. Vinoba Bhave, *Bhoodan Yajna* (Ahmedabad: Navajivan Publishing House, 1954), iv.

8. The five ashrams are: Samanvaya Ashram (Bodh-Gaya), Prasthan Ashram (Pathankot), Visarjan Ashram (Indore), Vishwa Needham (Bangalore), and Maitri Ashram (Lakhimpur). The journals that he published include: *Bhoodan Yajna, Gandhi Marg, Interdiscipline, Maitri, People's Action,* and *Sarvodaya.*

9. *The Overseas Hindustan Times* (New Delhi), 25 November 1982, 1 and 16.

10. Vinoba Bhave, *Swaraj Shastra,* 5th ed., trans. Bharatan Kumarappa, (Varanasi: Sarva Seva Sangh Prakashan, 1970), 3–5.

11. Tandon, 5.

12. *The Overseas Hindustan Times,* p. 8, reports 16, 77, 711.6 hectares (4, 143, 947.6 acres) were contributed with 5, 14, 294.2 hectares (1, 270, 306.6 acres) distributed. Some sources put these totals much higher (cf. R. P. Masani, *The Five Gifts* (London: Collins, 1957), 171f).

13. Raghavendra Nath Misra, *Bhoodan Movement in India* (New Delhi: Chand and Co., 1972), 108. Cf. Masani, *Five Gifts,* 171f, 173; and Sugata Dasgupta, *A Great Society of Small Communities* (Varanasi: Sarva Seva Sangh Prakashan, 1968), 24.

14. *The Overseas Hindustan Times* (New Delhi), 25 November 1982, 16.

15. Vinoba Bhave, *Democratic Values and the Practice of Citizenship* (Kashi: Sarva Seva Sangh Prakashan, 1962), 17.

16. Ram Suresh, *Vinoba and His Mission,* 3rd. ed. (Kashi: Akhil Bharat Sarva Seva Sangh, 1962), 515.

17. Bhave, *Democratic Values,* 98.

18. Shriman Narayan, *Vinoba: His Life and Work* (Bombay: Popular Prakashan, 1970), 350.

19. Bhave, *Democratic Values,* 235. Cf. Narayan, *Vinoba,* 344.

20. *Ibid.,* 26.

21. Babu Ram Misra, *V is for Vinoba: The Economics of the Bhoodan Movement* (Calcutta: Orient Longmans, 1956), 5. "Vinoba's target is 50 million acres of land. Since there are 300 million acres of cultivable land in India and an average family has five members, Vinoba felt that every family could give away one-sixth of its land holding, accepting the poor landless man as the sixth member of the family. This is the Bhoodan way of bringing about a peaceful revolution in the country." *Ibid.,* 31. Cf. Vinoba Bhave, *The Third Power,* trans. Marjorie Sykes and K. S. Acharlu, (Varanasi: Sarva Seva Sangh Prakashan, 1972), 37.

22. Bhave, *Bhoodan Yajna,* 24.

23. Dasgupta, *Great Society,* 15 and Misra, *Bhoodan Movement,* 21f, 23. These ideas could have come from the *Gita.*

24. Bhave, *Bhoodan Yajna,* 63f, 71; cf. Misra, *V is for Vinoba,* 57. No money actually changed hands. All funds were held in "trusteeship."

25. R. N. Misra, *Bhoodan Movement,* 26. These are called the five gifts *(pancadana),* and each has a didactic purpose. Bhoodan teaches to forsake the idea of ownership of property; Sampattidan teaches to renounce the accumulation of wealth; Shramdan teaches the dignity of labor; Premdan teaches one to love his neighbor as himself; Buddhidan teaches the power of knowledge.

26. Masani, *Five Gifts,* 91; Ram, *Vinoba and His Mission,* 515–16.

27. See Narayan, *Vinoba: His Life and Work,* 344ff for a full glossary of the concerns of Vinoba.

28. Vinoba Bhave, *Talks on the Gita,* 8th ed., (Varanasi: Sarva Seva Sangh Prakashan, 1982), 183. (Hereafter referred to as GT).

29. GT, 89.

30. GT, 16, 89.

31. GT, 1.

32. GT, 2. Vinoba Bhave, *Random Reflections,* trans. and compiled by Vasant Nargolkar (Varanasi: Sarva Seva Sangh Prakashan, 1971), 3. Vinoba Bhave, *The Steadfast Wisdom* 2nd ed., trans. Lila Ray (Varanasi: Sarva Seva Sangh Prakashan, 1973), 157 (hereafter SW). GT, 56; SW, 90, 95, 32, 33; GT, 8; SW, 90; GT, 10, 144, 157.

33. GT, 2, 16, 175.

34. SW, 32, 33, 38, 103.

35. SW, 44.

36. Bhave, *Random Reflections,* 36; GR, 2; SW, 151.

37. GT, 90, 175, 186, 187, 183.

38. SW, 113.

39. GT, 1.

40. GT, 5, 6, 8.

41. GT, 144.

42. GT, 56, 127, 143.

43. GT, 21. E. R. Sreekrishna Sarma, in *Gītā Samīkṣa* (Tirupati: Sri Vankateswara University, 1971, 169–174), argues that "The Essence of the Gita according to Vinoba" is *sthita prajñā.* Whereas this is a very important aspect of Vinoba's teachings on the *Gita,* much is overlooked if only this teaching is studied.

44. GT, 2.

45. GT, 143, 144, 16.

46. See Vinoba Bhave, *Commentary on Japji, Guru Nanak's Great Composition,* trans. Gurbachan Singh Talib, (Patiala: Punjabi University, 1973), for an example of Vinoba's hermeneutic on a less volatile text. The methodology of this section is based on an inductive study of Vinoba's two works on the *Gita.* As stated, Vinoba never explicitly articulates the rules which he is employing, but his usage of implicit rules is quite evident. The reader is referred to the place in the text where this rule was seen to be operative.

47. SW, 18, 34, 42, 54, 64, 65, 97.

48. SW, 17, 28.

49. SW, 7, 116, 121, 157.

50. SW, 75, 161.

51. SW, 12, 89, 130, 97.

52. SW, 81.

53. GT, 222.

54. SW, 7, 75.

55. SW, 160.

56. SW, 37, 110; GT, 46, 190.

57. GT, 9, 10, 78, 34; SW, 10, 14, 160.

58. SW, 12, 21, 77, 89.
59. GT, 90, 107, 179.
60. GT, 3, 8.
61. SW, 109.
62. SW, 35, 140, 141, 144, 150, 161.
63. SW, 90, 56, 58; GT, 58, 105.
64. GT, 27.
65. GT, 128, 33, 35, 99.
66. GT, 145, 216, 217.
67. GT, 189; SW, 77.
68. GR, 2, 21, 127, 144.
69. GT, 48, 183.
70. GT, 53; SW, 21, 77.
71. GT, 16, 92, 136, 139; SW, 71, 132, 140.
72. GT, 127; SW, 41, 44, 63, 64, 132, 162. Vinoba compares his interpretations with Shankara, Manu, Gandhi, and Tilak. He is not afraid to call these authorities wrong.
73. For a discussion of the methodological implications of a search for "real meaning" see Richard Robinson, *Definition* (Oxford: Clarendon, 1972), 149–192 and Robert D. Baird, *Category Formation and the History of Religions* (The Hague: Mouton, 1971) 11–14.
74. Bhave, *Random Reflections,* 68–69.
75. SW, 116, 120; GT, 33; Vinoba Bhave, *Vinoba on Gandhi,* ed. Kantilal Shah, trans. J. P. Uniyal (Varanasi: Sarva Seva Sangh Prakashan, 1973), 150.
76. SW, 81, 90, 42.
77. SW, 45, 125, 133; GT, 106. See Bhave, *The Dhammapada,* in which Vinoba rearranges an entire text in order to demonstrate his understanding and interpretation of the text.
78. SW, 41, 39, 123, 132, 162, 76, 80, 110.
79. SW, 110, 11, 12, 118, 160.
80. GT, 179. See Baird, *Category Formation,* 2–5, 11–14, 129–133 for a discussion of the methodological implications of a search for the essence of something.
81. GT, 2, 21, 127, 144, 175, 187, 217.
82. GT, 2, 91, 186, 214.
83. GT, 144, 145, 46, 93, 189.
84. GT, 90, 179; SW, 42, 37.
85. GT, 3, 205, 207.
86. GT, 90; SW, 105, 156.
87. SW, 31, 72, 74, 75, 98, 133, 89, 110, 120.
88. Bhave, *Random Reflections,* 36.
89. SW, 141; GT, 9, 63.
90. GT, 121, 126, 139.
91. GT, 128, 188.
92. GT, 188, 141, 175.
93. GT, 175.
94. GT, 9, 24, 27, 48, 58, 69, 105–107, 129, 139, 161, 176, 188, 200–201.
95. Bhave, *Bhoodan Yajna,* 39.

96. GT, 5, 93.
97. GT, 105, 182.
98. GT, 124, 118.
99. GT, 139, 145; SW, 3, 50, 129.
100. SW, 38, 42, 76.
101. GT, 192, 106, 42, 100, 108, 94, 184–185.
102. GT, 209, 211, 205; SW, 89.
103. GT, 127.
104. GT, 145; cf. SW; cf. *Gita Samiksa.*
105. SW, 59.
106. GT, 216–217.
107. GT, 187, 175, 188–189, 184–185.
108. In this section it is assumed that the reader is familiar with Gandhi and his concerns. A structural overview of Gandhian concerns is found in Boyd H. Wilson, "Ultimacy as Unifier in Gandhi," in *Religion in Modern India,* ed. by Robert D. Baird (New Delhi: Manohar, 1981), pp. 227–46.
109. GT, 151.
110. SW, 18; GT, 191, 33, 34, 194.
111. GT, 159, 55, 205.
112. SW, 109, 36, 45.
113. GT, 133, 224, 125.
114. GT, 183.
115. Bhave, *The Third Power,* 65.
116. Vinoba Bhave, *Revolutionary Sarvodaya,* ed. and compiler Vasant Nargolkar (Bombay: Bharatiya Vidya Bhavan, 1964), 36.
117. Bhave, *Bhoodan Yajna,* 42. Cf. Bhave, *Random Reflections,* 49f, 39; cf. Vinoba Bhave, *The Principles and Philosophy of the Bhoodan Yajna* (Tanjore: Sarvodaya Prachuralaya, 1955), 2.
118. GT, 58, 28, 29, 31, 45, 209, 130, 211.
119. GT, 186, 122, 130ff, 205.
120. GT, 183, 25–26.
121. GT, 71, 95, 85, 205.
122. GT, 204, 93, 74, 202, 97, 212.
123. GT, 201–205.
124. GT, 182, 179, 19, 180.
125. See, for example, Bhave, *The Principles and Philosophy of the Bhoodan Yajna* and Vinoba Bhave and Jayaprakash Narayan, *Gramdan for Gram-Swaraj,* trans. Suresh Ram (Varanasi: Sarva Seva Sangh Prakashan, 1967).
126. Bhave, *Commentary on Japji.*
127. Vinoba Bhave, *Thoughts on Education,* trans. Marjorie Sykes (Varanasi: Sarva Seva Sangh Prakashan, 1972), p. 17; Bhave, *Vinoba on Gandhi,* 131; Bhave, *Bhoodan Yajna,* 33; Bhave, *Random Reflections,* 12, 17; Bhave, *Thoughts on Education,* 13; Bhave, *Principles and Philosophy of Bhoodan Yajna,* 1.
128. Vinoba Bhave, *Christ: The Love Incarnate,* trans. Dilip Singhi (Varanasi: Sarva Seva Sangh Prakashan, 1964), 9f.
129. GT, 118, 182, 189, 179, 180, 186, 183.
130. Bhave, *Democratic Values,* 44; GT, 167.

131. GT, 167, 103.

132. GT, 93, 96; Bhave, *Bhoodan Yajna,* 58; Bhave, *Thoughts on Education,* 17.

133. GT, 224, 205, 151, 28, 85, 14, 125, 133.

134. Bhave, *Principles and Philosophy of Bhoodan Yajna,* 1; Bhave, *Revolutionary Sarvodaya,* 1; Bhave, *Bhoodan Yajna,* 42; cf. Misra, *V is for Vinoba,* 56.

CHAPTER SEVEN

1. Clark Kerr, Chancellor of the University of California in the early 1960's, wrote a book titled, *The Uses of the University,* which some criticized as espousing a service station model of the University, with no philosophical depth to his understanding of what the classic role of the University should be. To some critics, Vivekananda's usage may seem similarly vulnerable. I am suggesting, however, that his functionalism, regardless of any assessment of other such expressions, may have substance and may with some integrity represent key insights of the *Gita.*

2. Swami Nirvedananda, "Sri Ramakrishna and Spiritual Renaissance," *Cultural Heritage of India,* vol. 4, ed. by Haridas Bhattacharya (Calcutta: The Ramakrishna Mission, 1956), 693. For other details of the life of Vivekananda, in addition to other sources cited here, see my *The Swan's Wide Waters: Ramakrishna and Western Culture* (New York: Kennikat Press, 1974).

3. Romain Rolland, *Prophets of the New India* (London: Cassell and Co., 1930), 183.

4. Eastern and Western Disciples, *Life of Swami Vivekananda* (Calcutta: Advaita Ashrama, 1960), 297.

5. Earlier he seemed rather charmed by his experiences as a fund-raiser. Compare the accounts in Marie Louise Burke, *Swami Vivekananda in America: New Discoveries* (Calcutta: Advaita Ashrama, 1958), 95, 104, with those on 393, 423.

6. Swami Vivekananda, *Collected Works* (Calcutta: Advaita Ashrama, 1926), VII, 57.

7. *Ibid.,* III, 245.

8. An editorial on January 21, 1897, in *The Indian Mirror* offered this enthusiastic estimate of his achievements: "The tide of conversion seemed to have rolled back from the East to the West—the tables were completely turned—and the Hindu mission to the West was crowned with a greater and more glorious success than what ever has been vouchsafed to Christian mission in the East." The Rajah of Ramnad, one of those who had first given to Vivekananda the idea of attending the Parliament, interpreted his triumphs in the language of reverse imperialism: "Your Holiness has crossed boundless seas and oceans to convey the message of truth and peace, and to plant the flag of India's spiritual triumph and glory in the rich soil of Europe and America." Sankari Prasad Basu and Sumil Bihari Ghosh, eds., *Vivekananda in Indian Newspapers, 1893–1902* (Calcutta: Dineshchandra Basu Basu Bhattacharya and Co., 1969), 125, 134.

9. They may not have been so formal. The lectures in San Francisco were recorded in shorthand by Ida Ansell, with a number of acknowledged gaps, but with subsequent editing, apparently not by Vivekananda. The Bengal lecture, given in Bengali, is simply described as "a translation of the summary of the discourse as it was entered in the Math diary." Vivekananda, *Works,* IV, 102.

10. *Ibid.,* 106.

11. *Ibid.,* 104.

12. *Ibid.,* III, 260.

13. *Ibid.,* 50.

14. *Ibid.,* I, 455.

15. *Ibid.,* 464.

16. *Ibid.,* IV, 107.

17. Walter R. Houghton, Editor-in-Chief, *Neely's History of the Parliament of Religions* (Chicago: F. T. Neely, 1893), 65.

18. Joseph Cook, *Orient* (London: Ward, Lock and Co., 1885), 231.

19. *Ibid.,* 288.

20. J. H. Barrows, ed., *The World's Parliament of Religions,* two vols. (Chicago: The Parliament Publishing Co., 1893), 538, 540.

21. *Ibid.,* 971.

22. Vivekananda, *Works,* III, 468.

23. *Ibid.,* I, 44.

24. *Ibid.,* III, 470.

25. *Ibid.,* IV, 96, 97.

26. *Ibid.,* 94. For a further discussion of this possible indebtedness and its extent, see "Emerson's Discovery of the East" a chapter in Carl T. Jackson's, *The Oriental Religions and American Thought* (Westport, Conn.: Greenwood Press, 1981), 45–62. In his very detailed discussion, Jackson does not document the account of Emerson's meeting with Carlyle, but states that the *Gita* was Emerson's favorite Oriental text and that he often urged his friends to read it. He refused, however, to sponsor an American edition, excusing himself by saying that it would not do to "publish our prayers" in the daily paper.

27. Vivekananda, *Works,* I, 473.

28. *Ibid.,* 473, 474.

29. *Ibid.,* 469.

30. *Ibid.,* 478.

31. *Ibid.,* 479.

32. *Ibid.,* 470. Vivekananda might have cited his master's oft-repeated analogy to everybody's belief that his own watch is right. In fact, no one's watch is exactly right; all visions are partial. See M (Mahendranath Gupta), *The Gospel of Sri Ramakrishna* (Madras: Sri Ramakrishna Math, 1964), passim.

33. Vivekananda, *Works,* I, 468.

34. *Ibid.,* 456.

35. *Ibid.,* 117.

36. *Ibid.,* IV, 96.

37. *Ibid.,* I, 457.

38. Swami Nikhilananda, *Vivekananda, a Biography* (New York: Ramakrishna-Vivekananda Center, 1953), 66.

39. Vivekananda, *Letters of Swami Vivekananda* (Calcutta: Advaita Ashrama, 1960), 351.

40. Vivekananda, *Works,* I, 464.

41. *Ibid.,* 465.

42. *Ibid.,* IV, 402–403.

43. *Ibid.,* 405.

44. *Ibid.,* 404.

45. *Ibid.,* III, 242.

46. *Ibid.,* IV, 109.

47. *Ibid.*

48. *Ibid.,* I, 468.

49. *Ibid.,* VII, 199. The reader will note that such passages as are here referred to may as easily, perhaps more easily, support *bhakti* interpretations.

50. *Ibid.,* 237.

51. *Ibid.,* 272, 273.

52. *Ibid.,* VI, 264.

53. Eastern and Western Admirers, *Reminiscenses of Swami Vivekananda* (Calcutta: Advaita Ashrama, 1960), 162, 163.

54. Vivekananda, *Works,* VIII, 174.

55. Eastern and Western Disciplies, *Life,* 507. The controversy was resolved for the time, with the other disciples yielding to Vivekananda's pre-eminence. But the *bhakti* spirit was pervasive, and would gain a permanent foothold in the Movement along with the attention to Vivekananda's prioritized *jñāna* and karma yogic emphases. Even the shrine at Almora, which he had conceived as a purely Advaitic shrine, without symbol or image, could not be so maintained. Very early, he noted somewhat ruefully, an image of Ramakrishna had been installed for worship.

Perhaps the Bengali origins of the Ramakrishna Movement would have made the total exclusion of *bhakti* an unnecessary and arbitrary truncation of the tradition by the Movement. The devotional movements of Vaishnavism, in particular, had been particularly strong there, giving the devotee something of a special status competitive on occasion with general brahmin supremacy. This has been effectively detailed in a paper by Joseph T. O'Connell, "*Bhagavad-Gītā* in Bengal: Desacralizing the Polity," read at the American Academy of Religion, Atlanta, Georgia in 1971. He outlines a policy of theoretical denial of brahmin pretenses, supported by *Gita* citations, but without frontal challenge.

56. R. C. Majumdar, *Swami Vivekananda: A Historical Review* (Calcutta: General Printers and Publishers, 1965), 49.

57. Vivekananda, *Works,* I, 38. There is another strain of thought, however, more easily translated for non-violent dispositions, from the *Shanti Parva* section of the *Mahabharata,* where Yudhisthira, Arjuna's elder brother, reflects after the war, not on the eve of battle, on all of the destruction caused, along with his role in it. His reflection is complicated by the knowledge that he must now assume the role of kingship. In the face of what he has done and what he must do, Yudhisthira is torn by grief.

Yudhisthira said, "Indeed, the Whole Earth has been subjugated by me through my reliance on the might of Krishna's arms, through the grace of the Brahmanas and through the strength of Bhima and Arjuna. This heavy grief, however, is always sitting on my heart, viz., that through covetousness I have caused this dreadful carnage of kinsmen." (Protap Chandra Roy, *The Mahabharata*. 2nd edition, 12 vols. [Calcutta: Oriental Pub. Co., 1962], VIII, I, 1. See also VII, 9; VII, 11; and XVIII, 33, all in vol. VIII.)

The contrast between the assumptions of the *Shanti Parva* and the *Bhagavadgita* at this point are that renunciation, after the pattern of the *ashramas,* is apparently a more honorable choice in the former. The forest is the field in which one overcomes the senses. The *Gita* seems to ignore the classical pattern of the *ashramas,* believing that renunciation, through *nishkama karma,* may be attained in the midst of the battlefield and its equivalents as well as in the forest. One does not have to withdraw from life to renounce.

The *Shanti Parva,* however, would more naturally support a case for non-violence, which Gandhi and others had to take some pains to extract from the *Gita.* Why was its precedent less appealed to? Presumably, because it was not nearly so popular a text. If support were to be gained from the tradition for non-violence, it had to be secured from those sources which had most popular authority, and which were most readily available.

58. Vivekananda, *Works,* I, 38–40.
59. *Ibid.,* III, 245.
60. *Ibid.,* 246.
61. *Ibid.*
62. *Ibid.,* III, 294.

Chapter Eight

* This study was partially supported by a grant from the General Research Fund of the University of Kansas.

1. See Robert n. Minor, "Sarvepalli Radhakrishnan and 'Hinduism' Defined and Defended," in *Religion in Modern India,* ed. by Robert D. Baird (New Delhi: Manohar, 1981), 305–38.

2. Gerald James Larson, "The Song Celestial: Two Centuries of the *Bhagavad Gita* in English," *Philosophy East and West,* XXXI, No. 4 (October, 1981), 525.

3. "The Religion of the Spirit and the World's Need: Fragments of a Confession," in *The Philosophy of Sarvepalli Radhakrishnan,* ed. by Paul Arthur Schilpp (New York: Tudor, 1952), 9.

4. See note 1 above.

5. London: Macmillan and Co., 1920. The book's preface puts the intention succinctly: "This book attempts to show that of the two live philosophies of the present day, pluralistic theism and monistic idealism, the latter is more reasonable as affording the spiritual being of man's full satisfaction, moral as well as intellectual."

6. "Karma and Free Will," *The Modern Review* (Calcutta) III (May, 1908), 425. See Kashinath T. Telang, *The Bhagavadgītā with the Sanatsujatiya and*

the Anugītā (Oxford: Oxford University Press, 1882), 56. Cf. S. Radhakrishnan, "Indian Philosophy: The Vedas and the Six Systems," *Madras Christian College Magazine* III (1908), 34.

7. *The Ethics of the Vedanta and its Metaphysical Presuppositions* (Madras: The Guardian Press, 1908), 71.

8. *Ibid.*, 75.

9. *Ibid.*, 79.

10. *Ibid.*, 74.

11. *Ibid.*, 85–86.

12. *Ibid.*, 86n.

13. "The Ethics of the Bhagavadgita and Kant," *International Journal of Ethics* XXI, No. 4 (July, 1911), 465–6.

14. *Ibid.*, 467.

15. *Ibid.*

16. S. Radhakrishnan, *Occasional Speeches and Writings. Second Series: February 1956—February 1957* (New Delhi: Ministry of Information and Broadcasting, Government of India, 1957), 297. (Hereafter noted as *OSW*, II.)

17. "Tilak as a Scholar," *The Indian Review* XXII (December, 1921), 738. Cf. S. Radhakrishnan, "Hinduism and the West," in *Modern India and the West*, ed. by L.S.S. O'Malley (London: Oxford University Press, 1941), 352.

18. "The Ethics of the Vedanta," *International Journal of Ethics* XXIV, No. 2 (January, 1914), 168.

19. *Ibid.*, 168.

20. *Ibid.*, 183.

21. Minor, 308–10.

22. "The Ethics of the Vedanta," 174.

23. "The Ethics of the Bhagavadgita and Kant," 467. This verse, quoted first in "Karma and Free Will" above, is again quoted by Radhakrishnan from Telang's translation.

24. *Ibid.*, 469–70. Cf. "The Ethics of the Vedanta," 180, and Robert N. Minor, "In Defense of Karma and Rebirth: Evolutionary Karma," in *Karma and Rebirth: Post Classical Developments*, ed. by Ronald W. Neufeldt (Albany: SUNY Press, 1986), 15–40.

25. *Ibid.*, 466. Cf. "The Ethics of the Vedanta," 179.

26. "The Ethics of the Vedanta," 174–75.

27. *Ibid.*, 174.

28. *Ibid.*, 178.

29. S. Radhakrishnan, *Occasional Speeches and Writings: October 1952—January 1956* (New Delhi: Ministry of Information and Broadcasting, Government of India, 1956), 192. (Hereafter noted as *OSW*, I.) Cf. Minor, "Sarvepalli Radhakrishnan," 328, n. 3.

30. S. Radhakrishnan, *Indian Philosophy*, Vol I (London: George Allen and Unwin, 1923), 7.

31. *Ibid.*, 49–53.

32. *Indian Philosophy*, Vol. II (London: George Allen and Unwin, 1927), 771.

33. *Ibid.*, 780.

34. *Indian Philosophy,* I, 530.
35. *Ibid.,* 534.
36. *Ibid.,* 549.
37. *Ibid.,* 572.
38. *Ibid.,* 535.
39. *Ibid.,* 536.
40. *Ibid.,* 537.
41. *Ibid.,* 533.
42. *Ibid.,* 539.
43. *Ibid.,* 533–4.
44. *Ibid.,* 539, 542.
45. *Ibid.,* 543–4.
46. See Robert N. Minor, "Sarvepalli Radhakrishnan on the Nature of 'Hindu' Tolerance," *Journal of the American Academy of Religion* L, No. 2 (June, 1982), 275–90.
47. *Indian Philosophy* I, 520.
48. *Ibid.,* 521, 544.
49. *Ibid.,* 545.
50. *Ibid.,* 545–6.
51. *Ibid.,* 546.
52. *Ibid.,* 547. Cf. on 15.1ff, p. 548.
53. *Ibid.,* 532.
54. *Ibid.,* 554.
55. *Ibid.,* 521–2. These three paths are identified with three forms in which the Absolute reveals itself: "to those seeking for knowledge as the eternal light"; "to those emotionally inclined as Eternal Love and Beauty of Holiness"; and "to those struggling for virtue as the Eternal righteousness." (553) These elsewhere will be identified with the *trimūrti* doctrine, that the One Absolute appears as Brahma, Vishnu, and Shiva. See Minor, "Sarvepalli Radhakrishnan and 'Hinduism,'" 332, n. 45.
56. *Indian Philosophy* I, 554–5.
57. *Ibid.,* 557.
58. *Ibid.,* 556. Cf. 558.
59. *Ibid.*
60. *Ibid.,* 564.
61. *Ibid.,* 560.
62. *Ibid.,* 562.
63. *Ibid.,* 565.
64. *Ibid.,* 566.
65. *Ibid.,* 569.
66. *Ibid.* This manner of organizing the life of the religious individual in four stages may have been an attempt to combine the ascetic and householder ideals. In it the upper-class person's life moved through four stages: as a student *(brahmacārya),* householder *(gṛhastha), recluse or forest dweller (vānaprasthya),* and one who is beyond the ashramas *(atyaśramin),* later called a *saṃnyāsin.* In the modern period it is often affirmed as a model for all "Hindus."

67. See, for example, *The Hindu View of Life* (London: George Allen and Unwin, 1927), chapter four, though this is a common theme in Radhakrishnan's writings.

68. *Indian Philosophy* I, 575.

69. *Ibid.,* 578.

70. See Hein's summary of these books in "Hinduism" in *A Reader's Guide to the Great Religions,* ed. by Charles J. Adams (2nd ed.; New York: Free Press, 1977), 151; and Minor, "Sarvepalli Radhakrishnan and 'Hinduism,'" 321–7.

71. S. Radhakrishnan, *Religion and Society* (London: George Allen and Unwin, 1969), 74.

72. S. Radhakrishnan, *India and China: Lectures Delivered in China in May 1944* (Bombay: Hind Kitabs, 1944), 97. Cf. S. Radhakrishnan, *Recovery of Faith* (Delhi: Hind Pocket Books, 1967), 169. In *Indian Philosophy* I, 599, he said: "So far as Mahayana is concerned, there is practically nothing to distinguish it from the religion of the Bhagavadgita."

73. S. Radhakrishnan, *East and West in Religion* (London: George Allen and Unwin, 1933), III.

74. S. Radhakrishnan, *The Principal Upaniṣads* (London: George Allen and Unwin, Ltd., 1953), 9.

75. *Ibid.; The Dhammapada with Introductory Essays, Pali Text, English Translation and Notes* (Oxford: Oxford University Press, 1950); *The Brahma Sūtra: The Philosophy of Spiritual Life* (London: George Allen and Unwin, 1960).

76. Daya Krishna, however, questions the fact of Vedantin obligation to use the *prasthāna-traya* in "Vedanta—Does it Really Mean Anything?," *Conspectus* II, No. 2 (1966), 20–8.

77. S. Radhakrishnan, *The Bhagavadgītā with an Introductory Essay, Sanskrit Text, English Translation and Notes* (London: George Allen and Unwin, Ltd., 1948), 16.

78. Likewise the *Dhammapada* includes an introduction which reprints a previous lecture/article delivered as the Annual Lecture on a Master Mind to the British Academy, June 28, 1938: "Gautama the Buddha." To Radhakrishnan, the Buddha taught the doctrine of the *Upanishads,* though his emphasis was upon ethics rather than metaphysics. *Gautama the Buddha* (2nd ed.; Bombay: Hind Kitabs, 1946), 34–36. For other references, see Minor, "Sarvepalli Radhakrishnan and 'Hinduism,'" 335, n. 88, to which add *The Teaching of the Buddha* (Columbo: The Public Trust of Ceylon, 1933).

79. *The Bhagavadgītā,* 7.

80. Pyarelal, "Gandhiji's 'Krishna;'" in *The Radhakrishnan Number: A Souvenir Volume of Appreciations* (Madras: Vyasa Publications, 1962), 55.

81. Radhakrishnan, *The Bhagavadgita,* 11, 20.

82. *Ibid.,* 11.

83. *Ibid.,* 6.

84. *Ibid.,* 7.

85. *Ibid.*

86. One third of the total references to Indian authors is to Shankara, and the most often quoted western source is the New Testament, emphasizing

the Greek-European religio-philosophical tradition. See Robert W. Stevenson, "Historical Change in Scriptural Interpretation: A Comparative Study of Classical and Contemporary Commentaries on the Bhagavadgita," (unpublished Ph.D. dissertation, Harvard University, 1975), pp. 421–4.

87. For example see *OSW*, I, 394; *East and West in Religion*, 19.
88. *The Bhagavadgītā*, 66.
89. *Ibid.*, 20.
90. *Ibid.*, 31.
91. *Ibid.*, 254.
92. *Ibid.*, 325.
93. *Ibid.*, 301. See Stevenson's discussion, 412–439.
94. *Ibid.*, 25.
95. *Ibid.*, 26.
96. *Ibid.*, 7.
97. *Ibid.*, 20.
98. *Ibid.*, 158.
99. *Ibid.*, 159, 203.
100. *Ibid.*, 169.
101 .*Ibid.*, 210.
102. *Ibid.*, 335.
103. *Ibid.*, 340.
104. *Ibid.*, 160–1.
105. Even when commenting upon 18.41, he says: "The four classes are not determined by birth or colour but by psychological characteristics which fit us for definite functions in society." *Ibid.*, 365.
106. *Ibid.*, 161. See Stevenson's discussion, pp. 514–20.
107. *Ibid.*, 79. Cf., 50.
108. *Ibid.*, 146.
109. *Ibid.*, 184.
110. *Ibid.*, 184, 292. For Radhakrishnan's understanding of *ahiṣma*, see Stevenson, pp. 484–89.
111. *Ibid.*, 76. Cf. 69, 74, 139, 298.
112. *Ibid.*, 287.
113. *Ibid.*, 274.
114. *Ibid.*, 270–71. Cf. *Recovery of Faith*, 107, *et. al.*
115. *Ibid.*, 277, 272.
116. *Ibid.*, 274.
117. *Ibid.*, 289–90.
118. Minor, "Sarvepalli Radhakrishnan and 'Hinduism,'" 323.
119. S. Radhakrishnan, "Indian Culture," in *Reflections on Our Age; Lectures Delivered at the Opening Session of UNESCO at the Sorbonne University, Paris* (New York: Columbia University Press, 1949), 121.
120. *OSW*, II, 163. Cf. also *OSW*, I, 147; *President Radhakrishnan's Speeches and Writings May 1962—May 1964* (Ministry of Information and Broadcasting, Government of India, 1965), 171 (hereafter noted as *PRSW*, I.) S. Radhakrishnan, *Fellowship of the Spirit* (Cambridge: Harvard University Press, 1961), 20.
121. *OSW*, I, 120.

122. For example, see *Fellowship of the Spirit,* 16.

123. *OSW,* I, 392. Cf. 76, 194, 199–200, 217–218; *OSW,* II, 50, 75, 235–6; *Occasional Speeches and Writings. Third Series: July 1959—May 1962* (Ministry of Information and Broadcasting, Government of India, 1963), 241, 338 (Hereafter noted as *OSW,* III.) *PRSW,* I, 132, 163, 188, 231, 430; *President Radhakrishnan's Speeches and Writings. Second Series: May 1964—May 1967* (Ministry of Information and Broadcasting, Government of India, 1969), 227–28, 233. (Hereafter noted as *PRSW,* II.)

124. *PRSW,* I, 212.

125. *Ibid.,* 403.

126. *Ibid.,* 244.

127. *Ibid.,* 243.

128. *OSW,* II, 76.

129. *Ibid.,* 180, quoting *Gita* 9.1. Cf. *The Report of the University Education Commission* (Delhi: Manager of Publications, 1949), I, 35; *Recovery of Faith,* 100–101.

130. *PRSW,* II, 192.

131. *Ibid.,* 209; *PRSW,* I, 126, 210, 398.

132. *OSW,* I, 226–7. Cf. 245; *OSW,* II, 145, 261, 297; *PRSW,* I, 188; etc.

133. *OSW,* II 342. Cf. *PRSW,* I, 259.

134. *OSW,* I, 360.

135. *Ibid.,* 404.

136. *PRSW,* I, 174; *PRSW,* II, 201–3; *Recovery of Faith,* 104.

137. *PRSW,* I, 191. Cf. *OSW,* I, 197; *PRSW,* II, 203; S. Radhakrishnan, *Religion in a Changing World* (London: George Allen and Unwin, 1967), 98.

138. *Ibid.,* 210. Cf. *PRSW,* II, 101; *Recovery of Faith,* 104 (here with *kṛṣṇārjunasaṃvāda.*)

CHAPTER NINE

1. G. S. Ghurye, *Indian Sadhus* (Bombay: Popular Prabashan, 1964), 75.

2. Swami Agehananda Bharati, "The Hindu Renaissance and its Apologetic Patterns," *Journal of Asian Studies* XXIX, No. 2 (1970), 286.

3. Joel D. Mlecko, "The Guru in Hindu Tradition," *Numen,* XXIX, No. 1 (1982), 33–61.

4. For more detail see: David Miller, "The Divine Life Society Movement" in *Religion in Modern India,* ed. by Robert D. Baird (New Delhi: Manohar Publications, 1981), 81–112.

5. Swami Sivananda, *Autobiography of Swami Sivananda* (Rishikesh: The Divine Life Society Press, 1958). See also: Swami Venkatesananda, *Gurudev Sivananda* (Rishikesh: The Divine Life Society Press, 1960), and N. Ananthanarayanan, *From Man to God-Man: The Inspiring Life-Story of Swami Sivananda* (New Delhi: Indraprastha Press, 1976).

6. Sivananda, *Autobiography,* 4.

7. *Ibid.,* 11.

8. *Ibid.,* 22.

9. See Ghurye, 82–97 for a discussion of Dashanami suborders.

10. Venkatesananda, 129; Ananthanarayanan, 27.
11. Sivananda, *Autobiography,* 30–31, 35.
12. Ananthanarayanan, 54.
13. Swami Sivananda, *The Sri Bhagavad Gita* (Durban: Divine Life Society Press, 1962), 44.
14. *Ibid.,* 28.
15. Translation in Sarvepalli Radhakrishnan and Charles A. Moore, (eds.) *A Source Book in Indian Philosophy* (Princeton: Princeton University Press, 1957), 532.
16. Daniel H. H. Ingalls, "Samkara on the Question: Whose is *Avidya?*', *Philosophy East and West,* III, No. 1 (April 1953), 69.
17. Sivananda, *Gita,* 568–552.
18. *Ibid.,* 570–72.
19. Translation in Radhakrishnan and Moore, 543.
20. Sivananda, *Gita,* 548–552.
21. See Swami Sivananda, *Practice of Karma Yoga* (Delhi: Motilal Banarsidass, 1974), 195–198.
22. George M. Williams, *The Quest for Meaning of Swami Vivekananda: A Study of Religious Change* (Chico: New Horizons Press, 1974), 39–41.
23. Ludo Rocher, "Karma and Rebirth in the *Dharmasastras*" in *Karma and Rebirth in Classical Indian Traditions,* ed. by Wendy Doniger O'Flaherty (Berkeley: University of California Press, 1980), 61–89.
24. *Ibid.,* 63.
25. *Ibid.,* 66.
26. Louis Dumont, *Homo Hierarchieus* (London: Paladin Publishers, 1970), 81.
27. *Ibid.,* 90.
28. *Ibid.,* 145.
29. *Ibid.*
30. *Ibid.,* 113.
31. Sivananda, *Gita,* 173.
32. *Ibid.,* 750.
33. *Ibid.,* 553.
34. Dumont, 106–7.
35. Sivananda, *Gita,* 769–70.
36. Sivananda, *Practice of Karma Yoga,* 130.
37. *Ibid.,* 204.
38. Sivananda, *Gita,* 173–74.
39. *Ibid.,* 772.
40. Swami Sivananda, *Ethics of the Bhagavad Gita* (Rishikesh: The Divine Life Society Press, 1957), 77–78.
41. Sivananda, *Gita,* 557.
42. Sivananda, *Practice of Karma Yoga,* 186–89.
43. Sivananda, *Gita,* 562.
44. *Ibid.,* 564–65.
45. *Ibid.,* 523.
46. *Ibid.,* 539.
47. *Ibid.,* 602.

48. Ingalls, 72.
49. *Ibid.*
50. Sivananda, *Gita,* 559–60.
51. Sivananda, *Ethics,* 190.
52. Sivananda, *Gita,* 167.
53. Sivananda, *Practice of Karma Yoga,* 66–68.
54. See: George M. Williams, "The Ramakrishna Movement: A Study in Religious Change" and David M. Miller, "The Divine Life Society Movement" in Robert D. Baird, *Religion in Modern India,* 55–112.
55. Bharati, "Hindu Renaissance," 227.
56. *Ibid.,* 274.
57. Khushwant Singh, *Gurus, Godmen and Good People* (Bombay: Orient Longman, 1975), xii.

CHAPTER TEN

1. For a thorough discussion of introductory matters see Robert N. Minor, *Bhagavad-Gītā: An Exegetical Commentary* (South Asia Books, 1982), xv-lx.
2. R. C. Zaehner, *The Bhagavad-Gītā* (Oxford University Press, 1969), 153.
3. *Ibid.,* 153–54.
4. A. C. Bhaktivedanta Swami Prabhupada, *Bhagavad-gītā As It Is* (Collier Books, 1972) Complete Edition, 147.
5. *Ibid.,* 153–54.
6. *Ibid.,* 154.
7. *Ibid.,* 156.
8. *Ibid.,* 157.
9. *Ibid.,* 158–59.
10. *Ibid.,* 265.
11. *Ibid.,* 344.
12. *Ibid.,* 345.
13. *Ibid.,* 415.
14. *Ibid.,* 320.
15. *Ibid.,* 478.
16. *Ibid.*
17. *Ibid.,* 761.
18. *Ibid.,* 782.
19. *Ibid.,* 377.
20. Franklin Edgerton, *The Bhagavad Gītā* (Harper & Row, 1964, first pub. in 1944); Eliot Deutsch, *The Bhagavad Gītā* (Holt, Rinehart and Winston, 1968); also cf. Zaehner and Minor.
21. Bhaktivedanta, *Bhagavad-gītā,* 222–23.
22. *Ibid.,* 223.
23. *Ibid.,* 173.
24. *Ibid.,* 390–91.
25. *Ibid.,* 822.
26. *Ibid.,* 648.
27. *Ibid.,* 398.
28 *Ibid.*

29. *Ibid.*, 447–48.
30. *Ibid.*, 278–79.
31. *Ibid.*, 279.
32. *Ibid.*, 261.
33. *Ibid.*
34. *Ibid.*
35. *Ibid.*, 228.
36. *Ibid.*, 232.
37. *Ibid.*, 359.
38. *Ibid.*, 318.
39. *Ibid.*, 713.
40. *Ibid.*
41. *Ibid.*, 581.
42. *Ibid.*, 24.
43. *Ibid.*, 266.
44. *Ibid.*, 28.
45. *Ibid.*, 469.
46. *Ibid.*, 713.
47. *Ibid.*, 170. *Taittirīya Saṃhitā* 1.7.4 says, "the sacrifice is Vishnu" and Shankara quotes this at this point in his commentary.
48. *Ibid.*, 171.
49. *Ibid.*, 172.
50. *Ibid.*, 227.
51. *Ibid.*, 215.
52. *Ibid.*
53. *Ibid.*
54. *Ibid.*, 218.
55. *Ibid.*, 780.
56. *Ibid.*, 621.
57. *Ibid.*
58. *Ibid.*
59. *Ibid.*, 261.
60. *Ibid.*, 362.
61. *Ibid.*, 439.
62. *Ibid.*, 444.
63. *Ibid.*, 664.
64. *Ibid.*
65. *Ibid.*, 541.
66. *Ibid.*, 541–42.
67. *Ibid.*, 542.
68. *Ibid.*, 546–47.
69. *Ibid.*, 577.
70. *Ibid.*, 590.
71. *Ibid.*
72. *Ibid.*, 591.
73. *Ibid.*, 385.
74. *Ibid.*
75. *Ibid.*, 497.

76. *Ibid.*, 316.
77. *Ibid.*
78. *Ibid.*, 511–12.
79. *Ibid.*, 88.

CONCLUSION

1. "The Making of a Terrorist: From the Autobiography of Damodar Hari Chapekar," in *Nationalism in Asia and Africa* edited by Elie Kedourie (New York: The World Publishing Company, 1970), 457.

2. From his poem "An Echo from Andamans" in Dhanajay Keer, *Veer Savarkar* (Bombay: Popular Prakashan, 1966), 93.

3. *The Bhagavad-gītā with a Commentary Based upon the Original Sources* (Oxford: University Press, 1969), 303.

4. "The Bhagavad Gītā and the Methods of its Study," *The Vedanta Kesari* LVIII, No. 8 (December 1971), 346.

Contributors

ROBERT D. BAIRD
Professor of the History of Religions in the School of Religion of the University of Iowa.

HAROLD W. FRENCH
Associate Professor of Religious Studies at the University of South Carolina.

J.T.F. JORDENS
Reader in Asian History and Dean of the Faculty of Asian Studies of The Australian National University.

DAVID M. MILLER
Associate Professor of Religion at Concordia University, Montreal.

ROBERT N. MINOR
Associate Professor of Religious Studies at The University of Kansas.

RONALD W. NEUFELDT
Associate Professor of Religious Studies at the University of Calgary.

AJIT RAY
Asian Librarian at The Australian National University.

ROBERT W. STEVENSON
Associate Professor of Religious Studies at McGill University.

BOYD H. WILSON
Assistant Professor of Religion at Hope College, Michigan.

Contributors

ROBERT D. BAIRD
Professor of the History of Religions in the School of Religion at the University of Iowa

HAL W. FRENCH
Associate Professor of Religious Studies at the University of South Carolina

J. T. F. JORDENS
Reader in Asian History and Dean of the Faculty of Asian Studies of the Australian National University

DAVID M. MILLER
Associate Professor of Religion at Concordia University, Montreal

ROBERT N. MINOR
Associate Professor of Religious Studies at The University of Kansas

RONALD W. NEUFELDT
Associate Professor of Religious Studies at the University of Calgary

AJIT RAY
Asian Librarian at the Australian National University

ROBERT W. STEVENSON
Associate Professor of Religious Studies at McGill University

BOYD H. WILSON
Associate Professor of Religion at Hope College, Michigan

Index

Index of Bhagavad-gita Passages Cited